5 - '98

SILENT SCHISM
RENEWAL OF CATHOLIC SPIRIT AND STRUCTURES

THE SILENT SCHISM

RENEWAL OF CATHOLIC SPIRIT
AND STRUCTURES

Owen O'Sullivan OFM Cap.

GILL & MACMILLAN

Gill & Macmillan Ltd
Goldenbridge
Dublin 8
with associated companies throughout the world
© Owen O'Sullivan OFM Cap. 1997
0 7171 2560 2

Print origination by O'K Graphic Design, Dublin
Printed by ColourBooks Ltd, Dublin

A catalogue record is available for this book from the British Library.

1 3 5 4 2

To my sister, Maeve, and to her sisters in the congregation of St Louis.

They excel.

CONTENTS

PREFACE

This book is about power in the church—the goals it serves, and the manner in which it is exercised. Its contention is that the way in which power is exercised in the church is based substantially on secular role models, such as political ones, rather than on those which derive from christian faith and tradition. And that, if it is true, calls for change.

The challenge of the book is directed principally to the leaders of the church since it is they, in fact, who hold power in it. It challenges them to introduce the spirit and structures of dialogue; it calls on them to trust the christian faithful, and to have the moral courage and intellectual honesty to face issues squarely. It also suggests evangelical alternatives to the existing power structures by proposing that democratic ideas and institutions be joined to hierarchy in the service of community.

Much of what is in the book is a description of what is already happening in the church, but, in T. S. Eliot's phrase, 'We had the experience but missed the meaning.'[1] This book seeks to find meaning in some of the experiences of the church during the past thirty years or so.

In places, hard-hitting criticisms are made. I have weighed them carefully, and I think they are no harder than they need be if they are to serve the interests of truth and justice. There is no point in proposing an alternative if people see nothing wrong with the *status quo*; there is no value in offering a solution if people acknowledge no problem which needs to be solved. 'Looking on the bright side of things' is an exercise in self-deception if it means a refusal to look unpleasant realities in the face. Before making any criticism I asked myself: is it true? is it just? is it necessary or helpful to make it? And I have tried to criticise ideas rather than people. In short, I have tried to strike a balance between being an uncritical lover and an unloving critic of the church.

The genesis of this book lies in the response I received to two articles in *The Furrow*, namely 'A Candle in the Darkness' published in September 1993 and 'The Silent Schism' published in January 1994. I received letters in response to the latter article from eighteen countries in Africa, Asia, Australia, Europe and North America, from married and single men and women, religious sisters and brothers, and priests both within and without the active ministry. It was clear to me that I had struck a chord with others from different backgrounds; I had said what many were thinking.

Following this, Michael Gill of Gill & Macmillan invited me to develop some of the points in the article into a book. What follows is the result of my taking up his invitation and trying to present, in a positive and practical way, some development of those ideas.

It is my hope that the book will be read as it was written, that is with the intention of facing problems squarely, seeking to open up avenues of discussion, and searching for a theological framework within which spiritual renewal and structural reform can take place in fidelity to the Gospel and the best of christian tradition.

A term frequently used in this book is 'the Vatican'. By that is meant the Roman Curia, the Vatican City-State, and the College of Cardinals, considered collectively. It does not mean the papacy, the see of Peter, the bishop of Rome. The two are distinct.

I have thought a good deal about the use of inclusive language, such as using he/she and him/her instead of simply he and him etc. I have not always done so because I think that some people may find it distracting when reading. Despite this, I hope it will be understood that whatever relates to people in the book applies equally to women as to men, unless the context clearly identifies one or the other.

I wish to acknowledge my gratitude to the Rev. Ronan Drury, editor of *The Furrow*, for permission to use material from the two articles referred to above.

In conclusion, I am calling for a renewed church, and I believe that the way to achieve it is through dialogue with moral courage and intellectual honesty.

1

PERSPECTIVES

1.1 THE RIVER-BED AND THE RIVER

In the part of Africa where I live the rains usually finish about the end of March or early April. From then until late October or early November there is scarcely a shower. Gradually the level of the rivers and the streams drops until, in some cases, they dry up completely and nothing at all is left but an empty bed. Looking at one such, I'm reminded of the words of the psalm which speaks of 'a dry, weary land without water'. The land is indeed dry and weary and the people are weary along with it. That river-bed keeps coming back to me; it is dead, dry, empty, seeming to mock its purpose of being a channel of life. Sometimes whirlwinds come, blowing up dust and sand, turning them round in the air, and sending dried leaves and the ash of burnt grass showering on any passerby.

In October, the hottest month of the year, the level of humidity rises from day to day. Towards the end of the month clouds begin to gather, to darken, and then to send out immense, earth-shaking claps of thunder. When the heat is at its most intense, then you know that relief is near. Accompanied by powerful bolts of lightning the rains begin with large blobs, not mere drops, that carry with them the dust and grit that permeate the air.

There is a wonderful freshness about the first rains. The local people, the Malozi, have a word for them in their language, Silozi; they call them *maseulo*. Those first rains bring with them a heavy, heady scent that is suggestive of life and growth. When the *maseulo* come, people know that help is on the way, they can relax, crops will grow, the air will cool, and they will be able to sleep at night.

As the rains intensify, the water begins to run off a little and to send down rivulets to the streams that feed the rivers, and the annual cycle of regeneration of the rivers begins. The level of water begins to rise again, the current flows faster, carrying with it the accumulated debris of the previous half-year. In exceptional cases, say every ten or fifteen years or so, the rains are particularly heavy and they turn the rivers into powerful forces of destruction which burst their banks, wash away crops and houses, and leave behind a trail of waste and hunger.

The river is a kind of living parable. The dried-up river-bed is a structure without life or spirit. It is a framework which has potential, but which in the dry season is so dead that there seems no hope that it will ever be a bearer of life. But when the hot season is at its most intense, when rain seems only a distant memory, when it is hard to imagine what cool fresh air is like, then comes an about-turn. The new rains bring with them life, growth, freshness, clean air—a spirit of resurrection. The river-bed fills up, channels the new life and gives it direction and purpose. The villagers who live along the banks of the river have easy access to water, the crops grow, and the brown, grey and black colours of the earth give way to a blossoming of green.

But if the rains are too heavy the channel can no longer cope, the flood betrays the hope engendered in the people, and the result may be destruction, decay, and even death.

The parable says to me that both spirit and structure are necessary. Without the spirit, structures are lifeless; without a structure, the spirit may run wild and end by betraying people's hopes. It's not either-or, it's both-and.

I am reminded of what Martin Luther King, the American civil rights leader, wrote about his struggle in the 1950s and 1960s. He pointed out that there was a real change of attitude on the part of the American people at that time towards civil rights issues. There was a willingness to look at matters afresh and a determination to see to it that the evil legacy of discrimination on racial grounds was firmly and finally eliminated. But to bring that about legislative change was necessary. A change of attitudes by itself might never have got beyond the level of ineffectual goodwill; it might have remained merely wishful thinking. There had to be a change of structures as well.

What made the civil rights struggle in the USA in the 1960s so effective was that it combined the two. The prophetic leadership of John F. Kennedy combined with the tough political management of Lyndon B. Johnson ('I may not have style, but I get things done', he said) succeeded in changing the social and political landscape of the USA. It was an example of the effective union of spirit and structure, charism and management, *glasnost* and *perestroika*, renewal and adaptation.

Perhaps there is a kind of codicil to the parable of the river-bed: that sometimes it is necessary to wait until it appears that there is no hope, until a situation seems beyond recovery, for God to pull one of his surprises, and create something new out of a scene of desolation. God is good at surprises: creation out of nothing; the transcendent God of heaven and earth being born in a stable; the Son of God giving new life to humanity through his death; God the Holy Spirit coming in the form of a dove or tongues of fire.

God is still pulling such surprises: Pope John XXIII, seventy-six years of age when he was elected, seemed to some to be merely a stop-gap figure who would hold the fort for a few years until a younger man came along, but instead initiated a shake-up in the church, the like of which had not been seen for several centuries. Another surprise was that the USSR, which ground on relentlessly, seemingly immune to the upheavals which beset the Western world in the 1960s and 1970s, collapsed, imploded, in the space of a few years in the late 1980s and early 1990s, with scarcely a shot fired; like John XXIII, Gorbachev probably didn't fully appreciate the significance or power of the process he had begun. And, in South Africa, Nelson Mandela moved from prisoner to president in four years. In other countries, the one-party state has given way to a new situation with real political debate, genuine freedom of expression, and a sudden blossoming of variety where before there had been only sterility, conformity and the mindless repetition of slogans.

1.2 NOT EITHER-OR BUT BOTH-AND

Saint Augustine described words as 'those precious cups of meaning'. They are significant for relationships. Where words are corrupted there can be no dialogue, and discussion becomes mere verbalising. Just as the forging of a currency can destroy an economy, the 'forging' of language by semantic manipulation or its devaluation through laziness can render human discourse void.

I remember how, in my student days, I looked up the meaning of the word 'heresy' in a dictionary. I wanted to find out its original sense. It came as a surprise to find that it meant 'choice'. The Greek word *haeresis* means 'choice'. This surprised me because heresy is one of the 'bad' words of the christian vocabulary. 'What's wrong with choice?' I asked myself. 'Isn't the making of choices part and parcel of being human?' So how does a 'good' concept like choice come to be tagged with a 'bad' label like heresy?

Reflecting further on the matter, it occurred to me that what is involved in heresy is the imposition of unnecessary and unhelpful choices on people. In effect, a heresy imposes an either-or choice where the full truth of the matter might be best expressed in terms of both-and.

Some of the great classical heresies of history have been posed in terms of either-or choices. For example, is Jesus Christ God or is he man? What are the sources of revelation?—scripture or tradition? Are people saved by faith or by works?

If you ask the wrong question, you cannot get the right answer, and heresies ask the wrong questions. By demanding an answer in terms of either one facet or another of the truth they ignore the wider picture. They erect a partial truth into a pseudo whole truth. It could be added that it is a characteristic of heresies that they seek to give definitive answers to questions which are still provisional. In the case of the examples listed above, christian orthodoxy would reply that Jesus is both God and man; scripture and tradition are together the source of revelation; and people are saved by faith and by works. The same inclusive approach applies also to nature and grace, reason and faith, freedom and authority.

The either-or approach is deceptively attractive in its simplicity; it is simple to the point of being simplistic. It is helped by knowing what, or whom, you are against. And that is another of its weaknesses: it easily becomes a source of division between people, lending itself to the adoption of a them-versus-us approach to reality. In the years after the second Vatican Council (1962–5), there was a lot of debate in a conservative-versus-progressive mould, as there now is between restorationists and liberals. Labels came to be attached, people formed themselves into factions, and issues were sometimes discussed less on objective criteria than on subjective ones. None of this was helpful.

In contrast, a both-and approach to reality seeks to reconcile different emphases, to achieve a creative balance between positions which may seem to be opposed, but which in fact, may be complementary. It is a difficult balance to achieve since it lacks the fundamentalist simplicity of the either-or approach, but it is true to life as it is actually lived by most people.

An example of this is found in Saint Paul's letter to the Galatians, chapter 6. In verse 2 he says, 'Bear one another's burdens, and in this way you will fulfil the law of Christ.' In verse 5 of the same chapter he says, 'For all must carry their own loads.' One might ask, 'which is it to be?' Such apparent conflicts are upsetting to those with tidy minds who want life to be neatly labelled and pigeon-holed. Saint Paul, I imagine, simply saw that there was a truth in each statement and was not concerned about trying to define exactly how one related to the other. Life is larger than logic, and the ordinary business of day-to-day living does not require precise definitions at every turn.

The either-or approach is alive and well both in the church and in the world at large. For example:

1. Zambia (where I live) has abandoned Marxist economics and has assumed, apparently without much serious reflection, that since Marxism did not provide the solutions then capitalism must—if not one, then the other. But is this so?

2. The UN conference on population and development, held in Cairo in 1994, spent much energy arguing whether population control brings about development, or development brings about population control. It was often an either-or debate.

3. Evangelical christians seem to be perennially locked in debates over whether the christian faith is about individual salvation or about what they call 'the social Gospel'.

4. The Roman Catholic church seems to be polarising between those who wish the second Vatican Council had never taken place and want a return to the pre-conciliar past, and those who believe that a new start on radically different lines is now needed. Insofar as they still talk to each other (and some, for the sake of peace, have given up), it is a dialogue of the deaf. There is no meeting point, no common ground; instead, there is a silent schism.

One could multiply such examples. But the point remains the same: both-and is better than either-or.

2

MODELS OF THE CHURCH

When the American theologian, Avery Dulles, published his book on models of the church,[1] there were many who found the expression bewildering. What did 'models' of the church mean? The church was the church, and that was it. Growing up in an environment when it used to be asserted with full confidence that no matter who or what changed the Catholic church would never change, it took some time—with a little help from history and some experience of life—to learn that the church indeed does change. Had it not done so, it would have died a long time ago, as does everything that refuses to change.

2.1 THE IMPERIAL MODEL

In the early centuries of the christian era, once the initial period of persecution had passed, and the church moved from catacombs to toleration to establishment, and spread out beyond the Mediterranean basin, the question of an organisational model became a pressing one.

Broadly speaking, it can be said that the church in the east—that is, the one centred on Constantinople—adopted as its model the Greek city-state, while the Latin church in the west, centred on Rome, took the Roman empire as its model. One consequence of this was that the eastern church became and is to this day national in character, as for example in the Russian, Greek and Serbian Orthodox churches. By contrast, the Latin church in the west retained a more universal character (the word *catholic* means *universal* in Greek). It adopted the imperial organisational model.

The empire was divided into provinces led by consuls or pro-consuls, or governors, appointed by Rome and answerable to Rome. The church was divided into ecclesiastical provinces, led by archbishops, appointed by the pope, and answerable to him. The archbishops, in turn, set up a subordinate structure of dioceses led by bishops. Regional councils of bishops, sometimes presided over by a papal legate, were common. These were structures with which people were familiar and could relate to without difficulty.

As the Roman empire declined and eventually went into collapse, there was no supranational organisation in Europe, other than the Catholic church, which could give coherence and structure to a continent in danger of disintegration and anarchy. Nowhere else was there either the vision or the resources to fill the gap. Whether they liked it or not, the popes came to acquire a political role. At the end of the fifth century, Pope Gelasius I told Emperor Anastasius I, 'Two there are, august emperor, by which this world is ruled on title of original and sovereign right—the consecrated authority of the priesthood and the royal power.'[2] Not so long afterwards there was effectively only one—the pope.

The church had shown that it could survive the persecution of the pagan Roman empire; whether it could survive the patronage of a christian Roman empire was more problematic. For example: the persecuted christian church held that property should be held in common; the established christian church asserted the rights of private property.

But a greater challenge still was whether the church could take over the role of emperor and still be church. Popes from about the year 1000 held that the task of the church was to build Christendom, a unitary society based on the Gospel. It would be styled on the idealised Israel of the Old Testament, where the law of God was the constitution of society. The temporal would be subordinated to the eternal, the material to the spiritual, the king would be the servant of the Gospel, and society as such, not simply its individual members, would be christian.

This meant, among other things, that the pope would have the power to depose kings, and that they would rule in his name. It was said of Innocent III, pope from 1198 to 1216, that when he stamped his foot crowns rattled all over Europe. He intervened in the politics of Spain, Portugal, Poland, Hungary and Bohemia. He put England under interdict (which meant that the population was denied the sacraments and christian burial) for five years in support of his candidate for Archbishop of Canterbury as against the local choice; and he intervened in a disputed election to appoint a Holy Roman Emperor. Described by one Catholic historian as perhaps the greatest of all the popes, he was the first to call himself Vicar of Christ.

An agenda of such dazzling ambition as Christendom involves, however, a dangerous over-reaching on the part of the church. The kingdom of God is not of this world: Christ rejected the role of political Messiah; christians are 'aliens and exiles' (1 Pet. 2:11) on earth who have not here a lasting city (Heb. 13:14). The church's function is to be a leaven fermenting in society (see Lk. 13:20–21) rather than to absorb it or take it over, and an imperial Vicar of Christ is probably as near to being a total contradiction as anything can be. The church is nearer to its Christ-given role when it is a minority struggling within existing structures than when it is a powerful, settled, established institution in full control of affairs. The not so subtle seduction of power is a perennial threat to the church and constantly needs to be recognised as such.

Habits of mind die hard, and the imperial model of church remained in people's minds after the time when Christendom was still considered to be a desirable and attainable objective. The alliance of throne and altar, of cross and crown, when Christ and Caesar were hand and glove, led the church in Europe to be very sympathetic to royal government and, from the time of the French revolution until recently, more than a little hostile to the idea of democracy. The theory of the divine right of kings, though never formally taught by the church, was part of the common currency of christian belief and life for several centuries. (It was a way of saying that the monarch wasn't accountable to the people.)

Up to 1963, popes were crowned after their election. Cardinals were princes of the church. The Vatican operates, to some extent at least, within the mental framework of a royal court, using some of the thought patterns, vocabulary, ritual, ranking system, dress, titles, and paraphernalia of royalty. Nuncios and pro-nuncios are the consuls and pro-consuls of an ecclesiastical Roman empire, and the effective instruments of appointing bishops, often with only the most cursory consultation of local interests and personnel. Where there are humans there are politics, and it should not come as a surprise if the infighting, intrigues, power-games, careerism, and favour-seeking characteristic of royal courts were also to be part of the scene. And the 'divine right' of the bureaucracy means that the rest of the church is accountable to the Vatican while the Vatican is not accountable to anyone.

The imperial model of church seems to be undergoing something of a restoration at present. Since Vatican II (1962–5) there has been a constant and very successful effort on the part of the Vatican to win diplomatic recognition. It now exchanges ambassadors with almost every important country and most of the smaller ones as well, more than one hundred and fifty-five countries in all. The official rationale is that the Gospel needs to be inserted into the world of international diplomacy and politics. However, others believe that what actually happens is that the Gospel, and the church whose task it is to promote it, become part of the power game and inevitably become compromised by political manoeuvre.

Recent events in Mexico raise a question mark over the process. It had been an objective of Vatican policy to have diplomatic relations with Mexico, a country with a predominantly Catholic population, but also a history of intense anti-clericalism in some states of the Mexican federation. This anti-clericalism led to active persecution of the church in the 1920s, and the church responded with interdicts and excommunications. Under President Carlos Salinas de Gortari relations were restored in 1993, but with strings attached.

In the southern state of Chiapas, Bishop Samuel Ruiz Garcia of San Cristobal de las Casas was a strong supporter of the rights of the indigenous Indian population and for that reason became a thorn in the side of the local establishment. They wanted him out and asked the Vatican to do the job; the Vatican agreed. In the latter half of 1993 the nuncio in Mexico city began the process of removing the bishop from office. He won the support of the Mexican bishops. But then the plan began to unravel. On 1 January 1994 the Zapatista revolt in Chiapas took Mexico by surprise. The government, caught unawares, reacted clumsily by sending in the army with full military force, including air strikes, and sought a scapegoat. Who did they blame?—the bishop, of course; he had stirred up the people.

Then wiser counsels prevailed. The army was withdrawn and a process of mediation was decided upon. For that a mediator was necessary. Who could fulfil the role?—the bishop, of course. After that, there was no more from either the government or the Vatican about removing the bishop from office—at least for the moment.

Could the Vatican's role in this case be described as one of inserting the Gospel into the world of politics?

Similar questions may be asked about the role of nuncios in relation to the bishops of a country. Apart from their key role in the appointment and transfer of bishops, they exercise other powers also. They can, and do, exercise a veto on the appointment of representatives to the synod of bishops. They control, to a considerable extent, the flow of information between the Vatican and the bishops. (In *The Name of the Rose*, Umberto Eco has dramatised the power linked to control of information.) They sometimes impose themselves on meetings of conferences of bishops. In one east African country the bishops found their own way of dealing with a nuncio who came uninvited to their meeting. They greeted him in English, which he knew, gave him a cup of tea and a biscuit, and then continued their meeting for the rest of the day in Kiswahili, the *lingua franca* of east Africa, which he didn't know. The poor man must have been numb with boredom!

Another question worth asking is why nuncios, if they should exist at all, must be bishops? Is it right to use the sacrament of order as a means of bestowing status, of establishing that a man has a degree of clout? Are local bishops not able to ordain new bishops when the need arises? The official rationale for nuncios is that they are a sign of *communio* between the local church and the see of Peter. Could the chairman of the bishops' conference not fulfil this role? It is also said, from the Vatican's perspective, that nuncios are at the service of the local church. It often seems, however, from the local church's perspective, that they are a control mechanism, a symbol of the Vatican's fear that the locals will get out of control if it does not have its man on the spot to keep a watchful eye on them. They are symbols of a lack of trust rather than of *communio*.

2.2 THE CATHOLIC ALTERNATIVE SOCIETY

A model of church which has been dominant until very recently is what might be called the Catholic alternative society. A modified version of the medieval concept of Christendom, it calls on the church to stand apart from the world which is seen as a place of temptation and sin, under the control of powers hostile to the Gospel. One of the visual images used to illustrate the concept was that of a fortress standing on a hill, defying its enemies to do their worst, assured that God would give it the final victory.

This understanding began to develop in the wake of the failure of the concept of Christendom. It was a fall-back position, a second line of defence. The moral authority of the popes had been weakened by their active promotion of the crusades, and, paradoxically, it was the reform-minded popes who were their most active proponents. The intense political involvement of popes in political conflicts, coupled with the use of religious sanctions such as excommunication, sapped public confidence in the system.

Furthermore, the failure by six general councils of the church in the years between 1123 and 1274 to put into effect the reforms they enacted made it seem to some that the church was incapable of reforming itself. Then, in the mid-fourteenth century came the Black Death, the bubonic plague which killed about one third of the population of Europe. Itself a by-product of the crusades, it acted like a haemorrhage of the christian body politic, with the result that people were concerned more with survival than with the realisation of such an ambitious programme as Christendom. The great western schism, with rival claimants to the papacy living at Rome and at Avignon in France in the period from 1378 to 1438, could not but have diminished confidence in the papacy.

There were other factors in the wider world also which began to impinge on the christian community and to make it clear that if Christendom had ever been a viable option, that was no longer the case. For example, the Renaissance opened people's minds to a wider world of culture as they began to study anew the Greek and Latin classics. Perhaps they came to see that Greece's intellectual legacy to the world was respect for freedom of thought. Coupled with the development of printing, and the discovery of the New World (itself a by-product of the new technology which made long-distance navigation possible), it is not surprising that people began to take a fresh look at reality and to investigate, challenge and change existing modes of thought and behaviour.

It is possible that the church might have been able to ride the waves and emerge from the storm of new ideas reinvigorated and rejuvenated. However, the Reformation brought about an intense and prolonged period of reaction in which the church withdrew into itself, appeared to see only danger in new ideas and, almost as a matter of course, to go against whatever position the reformers held. The fact that the reformers, for their part, largely returned the compliment did not help matters; the either-or mentality was at work again. Anyone so foolish as to try and take the middle of the road would be knocked down by the traffic from either direction.

In the centuries which followed the Reformation, the church set itself apart from society; it multiplied its institutions, developing in many countries a network of Catholic schools, hospitals, newspapers, even political parties and trades unions, and a very large pattern of associations and clubs of all kinds. Ecumenism was a non-starter; marriage between a Catholic and a non-Catholic (the term 'non-Catholic' is itself revelatory of a them-versus-us frame of mind) was forbidden, and there was an array of laws to isolate

Catholics from the world around them—the index of forbidden books, abolished only in 1966, was an example. The index forbade Catholics under pain of excommunication to read a very wide variety of books, including such well-known works of modern literature as Graham Greene's *The Power and the Glory*. (Perhaps the whiskey priest was considered scandalous.) Running through it all was the certainty that we were right and others wrong. We confused certainty with truth. The idea that we might have anything to learn from others was suspect as suggesting a less than complete loyalty to the church.

The image of the church as fortress under siege by a hostile world gave Catholics a strong sense of identity. We knew who we were and what we stood for, and, most of all, we knew what and whom we were against. As a student for the priesthood I learned the theology of the Counter-Reformation, refuting the errors of Luther, Calvin, Zwingli and the rest, not really awake to the fact that the world was far indeed from fighting the theological battles of the Reformation and knew little or nothing about the issues involved. Our spirit of community came from a shared sense of being under attack by a world hostile to the church. We spoke a great deal about the church and a lot less about God. We revered Pius XII, the last of the Counter-Reformation popes (he was pope from 1939 to 1958), as the symbol of the church's resistance to the dangers of the modern world.

It is highly paradoxical that most of what the reformers sought did, in fact, come into being in the Catholic church in the following centuries, especially in and after Vatican II. The tragedy is that it took a division in the church to bring it about. If the Protestant dimension of christian faith and life—for example, the emphasis on individual responsibility for oneself before God, the use of the bible by the faithful, communion under the form of wine as well as bread, a vernacular liturgy and so forth—had been contained within the church through dialogue, the unity of the church could have been maintained and it would have been greatly enriched; the religious wars of Europe would never have taken place; and the history of Europe and the world would have been very different.

If we had been able to discuss issues on their merits rather than simply by reference to authority, to dialogue instead of merely argue, to see dissent as potentially creative rather than divisive, to see self-criticism by the church as healthy rather than as a betrayal, if the church had not interlocked its own interests with those of the power-games of the time, then the Reformation with all its division, hatred and even war, might never have happened.

The Catholic alternative society model of church is heavily institutional. It has the strengths of institutions: stability and continuity. It also has their weaknesses: rigidity, resistance to change, great cost in terms of personnel and finance, and also the risk that the institution comes to give its perceived interests priority over the goals and ideals it is meant to serve. It was this model of church which, substantially, was exported to mission territories, and which can claim the credit for having set the church on its feet in Africa, the Americas, and Asia. That was no small achievement.

It was a Eurocentric model, the limitations of which are becoming increasingly apparent, as the young churches formed in this mind-set (and it is a mind-set as much as an organisational framework) encounter great psychological difficulties in the task of inculturation: the task of relating the Gospel to their own culture and traditions, and their traditions to the Gospel. Trying to be African and christian at the same time is a severe challenge, and many Africans are really struggling to find a sense of identity, pulled as they are between the old and the new.

Another pressing fact for Africa is that the young churches are not able to meet the cost of these institutions without long-term dependence on foreign funding, with its concomitant effects of—at times—dependency, irresponsibility, childishness, and also corruption. The story (a true one) is told of a bishop in Southern Africa, the first local bishop in his diocese, who, shortly after taking over from his European predecessor, asked a development agency for a bulldozer. When asked what it was for, he replied that it was to bulldoze the many institutions with which his predecessor had burdened the diocese! The legacy of the Catholic alternative society is unsustainable in Africa. The effort at maintaining it is weighing down the church, making it difficult for it to respond flexibly to some of the new challenges, such as the proliferation of local sects.

The church appears to be clinging to this model as if it were identifiable with the inner reality of the church itself. There seems to be an inability to think of the church apart from the particular model in which we currently find ourselves. That model, it seems to me, is now in an advanced state of decay—which is no reason for anxiety. On the contrary, it is a normal development. But to spend more time, effort, personnel and money on trying to salvage it is a little like putting band-aids on a broken leg.

It might, perhaps, have been possible to salvage the mini-Christendom model of church in the years immediately after Vatican II when the institution was still in its heyday, if we had had the courage to revitalise it, but that would have called for a radicalness which proved to be beyond our vision or our courage. After Vatican II, we tamed and domesticated the council's impulse, and behaved as if all that Vatican II meant was giving the pre-Vatican II model of church a modest face-lift. But it was a lot more than that. Through our failure of nerve, the opportunity was lost, and is now, I believe, beyond recovery.

Indeed, when the history of the church from 1965 to the present comes to be written, I believe it will be seen mostly as a time of lost and even squandered opportunities. One example will perhaps be enough: just as the nineteenth century was the one in which the church lost the working classes, the twentieth century may be the one in which it lost its women. Without the active involvement of women on a large scale the church in Africa will lose out to Islam, as the church in north Africa did in the early centuries of the Christian era. And the church in other parts of the world will suffer equally grave losses.

The failure to revitalise the church after Vatican II may well have been a blessing in disguise. Had we rejuvenated the pre-Vatican II model of church, we might simply have prolonged a model which had outlived its usefulness, and thereby postponed a more far-reaching, penetrating and lasting renovation of the church.

The option of restoring the past is not now seriously open to us. Despite the wishful thinking and nostalgia for the *ancien régime* which are in the ascendant in the church's leadership at present, there can be no return to the position as it was before Vatican II. The attempt by the Vatican to bring about such a restoration and impose it on the church continues to have the effect of alienating the Vatican from the mainstream of Catholic life. The pope's visits to many countries, which were perhaps expected to strengthen the bonds between the papacy and ordinary Catholics, have, more likely, had the effect of reinforcing the widespread perception among Catholics that the church's leadership is out of touch with the grass-roots. A not uncommon reaction to papal visits is euphoria while they last, followed by disillusionment afterwards.

One of my fears for the church is that while its leadership continues on its present course, that leadership is more and more losing the confidence and perhaps even the goodwill of its members, including priests and religious brothers and sisters.

Many, I know, no longer listen to anything that comes from the Vatican, because they have given up hope of finding positive, creative thinking there that responds to people's real needs. At a more serious level, there are others who though clinging to faith in God have lost hope in the church and have quietly left it, at least at the formal level, and continue the search for human values elsewhere. But abandonment of religious practice, in terms of attendance at Mass and reception of the sacraments, is not uncommonly followed by loss of belief.

An unfortunate side-effect of this process is that it reinforces the conviction of those who wish to turn back the hands of the clock that they are the faithful remnant whom God has promised will always remain, no matter how many others may be unfaithful. If the present course continues, the church may find itself as removed from the mainstream of society in general as, for example, is the church in France. There the church's leadership persisted until 1945 in clinging to the unrealistic hope of an end to the Republic which it could never forgive for its origins in the revolution, and held out for a restoration of the monarchy. If the rest of the church were to become thus marginalised, it would no longer be the church of Jesus Christ; it would be merely a sect. That would be real infidelity.

Recent events in the former Soviet Union provide an example of what happens to an institution which refuses to change. When Brezhnev's period of stagnation was succeeded by more of the same under Yuri Andropov and Constantin Chernenko, the future of the Soviet Union became questionable. But when Gorbachev, convinced communist that he was, failed to read the signs of the times, and still continued—even after the failed coup attempt against him—to believe and to state publicly that the Soviet Union could be revitalised by a reformed communist party, he was seen by the public as having lost touch with reality and was swept away, along with the communist party.

A further illustration of how closed minds can help to bring about the downfall of a system comes from Gorbachev's predecessor, Chernenko, who enjoyed a brief spell at the top of the Soviet power pyramid. On one occasion his public relations people arranged an on-camera meeting for him with a group of young people. Apparently the intention was to show that he was alert and vigorous, contrary to rumour. All went well until the young people asked him some unscripted questions. He snapped at them peevishly, 'What's the point of these questions? Haven't they all been answered before?' His mind was locked into an ideology and he seemed to think that he had nothing to learn from life. There are people like him in the church too. They are not capable of entering into a dialogue, since they believe that all the questions have been answered before. By their intransigence such people contribute greatly to the destruction of the system which they claim to defend.

What the church needs now is not a modest course-correction, not a little fine tuning of the system, but a fundamental reorientation of the way it is run to bring it into line with the Gospel and the best elements of its own tradition. It needs to use power as an instrument of service, not of domination, and to exercise it in dialogue, not in dictation.

Those who have been blocking reform in the church since the end of Vatican II are preparing the way (unintentionally) for radical change. It was Arthur Schlesinger, I believe, who wrote that those who make peaceful evolution impossible make violent revolution inevitable. Reform, it has been said, is the worst enemy of revolution (because it makes it unnecessary). There has been no real reform in the way the church uses power. On the contrary, the movement has been in the opposite direction. Such a situation opens up several possibilities, of which I will examine three here.

Firstly, if the present trends in the church's style of leadership continue, one possible good may come from it, namely, that its folly and pointlessness will be so clearly evident to all but the wilfully blind that the need for radical overhaul will be accepted without serious challenge. But the price to be paid for that delayed recognition may be the loss of many of the church's most creative members, not because they will have lost faith in God but because they will have lost hope in the church.

Secondly, there may be a gradual decline into stagnation, a directionless drift leading nowhere. For public relations purposes such a situation would be dressed up as stability. Or it might be asserted that the church is taking on its evangelical role as a sign of contradiction (see Lk. 2:34), taking a stand against a sinful world. That would be to confuse obstinacy with strength, and its effect would be to marginalise the church from the world it has a mission to serve in the name of Christ. The fact that this has already happened in some countries means that such a possibility may not be dismissed as merely fanciful.

The film *Nicholas and Alexandra* about the end of the Romanov dynasty, is illustrative of this. It portrays Nicholas as a weak man who wished to be strong, but who instead became merely stubborn. His obstinate resistance to reform brought about the revolution which destroyed the monarchy that he had sought so strenuously to preserve by his refusal to change.

Thirdly, God may pull one of his surprises, as the resurrection was a surprise to those who saw Jesus die on Good Friday. Where there is Christ there is always hope.

God is the creator and redeemer of the universe, and mankind is the arch-bungler of his best plans. When Pope John XXIII called a general council of the church in 1959 for the purpose of— among other things—promoting the unity of christians, I believe that was one of God's plans for his people. That opportunity has now largely been lost or perhaps squandered, mainly through the timidity and lack of vision of church leaders at all levels. But God will get his way despite our best efforts to frustrate him. It may be that what God will do is to allow all the churches to go into terminal decline to the point of extinction in order to be able to build up out of the ruins a united christian church which will be a living symbol of unity in a divided world. Creation out of nothing is a speciality of God's. Have we faith strong enough to believe that?

2.3 THE ONE-PARTY CHURCH

I have lived in Zambia since the late 1970s. From 1972 until 1991 it was a one-party state on the model of the Soviet Union, grounding the party's claim to legitimacy on the Marxist-Leninist principle that the party represented the people and the government was its executive arm. The party in question, the United National Independence Party (UNIP), was always known simply as the Party, with a capital P like the capital C for Church. By definition, any other party was anti-people. Outside the party there was no revolution; the party was not accountable to anyone but itself; and it was united around one leader who held office from 1958 until 1992. It found its theoretical base in *Das Kapital*, the legitimate interpretation of which was entrusted to the guardians of orthodoxy, the ideologists, those grand inquisitors of the citadels of power.

For the ordinary party cadre, who might reasonably not be too conversant with *Das Kapital*, slogans were substituted. At party rallies, the cheer-leader would call out, 'One Zambia', and people would reply 'One Nation'. Then 'One Nation' with the response 'One Leader'. Then 'Who is that Leader?' to which the reply was 'Kaunda for ever and ever'. (Kenneth Kaunda was president.) And, for a time, the zealots of the UNIP Youth League used to raise their right arms in a fascist-style salute at appropriate intervals in the leader's speeches. I think it went unnoticed, that a party of the political left replicated the antics of the right. Hitler's party hacks used to chant *Ein Volk, ein Führer, ein Vaterland* (one people, one leader, one fatherland).

The party had its heroes and its martyrs, the revolutionaries who died in the struggle for independence. It had its annual festivals such as May Day, and it used ceremonial and ritual to cement loyalty to itself. It had its rites of initiation, such as entry into the party's Youth League. It placed a high premium on conformity and compliance. Criticism was equated with disloyalty, uniformity was seen as the guardian of unity, and passivity was preferred to an active, thinking mind. For the party, 'authority' and 'power' were interchangeable terms. To question or challenge the authority (i.e. power) of the party was the sin against the Holy Spirit. Anything else might be forgiven, but not that.

The result was a loss of personal freedom and initiative. The system operated on a kind of collective irresponsibility. No individual was responsible for anything. Since decisions were made collectively within the framework of an ideological strait-jacket, and new ideas were not welcome—quite the contrary—issues were not examined on their merits, but only by reference to what authority, namely the party and its government, had previously decided. Unquestioning acceptance of the party line was regarded as proof of genuine loyalty.

This could lead to farcical situations. Where the ideology was in conflict with the facts, the facts were suppressed and it was considered disloyal or subversive to draw attention to them. For example, where a rigid, centralised economic policy was driving the country into bankruptcy, the fact was simply denied. When the economic shambles had outrun the reserves of plausible deniability, then a scapegoat was found, and the president had a fixed ritual of denunciation, 'Colonialism, capitalism, zionism, racism, fascism, imperialism, and the exploitation of man by man', with the IMF and the World Bank thrown in for good measure. It was all good, clean fun; the problem was that it was meant to be taken seriously as a basis on which to run the country.

In the absence of solid information and facts, gossip, rumour and suspicion abounded. Any and every setback was blamed on 'sabotage' by an unnamed and therefore unchallengeable external Enemy (always spelled with a capital E like the capital D for Devil).

South Africa was hinted at darkly. Keeping things vague and muddled were an official tactic for throwing critics off balance. Thus, the president broke off relations with the IMF, then denied doing so and announced that negotiations were continuing as before. When the conflict between ideology and reality was so great that it could no longer be denied, then the party responded with a kind of mental flip in which a new line was promulgated, while affirming that there was perfect continuity between the old and the new. People were told that there had been no change at all.

Party ideology was, on the surface, fully democratic, always referring to the people who supposedly, were the source of power and the beneficiaries of the system. The reality, however, was that an authoritarian, hierarchical power structure held full control. An example of this was that the president was head of state, head of the party, head of government, chief of staff of the armed forces, and head of a holding company which controlled most of the country's industry, mining, commerce and agricultural marketing. He held power as a result of elections in which he was the only candidate, and was fond of saying he would continue in office only as long as the people wanted him.

The country's parliament was a rubber stamp which did what it was told to do. From time to time the president would remind it that it had no decision-making authority. Its function was to implement party decisions and no more. Only party candidates could stand for elections and the results were decided, in some cases at least, even before the election took place. As one government minister said to me before an election in which he was standing as a candidate, 'His Excellency has chosen me for this constituency.' When I asked how he could be sure since the election hadn't yet taken place, he just laughed and said nothing. He was elected.

The country was officially styled a 'one-party participatory democracy'. In reality, people's participation was limited to saying Yes to what the party had already decided in their name. The party was fond of pointing out human rights abuses outside the country's borders, and proclaiming its commitment to those rights at home. It was the 'Yes, of course, but . . .' type of commitment. For example:

'Should there be freedom of expression?'
'Yes, of course, but . . .'
'But what?'

'But subject to public order and morality.'
'Who decides about public order and morality?'
'Why the party, of course, who else?'

On that basis the party secured almost total control of the press, radio, TV and publishing. It did not accept that the best answer to criticism was an intelligent, well-articulated argument. It counted instead on its ability to ensure, either through control of the media or by silencing the critic through intimidation, that criticism would never be heard.

What was involved in this process was not simply political or even economic control. It was an attempt to control people's minds through the careful manipulation of language. Words became voided of meaning, mere sounds made with the mouth. Perhaps the best example of this was the use, or rather the abuse, of the word 'people'. Everything was done in the name of 'the people'. The phrase 'the people' was over-used to the extent that one no longer listened; the mind was numbed by boredom. The implied equation—the party is the people—fudged the fact that real power lay nowhere with the people, but with a self-perpetuating elite at the top, who lived in a closed circle immune to the ordinary pressures of life. When they said 'the people' they meant the party; and when they said the party they meant the president.

Along with this went a personality cult of the president. I can remember the two national newspapers, both owned by the party, publishing a sixteen-page supplement of birthday greetings to the president in the form of advertisements inserted by state-owned companies. And the one television channel, government-owned and operated, showing the president's birthday party on three consecutive nights, with the members of the central committee of the party gathered round smiling as they sang 'Happy birthday to you'.

In the end, the pretence became unsustainable. It was Abraham Lincoln, I think, who said that you can fool some of the people all the time, and you can fool all the people some of the time, but you can't fool all the people all the time. The point came when even those who professed to believe in the system could no longer stomach the lies, the hypocrisy, the sycophantic toadying, the empty sham of it all. When free and fair elections were held, under pressure from donor countries and international lending institutions, the party lost 83 per cent of its seats in parliament and the president gained only 19 per cent of the votes in the presidential election. He had made the mistake of believing his own propaganda and, as a result, seemed genuinely astonished that the people had rejected him. After the election he was a pathetic figure, hurt, alone, disappointed, living in a state of shocked surprise, unable to grasp what had happened. He had fooled only himself. It is worth mentioning in passing, that during the twenty-seven years of Kenneth Kaunda's presidency, the international media bestowed on him the image, the *persona*, of a gentle, liberal christian democrat, and that was how people saw him at international level.

The more that power was concentrated in the hands of one person, the greater the impact of his errors of judgment. Nothing could be done about education, health care, agriculture, or roads without political change because everything was politicised, and everything depended on one man. He had no intention of changing anything of substance lest he run the risk of losing control, and as a result the system gradually ground down to immobility.

However, it also needs to be said that the situation had gone on for longer than it need have done, because the people themselves had become accomplices in the system. For the sake of a quiet life, perhaps, the whole country had become involved in the lying and self-deception that were the indispensable props of the system. There were no prophets to speak a word of truth, to say openly what everyone knew was true. Absolute power had corrupted the party, and the people had allowed fear to corrupt them.

More recently, the Burmese Nobel peace prize-winner, Aung San Suu Kyi, has drawn attention to the corrupting power of fear. (She has also observed that the world is not so much divided between good people and bad, but rather between those who are willing to learn and those who are not.) In 1970, in his address on receiving the Nobel prize for literature, Alexander Solzhenitsyn pointed out that a dictatorship, no matter how seemingly secure, is vulnerable to truth, and that it is truly secure only when there is not even one person who will speak openly one word of truth. In the former Soviet Union, the scientists were the prophets of truth. Without the freedom to enquire and to discuss openly, there can be no science. The Soviet Union, based on scientific socialism, allowed a wide measure of academic freedom to scientists because it needed their services. But the human mind is or should be indivisible, and those who were free to discuss science openly also discussed politics openly. Dictatorships demand and depend on censorship, either the self-censorship of 'prudence' (for example, 'It might be wiser to say nothing'), or the censorship imposed by the power elite.

Marxism, despite its avowed atheism, has often been regarded as a substitute religion and in particular as a form of parasite on the christian faith . . . a parasite, and a parody, too. For example, Marxism parodies the messianic element in christianity by the hope that it engenders in the future—after the next five year plan, the workers' paradise; things will always be better in future so don't be distracted by the failings of the present. If christianity had never existed, would Marxism have come into being? Probably not: a cancer cannot grow without a living organism as its host.

In Zambia, as elsewhere, the Marxist party appropriated to itself religious language, symbols, and concepts. For example, the party's annual conference at a place called Mulungushi, came to be called the Mulungushi Rock of Authority, with the party's decisions handed down with quasi-divine authority as from an oracle. And those who fell foul of the party, but later succeeded in finding favour again, used to make what was in effect a public confession. They spoke of having 'repented' and being 'forgiven' by the president.

It is true, of course, as Lord Acton said, that the worst kind of corruption is when the best things become corrupt (*corruptio optimi pessima*), and the arrogation to themselves by Marxist parties of religious concepts is one such example. It is not christianity's fault if Marxism 'steals' some of its ideas, distorts them, and then uses them for its own purposes. But it is unsettling that there is a degree of similarity between the two systems, the party's and the church's, so that such mimicry becomes possible, plausible, and even (to some extent) persuasive. If one reads again the last few pages, substituting the word church for people, the Vatican for the party, and the pope for the president, it comes very close to the bone.

Consider the multiple meanings of the word 'church'. It may mean all of the baptised, or only Catholics, or the clergy, or the bishops, or the Roman curia, or the pope, or any combination of them. Canon law, for instance, states, 'The ordering and guidance of the sacred liturgy depends solely on the authority of the Church, namely, that of the Apostolic See and, as provided by law, that of the diocesan Bishops.'[3] In this context, the word 'church' is equated with the see of Rome and the bishops.

When someone says 'the church teaches such and such . . .' to whom does the word 'church' there refer? If only the pope, or the pope and bishops teach a particular doctrine, may it still legitimately be described as a teaching of 'the church'? If a doctrine is not in fact received by the great majority of the faithful, can it still truthfully be described as the church's teaching? By engaging in semantic sleight of hand as, for instance, by changing the meaning attributed to the word 'church' part-way through a discussion, anything may be proven or disproven as required. But while an argument may be won by doing so, the truth will be lost. And the church's task is to proclaim the truth.

Like a great many of my contemporaries, I am very glad to see the end of the one-party state. It was a rotten system, and it deserved the contempt it received. I would not like, however, to see a one-party church either. I have the feeling, and it unsettles me, that there are too many similarities for our own good between the one-party model of state government and that of the church today.

2.4 LIKE AN ARMY SET IN BATTLE ARRAY . . .

There have been periods in the life of the church when it has been influenced by a military model of leadership, when the church was likened to an army going out to battle. The christian was anointed as a soldier of Christ in confirmation and took his place in the church militant, doing battle with the enemies of the church and the forces of evil.

An especially vivid expression of this was in the period of the crusades, when christians were called by popes for two hundred years to take up arms and fight to free Jerusalem from the 'infidel' (the Moslems). The word 'crusade' itself comes from the word 'cross', and it recalls the words of Jesus: 'If any want to become my followers, let them deny themselves and take up their cross and follow me.' (Mt. 16:24) The crusade was presented as 'taking up the cross' in the following of Christ. One visual image used to represent it was that of the kneeling knight holding up his sword in offering to God. The fact that a sword in outline has the same shape as a cross was a kind of visual pun, just as the word 'crusade' was a verbal one.

The crusades themselves were botched from a military and political point of view. For example, Constantinople, the christian capital in the east, was captured and sacked by the christian crusaders from the west, while all of them presumably prayed to the one true God for victory over their common enemy, the Moslems. The economic interests of Venice were responsible for that blunder —Constantinople was Venice's main trading rival in the eastern Mediterranean.

However, there was a much more important issue at stake: the spiritual one. The crusades were a spiritual and moral victory for Islam on the day that the first christian soldier enrolled for battle, since they meant that the christian church had abandoned the methods of Christ for those of Islam—the *jihad*, the holy war.

In the teaching of Pope Boniface VIII on the text of Luke 22:38, an attempt was made to provide a theological basis for military involvement by the church. In the bull *Unam Sanctam*, published in 1302, the pope claimed that the two swords mentioned in the text represent spiritual and temporal power, and that both of them are in the hands of Peter, who represents the church. Therefore, he argued, the church has the right to exercise temporal power, including military force.

The pope's interpretation of the text has—for a very long time —been seen as far-fetched, indeed as an example of how not to interpret scripture, since what it does is to inject into the text a meaning which does not derive from it. It is best forgotten on the principle that a papal bull is not a sacred cow! It is better to remember what Jesus taught, that 'All who take the sword will perish by the sword.' (Mat. 26:52) A christian should be prepared to die for the faith, not to kill for it, since anyone who wishes to do the work of Christ should use the methods of Christ.

The church's occasional ventures into the area of linking the faith to military action have produced some of the oddest quirks in its history, some of them curiosities, some bizarre, some barbaric. There were military religious orders, such as the Knights Templars who defended Malta from the Turks. And in 1864 three battleships for the papal navy were launched from the Clyde in Scotland—of all places! In the 1930s, Cardinal Ildefonso Schuster, Archbishop of Milan, hailed the Italian invasion of Ethiopia, saying that Italy's army was carrying the cross of Christ over the plains of Ethiopia.[4]

These examples are a warning against allowing the Gospel to be subverted by being twisted to serve the interests of a party or an ideology. An instance of the latter was that the church in South America, until very recently, allied itself with some very unsavoury right-wing military regimes which walked hand-in-hand with the ruling oligarchy. As long as the regime professed to be anti-communist, its credentials were established and no awkward questions were asked.

In Argentina, the large-scale murders and 'disappearances' carried out by death-squads in league with the military junta did not bring any censure from the church in Argentina. Indeed, some bishops and priests gave passive and even active support to them.[5] This earned the bishops a public reproof from Pope John Paul II when he visited the country in 1982; he reminded them in his address that the good shepherd stays with his flock and does not run away and hide when trouble comes.

In Angola and Mozambique, the bishops did not oppose the savage repression of the people by the Portuguese military up to independence in 1975, repression carried out in the name of defending christian civilisation from communism. And what of Haiti in 1994? Its murderous rulers were recognised by scarcely any state, except the Vatican.

The military model of obedience expressed as 'Don't ask questions, just shut up and do as you're told' was the mentality which made possible the Gulag, Auschwitz and the Khmer Rouge. Would it be true to say that as many crimes have been committed in history in the name of obedience as in the name of revolt?

Within the church's own life, until recently, the type of obedience expected of members of religious orders was the 'ours not to reason why' type. Obedience was reduced to permissions and, with some exceptions, superiors were no more likely to consult their 'subjects' than generals were to discuss strategy with privates. Thanks to Vatican II, much of that mentality has gone, and obedience is now seen in religious orders more in terms of the person's responsibility for his or her actions, and on a community search for God's will in the light of the Gospel and the signs of the times.

Nonetheless, it is significant that the military model of church still finds favour with groups which seek a return to the past—such as the Blue Army, the Militia of Mary Immaculate, and to a lesser extent the Legion of Mary. Why Mary the mother of Jesus should be invoked as the patroness of reaction is a mystery. Her Magnificat (Lk 1:46–55) suggests a very different role.

As with any other model of the church, the military model needs to be examined and assessed critically in the light of the Gospel.

2.5 ASSESSING THE MODELS

The models of church considered in this chapter, and other possible ones as well, are not in any way exclusive. They can and do co-exist with each other, even when they might seem to be or are in fact in opposition to each other. Life is larger than logic, and people are able to live with situations which if considered in an abstract academic way might seem to be untenable. Neither does one model necessarily lead to another in any kind of sequence. Life is an untidy jumble, and so is life in the church—and it is all the more interesting for that.

Like Jesus, the church is both divine and human. (Did Jesus *found* a *church*, or would it be more accurate to say that he *called* a *community* into being?) And, like Jesus, the church is in this world and part of it. It cannot but take on some of the characteristics, good and bad, of the world in which it finds itself, since it does not live in the abstract but in ordinary everyday life.

The story is told of a Jewish rabbi who visited Rome during the time of the Renaissance popes. He saw all the politicking, the rackets and fiddles, the wine, women and song of the papacy, and promptly became a Catholic. When questioned by his astonished friends he replied, 'Any church that can survive that sort of leadership must be divinely inspired.' And he was right.

Jesus, as recorded in Matthew's Gospel, told his followers that he had not come to abolish the law but to fulfil it (Mt. 5:17–19). Yet was there ever a religious leader who criticised the religious establishment of his time as trenchantly as he did? The Gospels are full of vigorous denunciation by Jesus of the religious leaders of his people. In particular he denounced hypocrisy, the proclamation of one standard while living by another. And a second major element of his judgment on them was related to their harsh spirit of condemnation, their unwillingness to show compassion towards those who did not live up to their exacting standards. Jesus not only comforted the afflicted, but he afflicted the comfortable.

It is a healthy sign in any society when it is capable of self-criticism. It means that it has confidence in itself, and is able to stand back, have a look at itself, and be willing to change. If a society is no longer willing to change, it means that a process of ossification has begun. Whether motivated by pride or fear or whatever, it means that such a society is on its way to the grave. That is something which needs to be remembered by those in the church who regard any and every criticism as evidence of disloyalty. They should try to take on board the message that discomfiting truths are preferable to comforting half-truths.

Every model of the church needs to be assessed in the light of certain basic criteria, such as the following:

1. How does it relate to the life and teaching of Jesus as revealed in the Gospel?
2. What human needs does it attempt to serve? Do its structures, in

fact, help the achievement of its stated goals?

3. How does it relate to the signs of the times, to those diverse movements, attitudes, structures, etc. which arise from time to time, and which may contain in them a hint of the divine?

Examining a model in some greater detail may involve trying to answer such questions as these:

(a) What pattern of communication exists in this or that model? Is there provision for a ready interchange of information and ideas in all directions?

(b) What structures of authority and leadership are implicit in it? Are they shared, or only from the top down, or what?

(c) How does a given model cope with the challenge of change? Can it change itself if need be in a quasi-organic way?

(d) What kind of visual image would be used to represent it? Would it be, for example, an army marching into battle singing 'Onward, Christian soldiers', or the fortress on a hill hurling back the attackers, or a ship riding the waves, or a pilgrim people like the Israelites in the desert searching for the promised land.

Looking at the four models considered in this chapter, I can see that they have some basic characteristics in common. Their structures, their channels of leadership, authority, and communication are essentially of the top-down variety, without an adequate complementary element from the bottom up. And that is a major flaw.

At a still more serious level, I have the uneasy feeling that what we have done in these models is to make the church a substitute for the Holy Spirit. If I may coin a term, we have fallen into 'ecclesiolatry', the worship of the church. On a bookshelf near me as I write, I have about a metre or so of official church documentation from this century—and I have read it. A great deal of it consists of the church talking to itself about itself. There is not a lot in it about God, with the honourable exception of Pope John Paul II's three encyclical letters on God the Father, the Son, and the Holy Spirit.[6] There's something basically wrong with such a situation, like a compass that is off true north and therefore gives a wrong direction, skewing everything else.

There is also, in church documentation of recent years, a not-so-hidden agenda of power and control, the desire to limit, to restrict, to haul in the reins and keep them in the hands of those at the centre. There is no need to be afraid of the concept of power, or to think of it as somehow inherently unchristian. Power is a necessity; without it, the best ideas would never get beyond wishful thinking. What matters is the goal to which it is directed, and the manner in which it is exercised. Is the goal one of service or one of control? And is power exercised in dialogue or in dictation? To speak plainly, I am not too happy about the answers life gives me in answering those questions as they apply to the church.

Along with 'ecclesiolatry', we have also fallen into 'papolatry', the worship of the pope. I recall the pope's visit to Ireland in 1979. It generated a great wave of enthusiasm which sometimes carried away common sense. In one church, after the visit, a person with more zeal than intelligence placed a photo of the pope in front of the tabernacle containing the Blessed Sacrament. Fortunately, someone with sense removed it quickly. But it was illustrative of a mood which carries with it the risk of turning the Vicar of Christ into a substitute for Christ.

Why is it that we can accept, without difficulty, that popes are human, and therefore liable to imperfection—all, that is, except the incumbent, whom it is disloyal ever to treat or speak of as anything less than a paragon? When criticism from within is seen as letting the side down, or even siding with the 'enemies of the church', when dissent is put on a par with sabotage or a kind of fifth column, the result is timidity, sycophancy, deviousness, or, worst of all, playing games of political calculation with the truth. Have we made political correctness a substitute for truth?

Have we so centralised power, or, more accurately, allowed so much power to be centralised around the popes that, with every new holder of papal office, there is a lurch off in a new direction in keeping with the psychological, cultural and theological make-up of the incumbent? It seems to be so; but it is not good that it be so. It is possible and also desirable that we do things better.

2.6 POPE JOHN PAUL II

Pope John Paul II has exercised enormous influence in shaping the present life of the church, and it is impossible to understand that life without reference to his personality and policies. Some knowledge of his background is helpful.

He grew up in Wadowice, a small town in Poland, in the period between the two world wars. His father was an army officer; his mother died when he was still a child. An older brother died while studying medicine.

The church in which he grew up and became a priest was one which gave high priority to unity in the face of the threats posed first by six years of Nazi occupation and then by some forty years of communist rule. Discipline and uniformity in the face of the common enemy were seen as essential.

By 1978 when Pope Paul VI and then Pope John Paul I died, there was a shift to the right in the Western world. The liberal swinging sixties were a spent force, there were signs of social disintegration, and the 'Me generation' did not offer a viable way forward. Signs of this shift could be seen a little later in the choice of Margaret Thatcher as prime minister of Britain in 1979, and of Ronald Reagan as US president in 1980.

In the church, too, there was a similar shift of opinion. The latter years of the pontificate of Paul VI had been characterised by a sense of drift. In addition, some bishops were scared by the excesses which had taken place here and there after Vatican II— such as priests celebrating 'Masses' using cream crackers and coca-cola instead of bread and wine, with the idea of making the Mass 'relevant' to youth. Perhaps what happened when the cardinals gathered in conclave in 1978 was that they were worried, frightened men who muddled their way towards changing horses in mid-stream by opting for a strong figure who would give them the reassurance they sought, a firm hand on the tiller of the barque of Peter. They wanted a strong charismatic conservative who would lead the church back to the safe haven of the past, and they chose someone who would do that job. The cardinals' choice was one which reflected most of all their fear, but also their loss of faith in the vision of Vatican II, even though it was they, substantially, who had brought it about.

I believe it was the agenda of John Paul II when he became pope to bring about a return to orthodoxy seen in pre-Vatican II terms, even though such a return would borrow the language of Vatican II. An example of this is the encyclical letter *Veritatis Splendor* of 6 August 1993, which uses Aristotelian ethics as the methodological framework of the church's official moral teaching. (Perhaps this was because the pope's early training was as a philosopher rather than as a theologian.)

Underlying this move was a great element of fear: fear for the future of the church, since it appeared to some of its leaders that a sense of Catholic identity was being lost, and that the church was being invaded by the sexual revolution of the 1960s and 1970s. By contrast, the church from 1945 to the beginning of Vatican II in

1962 must have appeared to be safe, solid and secure. Prudence seemed to demand a return to the past. It seems that the newly-elected John Paul II, who almost certainly endorsed the views of his cardinals, set himself to this task by using the means he had already applied and seen applied by others in Poland, namely, to centralise authority, insist on uniformity and discipline, tolerate no dissent within the ranks, and confront the perceived challenge with a united front.

A key element in this process of centralisation of power in the Vatican were (and are) the nuncios. At the time of Vatican II diplomatic relations existed between the Vatican and some forty or fifty states. In the new climate of openness to the world created by Popes John XXIII and Paul VI, very many countries moved to establish such relations in the 1960s and 1970s. In each case a nuncio was appointed who then became the kingpin of an operation to control the episcopate by hiring and firing bishops. (How sad that the openness of John XXIII and Paul VI should be used in such a way!)

In regard to the appointment of bishops there has been a steady tightening of the screws of bureaucratic centralism. Processes of consultation have been severely eroded so that, by now, a common procedure is to present the local church with a *fait accompli*, the acceptance of which is then made a test of loyalty. Such a manner of proceeding severely strains the very loyalty on which it rests, and undermines respect.

Bishops themselves are experiencing a sense of being excluded from decision-making in the church. In some cases, far from being consulted, they are not so much as informed even after the event of decisions taken by the Vatican about their dioceses. For example, some bishops, on retirement at the age of seventy-five, or on transfer from another diocese, have not been consulted about possible successors. It is as if their opinions were not worth asking for. Or the reported case of the bishop who, while on holidays, discovered when listening to the radio that he had been transferred to another diocese.

Pope John Paul II has fought a battle to restore centralised control of the church. He has won it through force of personality, determination, hard work, and tough political management. He has led the mass media a merry dance, using his skill as an actor (he was an actor and playwright in his youth) to full advantage, projecting through them an image of gentle firmness. (But Pope Paul VI, a truly liberal man, was hanged, drawn and quartered by the media following his 1968 encyclical letter *Humanae Vitae*, and nothing he said or did subsequently received any credit from them!)

There is also clear evidence of a personality cult around John Paul II. His secretary of state, Cardinal Angelo Sodano, has forecast that John Paul II will pass into history as 'the Great', like Popes Leo I and Gregory I, the only two popes to be so honoured.[7] And if one looks at videos of the pope's pastoral visits, it is clear that he encourages the adulation of the crowd.

The pope has won a battle—but was it the right battle in the first place? I think it was the wrong one, and I will return to that later. Furthermore, consider the casualties. The bishops, as a body, are intimidated. If they have a vision for the church, they seem afraid to articulate it. They are caught in a squeeze between the rank and file (including the clergy) saying, 'Too little, too late', and the Vatican saying 'Too much, too soon'. They are paralysed into inertia, and seem not to have the leadership ability to break free of the squeeze. They cannot be helped by the knowledge that the manner in which they were chosen has often isolated them from the general body of believers.

In addition, many priests and members of religious orders are demoralised, their loyalty to the papacy stretched to the limit. Their silence does not mean acquiescence in the present course of the church; more often it is simply despair, the product of the feeling that there is no point in speaking because the Vatican 'listens' with cotton wool in its ears.

Among the lay men and women of the church there is a widespread sense of directionless drift. It is not simply that they *think* they are not being listened to; they *know* it. Appeals to them to stay with the church and change it from within ring hollow: at best, they are meaningless, because the power to make changes resides at the top, and there is no indication that those who hold that power have any intention of sharing it; at worst, they mock people by inviting them to undertake the role of Sisyphus, the legendary figure of Greek mythology sentenced by the gods to push a rock up a hill, only for it to slip from his grasp as he reached the summit and roll all the way down to the valley below.

The young, in more than a few countries, have simply left the church and gone elsewhere: drawn off by a popular culture without substance or content; or to the sects; or to simply abandoning formal links with any christian church, while, at the same time, often retaining a residual sense of loyalty to the christian faith itself in an undefined, inarticulate way, so that there is still a germ of hope.

At a wider level, the image of the church *vis-à-vis* the world has changed. In the years after Vatican II it was seen as being open to the world, ready to engage in dialogue with it, prepared to see the world as a potential partner for the sake of humanity. Now it is seen as having reverted to its true reactionary type, back in the trenches, slinging grenades over the top at its adversaries.

Within the church, trust has been replaced by fear, and dialogue by dictation. The path of the pilgrim church over the past twenty-five years or more is littered with the debris of shattered hopes and lost or even squandered opportunities. We have lost a sense of priorities to such an extent that Catholic identity, instead of being focused on love as Jesus taught (Jn. 13:35), centres instead on secondary issues like contraception.

The church at the end of the second millennium is more polarised, alienated and divided than it has been for a very long time, perhaps since the Reformation.

Where does one go from there? It should be obvious to all but those who refuse to see, or those too scared even to think, that radical change is necessary if the pilgrim church is to be lifted out of its slough of despond. The survival of the church is not in question; we have Christ's assurance on that (see Mt. 28:20). The question is rather whether the church is being faithful to the mission given to it by Christ. It cannot be faithful if it is not being true to itself. And it is not being true to itself where the pursuit of power for the sake of control remains the priority of its leadership. There is a world out there which needs the Gospel, but it does not hear or see it in the life of the church. Instead it sees a power struggle in which one side has won a (Pyrrhic) victory. It needs the Gospel, and it is offered a theology which sometimes is no more than a semantic instrument for the control of language, and therefore, of thought. The world also recognises that fear is the motive and fear is the method; and no souls are won by fear.

What about a new pope or a new council of the church? That approach is a *cul de sac*: to start at the level of pope or council is to start in the wrong place and from the wrong perspective. If the end in view is a renewed community, then renewal must start with the community, that is, with the grass roots. It is unrealistic to imagine that renewal from the bottom up can be led from the top down. To quote Gandhi again, 'The end must be prefigured in the means.' If lay people lead, as they are doing already in many respects, the clergy will follow eventually. If the clergy will not lead then the least they can do is to get out of the way and let the laity lead—an example being the present movements in Austria and Germany. Such movements offer more hope for renewal than do, for example, the synods of bishops. And yet the response of some Austrian and German bishops seems to be mainly a rearguard action, stalling and delaying, while aiming at a Kennan-like policy of containment. Small wonder that in Austria 28 per cent of Catholics in a recent poll said they saw the church as irreformable.[8]

2.7 THE KINGDOM OF GOD

The scriptural concept and symbol of the kingdom of God provides an alternative context for looking at the church, its nature and role. In the Old Testament, the kingdom of God denotes God's sovereign rule over all peoples through events, words, and people. It serves as a constant reminder to a self-centred humanity that, ultimately, it is God who is in control of past, present and future. Although the kingdom is a present reality which impinges on ordinary life, it cannot be limited to, or identified with, any earthly condition or institution. The people of Israel made the mistake of coming to think of the kingdom of Israel as the kingdom of God. It took their defeat, the destruction of the kingship, and the experience of exile in Babylon to open their minds to look at wider horizons.

The kingdom of God, also called the kingdom of heaven, is the central theme of Jesus' mission. He is the king, and he calls people to him through repentance and conversion (Mt. 4:17). It is presented as good news to outcasts, the poor and the alienated by offering them reconciliation. The signs that God's kingdom is present are that 'the blind receive their sight, the lame walk, lepers are cleansed, the deaf hear, the dead are raised, and the poor have good news brought to them.' (Mt. 11:4–6)

The kingdom is a reality which breaks down traditional distinctions between Jews and gentiles, insiders and outsiders. To the man who said to him that to love God with all your heart, with all your mind, and with all your strength, and to love your neighbour as yourself, is much more important than any offering or sacrifice, Jesus replied, 'You are not far from the kingdom of God'. (Mk. 12:33–4) Later on, Peter began to understand the full significance of this, saying, 'I truly understand that God shows no partiality, but in every nation anyone who fears him and does what is right is acceptable to him.' (Acts 10:34–5) The key conditions for entering the kingdom are submission to God and love of the poor (Mt. 25:31–46).

The parables of the kingdom in Matthew 13 present it as a dynamic rather than a static reality, one which has its fulfilment in heaven, and for which life on earth is no more than a step on the way. It is a present and future reality: present in Jesus (and in the Eucharist), and awaited in Christ's coming in glory at the end of time.

If the word 'kingdom' suggests power, pomp, and self-aggrandisement, the Gospels make it clear that such is not the way of Jesus. Before he even began his public ministry, Jesus experienced the temptation to use power and display as instruments of his work. His final answer to the tempter was to say, 'Away with you, Satan! for it is written, "Worship the Lord Your God, and serve only him."' (Mt. 4:1–10) And Jesus said of himself that 'The Son of Man came not to be served but to serve, and to give his life as a ransom for many.' (Mt. 20:28) And elsewhere the Bible says: 'by his bruises we are healed.' (Is. 53:5)—not 'by his power'. It was through suffering and dying that Jesus brought about the salvation of humanity.

How does this relate to the church? The kingdom and the church: what is their relationship? The church is a sign of God's kingdom; its mission is to point beyond itself to God. But to equate the church and the kingdom is to repeat the mistake of the people of Israel and to fall into the temptation that Jesus rejected in the desert.[9] It is a mistake that Jesus warned his followers against in the parable of the tenants who began to act like owners and set about taking over the vineyard as if it were their own (Mt. 21:33–46). A similar message is repeated in Mt. 23:9–10, where Jesus warns, '. . . you have one Father—the one in heaven . . . you have one instructor, the Messiah.' Matthew 23 has a message for scribes and pharisees of the present as well as the past. It calls the church, collectively as well as in individuals, to self-examination, especially on the temptation to possess, to control, to manage the kingdom of God.

The temptation to equate the church with the kingdom at the practical level, even if not in formal doctrinal statements, is a real one; to fall into it is to turn the Gospel on its head. 'In spite of the reverence in which the Apostles were held, early christian writings quote no sayings of or stories about them; Christ is the only authority and centre from whom all teaching is drawn.'[10]

It is worth noting a few facts and figures which should raise a question mark in the mind on this subject. The New Testament uses the phrase 'kingdom of God', or its equivalent the 'kingdom of heaven', more than one hundred and fifty times; of those, more than one hundred are in the Gospels. The term 'church' is used in the Gospels twice. By contrast, in the *Catechism of the Catholic Church*, the term 'church' runs to over two hundred lines of listings in the index, while the 'kingdom of God' merits only 11 lines.[11] When the central theme of Jesus' mission gets such scant treatment, while something which is meant to be a sign pointing to it receives such substantial treatment in a major work of church teaching such as the catechism, it points to something fundamentally wrong, if not in matters of orthodoxy, then in orthopraxis—something no less important. That the church is the kingdom of God is not taught, but it does seem to be thought, and that is a form of ecclesiolatry.

Where does this reflection lead? To begin with, we need to have less institution and more community, to be a little less Catholic and a little more catholic, and to introduce into the life of the people of God credible and effective structures of popular participation. We need the spirit and structures of democracy, as a complement to hierarchy, in the service of community.

Democracy in the church is an opportunity to be seized, not a danger to be warded off. That view is not shared by all. A Vatican document warned priests that what it calls 'democratism' (shades of 'Americanism' and 'modernism', perhaps?) is a grave temptation 'because it leads to a denial of the authority and capital grace of Christ and to destroy the nature of the church; it would be almost just a human society'.[12]

Perhaps we can learn from the Jews. For them, the focus of religious life is neither the synagogue nor the school, but the home. They start from the bottom up, and that sounds like a good idea. And they do not have theology; they tell stories—another good idea.

What matters most is to keep in mind the life and teaching of Jesus Christ who came that we may have life, and have it abundantly (Jn. 10:10).

3

DEMOCRACY IN THE SPIRIT
OF THE CHURCH

3.1 SHANGOMBO

Shangombo: it is not a household name, but it is a name which stands written in the book of life. It is a small settlement on the border between Angola and Zambia, beside the banks of the Mashi river. Most of the people who live there are Angolans who took refuge in Zambia from the war of independence against the Portuguese from 1962 to 1975, and from the civil war which followed.

Like most refugees, these people came into their new situation penniless. Their herds of cattle had to be left on the west bank of the river, their other possessions mostly abandoned in the rush to get away in dug-out canoes. Some never made it; crocodiles got them. Many have witnessed atrocities committed by Portuguese forces in the name of defending christian civilisation against communism, and have seen or experienced more atrocities in the civil war which followed from 1975 to 1994.

One possession they did not leave behind them was their faith. They received it through the Portuguese Benedictines at the mission of Santa Cruz in the town of Rivungu, now abandoned for about twenty years. They gathered for prayer and religious instruction. The nearest mission was about 175 km away, on the Zambezi river, at Sioma. The refugees, Kwamashi and Mbukushu by tribe, sent a delegation to the parish priest there and asked him for help in building a church. He shared the work with them and in 1974 the church, dedicated to Saint Anthony of Padua, was opened.

For the refugees the completion of the church was not a signal to rest on their laurels; it was a starting-point for greater efforts. A priest could visit them only three or four times a year because of road conditions, so the people had to become self-reliant. They chose a church council, appointed people to various tasks, and got to work. For example, some led a prayer service on Sundays; some prepared adults or children for the sacraments. Perhaps most importantly of all, others went out to the villages in the surrounding areas and began to spread there the Gospel of Jesus Christ.

One lasting memory I have of a visit to that area in 1978 was of an elderly voluntary catechist, Nicolao Chabiye, taking the parish priest to task for admitting to baptism people who were not properly prepared. He was one of those proven men, those *viri probati*, who had enabled the christian community to grow from one church in 1974 to four in 1978.

And then, it seemed, things began to go wrong. The South African army and air force, at that time engaged in a guerrilla war against SWAPO (who wanted independence for Namibia), began to strafe the roads, to bomb vehicles they found on them, and to lay land-mines. They helicoptered troops into an area south of Shangombo and set up camp, carrying out raids on villages and destroying canoes so that guerrillas could not cross the rivers. The people advised the priest not to come to them because of the danger, and so they remained without a priest for about four years.

But the Holy Spirit had been at work. When I returned to visit the area in 1982, the number of churches had grown to twenty-one. In each case, a church council had been chosen by the people, and the work of instruction in the faith had begun. In some cases even the leaders themselves were catechumens preparing for baptism. Few of them were literate, and the few books available to them were almost all in languages other than their own, making it necessary to translate the text as they used it.

All of this was the work of grace and the also the work of human hands. The churches were built by hand—literally. There are few shovels and no block moulds in the villages, much less cement mixers, or even cement. Walls were built of mud dried in the sun and smoothed out to form an even surface on a framework of wattles. The water for this was carried by women and children by the bucketful on their heads from a stream or well which could be up to 1km away. Then the roof was built of grass, long shoots of 2 or even 3 metres, tied to laths with strips of cattle hide, or the inner bark of trees.

None of this is to pretend that they were all perfect christians; they weren't. They have problems stemming from their culture, such as polygamy and divorce. Sometimes there is friction between the different tribes, or between the refugees and the settled people. And the fear engendered by witchcraft runs like a raw nerve through their lives. And yet, through it all, there is growth. The power of God is there.

Shangombo brings back many memories and emotions. I remember a small girl offering to share her supper with me—a rat; the bushman who gave me his hut to sleep in for the night and the bed was so short that my legs from the knees down dangled out over the end, even when I lay diagonally across it; the magnificent sunset looking across to Santa Cruz; the choir-master who led the congregation through a Latin Mass, using a dog-eared, coverless *Liber Usualis*, probably left by the Benedictines; the night the people put on a dance for me, that pitch black night when the only brightness seemed to be the reflection of firelight on eyes and teeth, until a messenger from the twentieth century, a satellite, cut an arc across the sky; the violence of a sand-storm so enveloping that even the lights of a vehicle could not penetrate it; the faith of men who spent five days walking 200 km or so to go to a course to improve their Sunday services.

Shangombo, whatever its name means, is surely a place of blessing.

3.2 WHAT IS DEMOCRACY?
In the closing months of the second world war, the French philosopher, Jacques Maritain, wrote that democracy has four characteristics which are essential to it. It should be:

1. personalistic: it should respect the rights of individuals because of the inviolability of the human person;
2. communal: the public or common good should be its aim;
3. pluralistic: it should respect and foster lesser societies;
4. theistic: it should be based on belief in God, a belief permeating the lives of its citizens.[1]

Maritain, of course, was writing of civil society; it was not the church that he had in mind. But could those ideals not be applicable to the church also—to its benefit?

It was another Frenchman, Pierre Mendes-France, who wrote that there is no democracy without democrats.[2] The truth of that observation is illustrated daily in several of the countries of the former Soviet Union where people have set up democratic structures such as a constitution, elections, a parliament, and so forth, but are experiencing great difficulty in making them work because of the absence of a democratic tradition. Their culture has been substantially unaffected by elements such as the Protestant Reformation, the Enlightenment, and the French Revolution. The absence of the positive features of those movements is a major *lacuna* in the formation among those peoples of the spirit of democracy.

At the practical level there is constant interaction between the spirit and the structures of democracy, and one will not last long without the other. It is worthwhile examining some of the basic components of a democratic system to see what spirit might imbue it so as to enable people to be full, conscious, and active participants in decision-making processes, thereby realising their full humanity in community.

3.3 THE FREE EXCHANGE OF INFORMATION AND IDEAS

'In the beginning was the Word, and the Word was with God, and the Word was God.' (Jn. 1:1). Jesus Christ is the Word of God; he is God's communication of himself to humanity. God takes the initiative in communication, and what he communicates is not an ideology or a system, but himself. Jesus did not say 'I teach the truth,' but 'I am the truth' (See Jn. 14:6). Knowledge that really communicates must be personal, and it communicates most effectively to the extent that it is personal. There was a truth in the older biblical translations in English which, when writing of sexual relations, said that a husband and wife 'knew each other'; they communicated at the most intense personal level.

In contrast to this, scientific knowledge is today presented as being at its best when it is detached and impersonal; only then will its claim to be objective be taken seriously. For a scientist to be personally involved is a big *no-no*. Maybe that is why some scientists profess to have no qualms about their involvement in the development, say, of new weapons. They say it is the right of the scientist to develop new technology, while the responsibility for deciding whether or how to use it rests with society. This separation of know-how from know-why is, it seems to me, an abdication of the human challenge to exercise freedom responsibly. Rights and responsibility are reciprocal.

On a different note, it should be recognised that science itself begins with an act of faith. More accurately, it begins with two acts of faith: firstly, an act of faith in the intelligibility of the universe, with the belief that the world out there makes sense, and that, therefore, it is not nonsensical to begin to examine it, or to presuppose that scientific enquiry is not a meaningless pursuit of irrationality; and secondly, science begins with an act of faith in the validity of human reasoning. One cannot use reason to prove reason. It is something that one takes as given to begin with.

It is not only the empirical scientists who find themselves caught in thorny dilemmas. Social scientists and those involved in the humanities have similar experiences. A writer, for instance, who draws on personal experience either to illustrate or to prove a point may be accused of generalising from subjective anecdotal evidence. But if he does not draw on such experience he may be accused of dealing with abstractions unrelated to human existence.

All human communication is limited and ambiguous. To take one example: banter is quite frequently a way of evading communication, it is a safe way of keeping people at a distance. But communication is at the heart of any human community. The similarity between the words 'communication' and 'community' is no coincidence; there is common ground, commonality, *communio*, between them. In short, there is no community without communication; and communication, of its very nature, is a two-way process.

The above is intended to make the point that it could benefit humanity to re-examine what we mean by knowledge and by communication, and to try, for example, to break out of the narrow confines of the analytical strait-jacket woven by Aristotle, Aquinas, and Francis Bacon, among others. This recalls again Jesus communicating himself: 'I do not call you servants any longer, because the servant does not know what the master is doing; but I have called you friends, because I have made known to you everything that I have heard from my Father.' (Jn. 15:15) Jesus is the message and the messenger.

The exchange of information
Consider the following quotations:

> 'If public opinion is to be properly formed, it is necessary that, right from the start, the public be given free access to both the sources and the channels of information and be allowed freely to express its own views.'

> 'Modern man cannot do without information that is full,

consistent, accurate and true.'

'When . . . authorities are unwilling to give information, or are unable to do so, then rumour is unloosed, and rumour is not a bearer of truth, but carries dangerous half-truths. Secrecy should therefore be restricted to matters that involve the good name of individuals, or that touch upon the rights of people, either singly or collectively.'

'[We] . . . are bound in duty to give complete and entirely accurate information to the news agencies so that they, in turn, can carry out their task.'[3]

Who made those wonderful statements, one might ask? Who has thus expressed commitment to freedom of information, access to sources, facilitating news agencies, and so forth? Was it the Civil Liberties Union? No, it wasn't—all of them come from a Vatican document. Readers will be able to judge for themselves how well the Vatican lives up to them.

The church has missed out on an opportunity by the ambivalent (at best) attitude of its leaders to the mass media. If the 1970s were the decade which measured influence in barrels of oil, the 1990s are the decade which measures it in bytes of information. But that opportunity is being lost, even squandered. Church leaders' attitudes towards the media are characterised by mistrust, and mistrust begets mistrust. The lack of openness towards the media is a by-product of suspicion, of a siege mentality, of seeing the world as them-versus-us. Evidence of this is to be seen in the low level of credibility enjoyed by the Catholic press, even among Catholics, who commonly see it as tame and toothless, clerical and ecclesiastical rather than christian, and living in a ghetto rather than going out to the world. 'Bad' reporting of church affairs is sometimes the product of simple laziness, either on the part of journalists or of church officials, but more often the result of mistrust growing out of the suspicion that church officials when they deal with the media give them truths, half-truths, and 'doctored' information all together in one package.

Journalists also have a point when they say that the church comes to them when it wants publicity, but when they go to the church for information, all they get is a 'no comment'. While the technology of information transfer is expanding exponentially, the level of human communication between the church and the world, and also within the church itself, seems paralysed by a mood of reaction. This sometimes applies even at the simple level of an exchange of information.

Reaction differs from conservatism, which may be a well-reasoned choice, carefully thought out; it is rather a reflex conditioned by fear—the fear, above all, of losing control (because information gives control), and also the fear of trusting people. Church leaders are afraid to trust ordinary church members, including priests. It is as if they are saying, 'We must keep a tight hold on the reins; give them an inch and they'll take a mile; then God alone knows where they'll end up.' But that is the reaction of a tired and frightened power structure, where the institution, in its own estimation, has become more important than the message which it is its stated goal to proclaim.

The experience of a journalist acquaintance of mine covering the 1994 synod of bishops on Africa illustrates these points. He found bishops open and easy to talk to, willing to express their opinions as long as they were assured it was off the record. But once asked if they could be quoted, they either closed up altogether or else adopted an 'official' stance and gave the party line.[4] His impression was that they were afraid of official disapproval of some of their opinions. What kind of *communio* does that fear speak of? And what kind of *progressio* can be expected in a church where bishops look over their shoulders to the Vatican in self-censorship before they speak?

Change in this area is both possible and desirable. If the church had the courage to implement its own policy, as expressed in the above quotations from *Communio et Progressio* it would be a stronger, more credible, more united and more creative community than it is. It would see opportunities where, at present, its leaders seem to see little but danger. It would be closer in spirit to the octogenarian friar who said to me when I was a novice, 'The man who never made a mistake never made anything.'

The exchange of ideas

'Catholics should be fully aware of the real freedom to speak their minds which stems from a "feeling for the faith" and from love.'[5] Late in 1994 the Vatican insisted that the Gregorian University in Rome withdraw the invitation it had issued to the Peruvian theologian Gustavo Gutierrez to address it.[6] And the American theologian Rosemary Ruether has had similar experiences. It is reminiscent of Humpty Dumpty in *Alice through the Looking-Glass*, where he said, 'When I use a word it means just what I choose it to mean—neither more nor less.'

What does the Vatican mean by the freedom to speak one's mind? Is its newspaper, *L'Osservatore Romano*, an example of such freedom in action? It has no discussion or debate, no opinion columns, no letters to the editor, and no editorial. Compared to it, pre-glasnost *Pravda* was a bubbling pot of intellectual ferment. If there was a prize for the world's dullest propaganda sheet, *L'Osservatore Romano* would win it—annually. People buy it, probably out of a sense of loyalty, but if the number of unopened copies still sealed in their plastic wrappers that I see in convents and priests' houses is any indication, its readers are few indeed. Even a letter from the nuncio to priests telling them they could pay for it with Mass stipends failed to win back any lost readers. However, all is not lost—it does have one redeeming feature: the old men in the villages near the mission in Malengwa where I live, swear by it—they say it is great for rolling tobacco in!

And what of Vatican Radio? As a missionary living in a rural area of Southern Africa, I know missionaries who listen on short wave radio to the BBC, Voice of America, Radio France International, Deutsche Welle, Channel Africa and both local and national radio stations. I do not know even one who listens to Vatican Radio, although every religious house is sent a programme schedule. The problem is not a technical one about audibility; it is a human one about credibility.

This problem is symptomatic of something much wider and deeper than merely Vatican Radio's difficulty in retaining listeners. Communication is a two-way process, and if people are not listened to they stop listening. There is a widespread perception in the church that the Vatican does not listen to people, is not interested in listening to them, has isolated itself behind a wall of indifference to public opinion in the church, and makes its decisions regardless of the rank and file. And so people stop listening to it, not as an act of defiance or retaliation, but simply because that is the way human communication works. If you want to be listened to, you must learn to listen.

There is another no less important factor at work also. The intellectual climate in the church at present is characterised by fear.[7] People are often afraid to say what they think, though that does not stop them from thinking. There is a renewal of censorship in the church and that is both a source and a sign of fear. It is at once both cause and effect.

But the cost of censorship must be counted. It calls into question the integrity of dialogue within the church, and between the church and the world, creating the suspicion that participants in the dialogue may, perhaps, not be speaking their minds but simply toeing the party line out of fear. Censorship undermines the credibility of the church's calls for respect for human rights. It rewards opportunists, careerists, flatterers, and hacks.

More than any of these pragmatic considerations, does censorship not betray a lack of confidence on the part of the church's leadership in the mission, the message, and the methods of the Gospel? More importantly still, is it not simply wrong, that is morally wrong, to prevent people from speaking their minds, or to penalise them if they do so? Does censorship not constitute an attempt to 'coerce the spirit', which Pope John Paul II condemned in his encyclical letter *Veritatis Splendor* as one of those acts which '*per se*, and in themselves, independently of circumstances, are always seriously wrong . . .'?[8] And another question worth asking is this: what master does censorship serve?—truth or power?

For those who may be tempted to shrug off considerations of principle as one of those luxuries which only naive and high-minded idealists can afford, there remain some pragmatic questions. Is censorship effective? Does it work? In the age of the telephone, the fax, the photo-copier, the floppy disc, the Internet, the laser beam and fibre optics, can a muzzle still silence people? People can use pseudonyms, as Pope John Paul II did in his youth in communist Poland; they can publish in theological *samizdat*. Does the external conformity produced by censorship face problems, or does it merely ignore or suppress them, so that they remain like a land-mine, ready to explode at any time? And who censors the censors? Have they a hot line to wisdom or are they fallible human beings like everyone else? Job's retort to his well-meaning but officious counsellors comes to mind: 'No doubt you are the people, and wisdom will die with you.' (Job 12:2) It is worth remembering that the censors who worked for Czar Nicholas II banned Adam Smith's *The Wealth of Nations*, but allowed through Karl Marx's *Das Kapital!*

The alternative to censorship is not license but responsibility. A communicator, of whatever sort, has a human responsibility to truth and to people's rights and sensitivities. In a church whose teaching is based on revelation, bishops have a responsibility to see to it that such revelation is not distorted or misrepresented. When the bishops of the church believe that a particular teaching or set of ideas is contrary to the christian faith, they have a right, and perhaps a duty, to say so. But it is quite a different matter to go a step further and start issuing bans, dismissals, and so forth. It would be a measure of real *communio* and real *progressio* in the church if its leaders could accept calmly and without anxiety that the best answer to bad theology is good theology, not a ban on the theologian.

In this matter, as in others, there may be something to be learned from our older brothers and sisters in revelation, the Jews. In the United States and in Israel, Jewish intellectual, cultural, and religious life operate under different conditions. The United States are pluralistic, there is no state religion, and no censorship of ideas. In Israel, by contrast, the state is officially Jewish, and orthodox Judaism, in particular, receives substantial state patronage. Religious political parties exercise powerful lobbying in parliament and frequently hold the balance of power, a balance which they use without hesitation to advance their sectional interests. Not to be a Jew puts one at a disadvantage in Israel. A comparison of the two societies brings out the differing consequences which flow from the varying conditions that prevail: Jewish life flourishes in the USA, while in Israel it is stagnant and divided. Freedom provides the catalyst for vitality, while its absence leads to a slow strangulation of the mind.

May the day soon come when the church's leaders will have the courage and the vision to do away with repression; when people will no longer, out of fear, stifle their creativity by self-censorship; when theological diversity within the framework of a common commitment to the one faith will be welcomed as a blessing.

3.4 DEALING WITH DISSENT: DIALOGUE OR DICTATION?

The Christian faith is based on a revelation. Unlike a philosophy, it is not simply a creation of the human mind. How does the question of dissent fit into this context, and the question of free exchange of information and, especially, of ideas?

It is worth looking for a while at an official church document to see how it deals with the question of dissent. In 1990, the Congregation for the Doctrine of the Faith, the Vatican's guardian of orthodoxy, produced the document *Donum Veritatis*, which dealt with this point among others. It describes dissent (in n.32) as 'public opposition to the magisterium of the church', the word *magisterium* being understood to mean the teaching authority of the church considered as residing in the pope and bishops. It goes on to describe such dissent as a 'temptation' and 'infidelity to the Holy Spirit' (n.40).

It rejects the idea that conscience can justify dissent: 'Argumentation appealing to the obligation to follow one's conscience cannot legitimate dissent' (n.38), and 'the freedom of the act of faith cannot justify a right to dissent' (n.36).

When difficulties arise, theologians may ask questions regarding 'the timeliness, the form, or even the content of magisterial interventions' (n.24). Such questions should be addressed to the responsible authority (presumably the Congregation) and not to public opinion (n.30).

The document acknowledges its own limitations: 'When it comes to the question of interventions in the prudential order, it could happen that some Magisterial documents might not be free from all deficiencies' (n.24). In regard to questions not in the prudential order there is a different standard: 'The willingness to submit loyally to the teaching of the Magisterium on matters *per se* not irreformable must be the rule' (n.24).

It also asserts that 'documents issued by this Congregation expressly approved by the Pope participate in the ordinary magisterium of the successor of Peter' (n.18).

Such a view of dissent does not meet with universal approval within the church. Nor is the question a merely academic one. While I have been writing this section of the book, a bishop has been dismissed from a diocese in France, a theologian from a seminary faculty, and two priests from the editorship of magazines in Africa and Europe.

Dissenters are difficult people. They refuse to shut up and toe the party line. They are a pain to those in authority. Like pain, they draw attention to a problem which needs to be taken account of. They are a warning signal, alerting against complacency or self-satisfaction. They cause alarm to those in the church who are fretful, anxious and harried about its future, who feel that without tight control from the centre things will get out of hand and end up God knows where. They are offensive to those with tidy minds who want no loose strings anywhere, but want all opinions to be bound together firmly in a single tapestry.

I am reminded of the story of Procrustes, the mythological innkeeper who had a passion for neatness and order in his one-bed inn. If a guest was too short for the bed he stretched him on a rack until he conformed exactly to the dimensions of the bed; if he was too tall, he chopped off whatever portion of his feet was necessary to bring him into line. Sometimes, to his dismay, he found the guest dead in bed in the morning, never thinking for a moment that his stretching and trimming of the night before might have had anything to do with it. 'But never mind', he thought, 'we live in an imperfect world, and a little loss here and there can't be set against the perfect tidiness of the bed with its perfectly fitting guest.'

An alternative view sees dissenters as an asset to a community, as those necessary nuisances who challenge, stimulate, question, and object, thereby broadening and deepening discussion, and making a community's perception of a problem more comprehensive. This, in turn, makes it possible to develop a broader base of support for dealing with a problem.

The capacity to live with dissent is a sign of strength in a community. To accept differences and respond to them creatively is an increasingly pressing need in a world sometimes savagely at war with itself whether in Bosnia, Somalia, Rwanda or elsewhere. We live in a pluralistic world, and it is an ever more urgent requirement of humanity that people learn to respect and accept each other despite differences, even basic ones.

Dissent is, in the first place, an affirmation of a truth, and 'all truth, by whomsoever it is spoken, is of the Holy Spirit.'[9] Dissent is a necessity for the development of doctrine and of life. Where there is no dissent, wrongs can be perpetuated indefinitely until they acquire the status of unchallengeable truth. History provides many such examples.

Take, for instance, the case of slavery. For centuries it was accepted as part of the natural order of things, an institution which had existed in every society and in every age, and which therefore seemed as much a part of 'nature' as the law of gravity itself. The church's efforts were directed, not to its abolition, which was regarded as too radical, too likely to rock the boat, possibly subversive, but rather to alleviating its worst excesses, thereby making it less unpalatable. Even Peter Claver, the 'saint of the slave trade', did not question the institution itself; he accepted it as part of life. Where were the christian dissenters in those days? Why was there no one to raise a voice and tackle the question at its roots, and say that slavery itself was simply wrong, quite apart from individual cases of excess here and there? Why was it that such an evil practice persisted in the life of the christian people, and with the church's active support and complicity, for so long?

Before the civil war in the United States, presbyteries and

religious houses in the south owned slaves; they traded, bought and sold them like their planter neighbours. Why was it that the challenge to slavery came from technological change, with the invention of machinery that could pick cotton more efficiently than the human hand, rather than from the christian conscience? In the Protestant tradition, with its greater tolerance of dissent, there was the voice of William Wilberforce who succeeded in bringing about the abolition of slavery in the British Empire in 1833. But where was the Catholic Wilberforce with the imagination, the vision and the courage to take the flak? In the matter of the abolition of slavery the Catholic church did not lead; it followed at a distance, slowly, 'prudently', where others had taken the risks and led the way. The final parting of the ways between the church and slavery came only with a decree of Pope Leo XIII in 1881.

But perhaps I am being unfair. Maybe there were Catholics who thought slavery was wrong and tried to act against it. But what happened to them? Were they silenced by those in authority? Where were the moral leaders of the church who were prepared to challenge the *status quo*? Why were they silent, or silenced? Was it fear that held them back? Fear of what? Of change? Of loss of power? Of taking a risk? Was it lack of faith in the presence of God in the church, as if its security depended on unyielding resistance to everything new? 'Perfect love casts out fear' says Saint John in his first letter (Jn. 4:18). Where was the love that showed itself in dissent on the issue of slavery? If we believe that the Holy Spirit not only *was* in the church but *is* in it, why is there so much fear in the church?—fear on the part of those who hold power that they will lose it if they slacken their grip on the reins, and fear among the rank and file of saying what they believe to be true without the crippling restraint of self-censorship?

There are pragmatic considerations also. If the church argues for pluralism, as for instance in claiming state aid for Catholic schools, why is it then so reluctant to admit the principle of pluralism in its internal life? Running with the hare while hunting with the hounds on matters of right and wrong is not the way of the Gospel. Rather the way of the Gospel is to recognise that authority in the church is the servant, not the master or the owner of truth. Christian authority is the power to serve, not to dominate. And if church authority is sacred, then its abuse is sacrilegious. A teaching church must also be a learning church, since both teaching and learning have their roots in discipleship.

How would Jesus of Nazareth look on the question of dissent? He himself can be considered the first and foremost of all religious dissenters. Was there ever a religious leader who criticised the religious establishment of his day so severely, even savagely? When he called them 'blind guides' 'hypocrites', (Mt. 23:13–33) and so forth he was using language of a kind which makes modern critics of the church seem toothless by comparison. And yet church leadership today appears to have become so thin-skinned that the smallest whisper of criticism or dissent evokes pained protests about disloyalty and infidelity.

Jesus targeted his criticism with great accuracy. He made it clear what he was not attacking—he said specifically that he had not come to abolish the law but to fulfil it (Mt. 5:17–19). Nor did he challenge the authority of the scribes and pharisees to teach. (Mt. 23:1–3)

He challenged the religious leadership of his time when they did not practise what they preached (Mt. 23:2–3); when they had deviated from teaching which came from God, as when he said to them, 'You have heard that it was said . . . but I say to you . . .' (Mt. 5:21–48); for putting the institution, the 'system' above the person (Mk. 2:27); and, perhaps most of all, he challenged them about their abuse of power. This is one of the recurring themes of his preaching. He made it clear that when power becomes self-serving rather than other-serving, when it dominates rather than enables, when it becomes an end in itself rather than a means to a higher end, then it has lost its bearings and corrupted its purpose. Jesus denounced such abuse of power in some of the most vigorous condemnations in religious writing.

How did the religious establishment of his day react? Were there some who said, in effect, 'Maybe this man has a point. Perhaps he's right. Let's take stock of ourselves and see if there's some truth in what he's saying.' Maybe there were such, but if there were the Gospels say nothing about them, except perhaps for Nicodemus the Pharisee, who was so frightened that he would come to see Jesus only by night (Jn. 3:1–2).

Overwhelmingly the reaction of the religious establishment was to seek to trap him, whether by devious questions, or by deliberate misrepresentation of his position, for example, in Mt. 22:15–33. They showed that they didn't mind losing the truth as long as they were not seen to lose an argument; they lost both. What was at stake for them was power, and to preserve what they perceived as their power base they were prepared to go to any length. The high priest

Caiaphas summarised it perfectly: '. . . it is better for you to have one man die for the people than to have the whole nation destroyed' (Jn. 11:49–50). The individual was to be sacrificed for the sake of the perceived interest of the institution, and the message was to be similarly sacrificed even though it was for its promotion that the institution was meant to exist. Ends became means, and means became ends.

The establishment got its way. They held a show trial; Jesus was found guilty on a trumped-up charge of wanting to be king, though they knew he had often specifically rejected the efforts of his followers to make him one (Lk. 23:1–3; Jn. 6:15). And he was crucified with the charge nailed to the cross, 'Jesus of Nazareth, King of the Jews'. They could have added the sub-title, 'Dissenters, take note.'

So where do we go in the church of today, as we become aware of the (probably inevitable) tensions between the leadership and the rank and file? To begin with, it can be said that tension can be either creative or destructive, depending on how people respond to it. It seems that, as things stand now, a great deal of the tension in the church is, in fact, destructive—though it need not be. Many people are leaving the church over this issue because they have come to read the choice facing them in terms of an either-or situation. They see it as God or the church, or perhaps the Gospel or the church. And this is a tragic situation: with the result that many who reject the church because they see it as an oppressive power structure go on to reject or to abandon what the church is meant to stand for, namely, Christ and the Gospel. Of those who drop away quietly from the church while still retaining faith in Christ and the Gospel, how many will still have that faith in five or ten years' time, without the support of a community of faith? Not many.

The most pressing need in the church at present is for the restoration of the spirit and practice of dialogue. It does not exist at present; instead there are many monologues at all levels. Everyone is talking and no one is listening. Here are two examples:

a) The document *Donum Veritatis* asks for dialogue, but does so in terms which make dialogue impossible. The tone of that document recalls the old saying '*Roma locuta est, causa finita est*' (Rome has spoken, the matter is closed). You cannot dialogue with someone who thinks he already has the answers, and whose attitude is that if you want to know what is right all you have to do is ask him. Besides, I tried it. About twenty years ago, I had a disagreement with some of my confreres on the application of the encyclical letter *Humane Vitae* which dealt, among other things, with the question of birth control. I had argued that a woman who had been advised by her doctor to avoid further pregnancies because of a heart condition could legitimately use a contraceptive within the terms of n.15 of that document which deals with the use of contraceptives for therapeutic purposes. They disagreed and suggested that I take the matter higher. I wrote to the Congregation for the Doctrine of the Faith; there was no reply.

b) In 1993, the priests' deanery of which I was then chairman unanimously expressed the wish that the upcoming synod of bishops on Africa consider the introduction of a married clergy working with a celibate clergy. I have heard nothing further about it since then, but I have very little doubt that the request was sent by the shortest possible route into someone's wastepaper basket.

Church leaders are highly sensitive to any criticism of the church by priests which appear in the mass media, and usually respond by asking why the issue was not brought up in the church's own internal channels. One could legitimately respond by asking, 'What channels are there that work?' When there is a scandal we cover up instead of cleaning up. When there is a controversy or a difficult issue that needs discussion, we do not face it; we fudge it, smothering it with piosities and platitudes. If issues are brought up at church meetings, as often as not the response will be on the lines of 'This is neither the time nor the place . . .' If an attempt is made to discuss them in church journals, either the editor will not print them, or if he does he risks dismissal. So what options are left? One can either allow important issues to lie dormant by doing nothing about them, or else take them to the mass media who will, at least, give them an airing. If church officials don't like that, they can blame themselves for it.

In dealing with tension in the church there is the way of denial. One can suppress information and discussion, tell half-truths and outright lies, one can censor, ban, prohibit, or threaten. One can launch witch-hunts, though I know from having lived in Africa that the real enemies of the community are not the alleged 'witches' but the diviners, the witch-hunters who pose as the deliverers of the community from harm. It is they who divide people from one another while posing as the benefactors of society. Witch-hunting is the way of dictatorship, it is one of the hallmarks of dictatorship, and it is a denial of the spirit of Christ. The way of suppression is the way of a power-structure that has become blind to its stated goals and drunk with power for its own sake. It is also a prelude to the downfall of that structure, as the recent history of the Soviet Union and one-party states illustrates.

As an alternative, there is the way of Christ. Consider the incident recorded in Mt. 16:21–3. Jesus had told his disciples that he would have to suffer and would be put to death. Peter, with his love for the ways of power, protested vigorously, perhaps because he had expected from Jesus a display of power which would dramatically rout all opposition. Jesus' answer must have shocked him: 'Get behind me, Satan! . . . you are setting your mind not on divine things but on human things.' For Jesus, the assertion of triumphalistic power was the antithesis of what he was about. For his part, Peter seems to have learned nothing from the incident; at the time of Jesus' arrest he wanted to defend him with a sword. (Jn. 18:10–11)

The lesson for the church today is that we must once and for all put behind us bans, dismissals and witch-hunting as servants of orthodoxy. Along with them should go the slave mentality and the slippery semantics which seek to justify them. They belittle, demean, degrade and humiliate the church; they are unworthy of it. In the same clean sweep should go that combination of cunning, calculation, cowardice, cop-out and cynicism that so often passes for prudence in the church.

The way forward is the way of dialogue. It was outlined with great clarity by Pope Paul VI in his first encyclical letter, *Ecclesiam Suam*, published in 1964. Two short quotations will serve as indicators of its general trend, though they by no means do justice to the full text. 'Our dialogue should be as universal as we can make it. That is to say, it must be catholic, made relevant to everyone, excluding only those who utterly reject it or only pretend to be willing to accept it.'[10] And dialogue 'is demanded by the pluralism of society, and by the maturity man has reached in this day and age. Be he religious or not, his secular education has enabled him to think and speak, and conduct a dialogue with dignity.'[11] Those statements, and, even more, the spirit they express, come like a breath of fresh air; above all, they express hope and confidence in humanity. They will be remembered long after the hand-wringing anxiety of frightened church bureaucrats is forgotten.

3.5 POWER AND THE PEOPLE

Lest old Aquinas be forgot: 'Two points should be observed concerning the healthy constitution of a state or nation. One is that all should play a responsible part in governing; this ensures peace, and the arrangement is liked and maintained by all.'[12] And what of the healthy constitution of the church?

The Catholic church in the western part of Zambia began in the 1930s, almost exclusively in rural areas, because of the policies of the then colonial administration. I spent some years as parish priest of a mission which provided a fairly typical example of standard missionary practice.

The focus of the mission's efforts was on schools. The mission built and maintained some twenty schools in a parish of about 15,000 sq.km.[13] On the mission itself there was a large boarding school for primary school boys and girls. A boarding system had to be used as otherwise many children, living in small villages scattered over a wide area, would never have had the chance of attending school at all. The fees for boarding were ten shillings a year for boys, and eight for girls. The lower fee for girls was part of a determined effort to persuade parents to allow their daughters to go to school. It succeeded in the long term, but only with a lot of effort and many setbacks. The children, who were mostly in the seven to sixteen years age bracket or thereabouts learned the three Rs, or perhaps one should say the four: reading, writing, arithmetic and religion. They also learned technical skills, the girls being taught domestic science, basket-making and leather-work, while the boys learned carpentry and block-making.

Later on a hospital was built. It concentrated a lot of effort on maternity care, and also on immunisation and under-five work. In addition, there was a small hospital and village for lepers. These institutions were looked after by sisters who also cared for children in an orphanage, taught in the school, looked after the boarders, helped women in the villages with various programmes, and ran a domestic science school.

The mission had an electricity system and the only motorised transport in the area. It built a canal to carry water to a hydraulic ram which supplied all the institutions. The canal was built without technical assistance or specialised equipment such as a theodolite, and it took three attempts to get it right, each attempt involving about 1.5 km of digging. The priests and brothers worked together with local men on all construction projects, including the clearing of new roads and some bridge-building.

In addition, the mission provided the postal service, the bank, a credit union, the guest-house, a repair shop, and the only significant source of local employment.

Looking back on it, you wonder how they did it all. There were never more than seven or eight sisters at a time, and three or four priests and brothers. They were highly motivated, being driven by the desire to bring people into the life of the church and thereby lead them to salvation.

Symbolic of this commitment was the church building, which occupied the central place among mission institutions. It was central both in its physical location and in its spiritual significance. It represented both the symbol and the source of people's commitment to God.

What was it all for? The missionaries of the time would have explained it in different ways: the establishment of the church; winning souls for Christ; bringing pagans to conversion; building christian community; saving souls; and so on.

Why did they do it the way they did it? Perhaps they would have said they were building a new Christendom in Africa, albeit on a tiny scale. They would have said that it was unrealistic to expect people, individually converted to christianity, to be able to remain faithful without the support of a strong community life. The missionaries were creating an alternative Catholic society, one which was different from and also apart from the local traditional society. It did, in fact, constitute a strong support base for new christians to grow in faith.

How successful was it? It implanted the church in African life. It set it on its foundations and enabled it to grow. In addition, it promoted human advancement hand in hand with the spread of the Gospel; the two went together. It contributed significantly to the enhancement of the status of women, and set up systems of education and health care where none had existed before. It also began and carried on the task of training local people to take over all these responsibilities.

What were its weaknesses and failures? It is difficult to give definite, clear-cut answers to such a question. How does one measure spiritual growth? How is conversion measured? The Gospel says, 'By their fruits you shall know them.' If that test is applied, then there appear to be severe limitations on 'success' anywhere. For example, in Zambia:

1. The impact of christian faith on marriage and family life would appear to be small, if the divorce rate, polygamy, and the scarcity of sacramental marriages are considered.

2. There is little tradition of passing on the faith in the home.

3. There appears to be little individual prayer, though there is group prayer, and also Bible reading.

4. Society, despite the appearance of being communitarian, is deeply individualistic, and riven by fear, suspicion, jealousy and the threat of witchcraft. And yet, the individual has not yet discovered him or herself apart from the group.

5. There has not been a serious effort to think through the relationship between the Gospel and the prevailing culture. They are like railway lines; no matter how far they go, they never meet.

6. Many people lack a sense of identity, and the self-esteem that goes with it.

7. A sense of the sacred and a commitment to the spiritual seem to be absent even in some cases where one would reasonably expect to find them.

On the part of missionaries, we made several mistakes. One was that of not adequately relating means to ends. We became so preoccupied with the day-to-day tasks that we did not stop to ask where it was leading, or whether the many activities were, in fact, achieving the goals we had set ourselves. Perhaps we did not want to ask those questions because we knew what the answers would be if we faced the questions honestly. And because we did not like— perhaps even feared—the anticipated answers, we did not ask the questions. We just kept going and hoped it would work out all right in the end. That wasn't a 'leap of faith' so much as a retreat from reality.

In retrospect, it is astonishing how little the person, life, and work of Jesus Christ served as a role model for missionary life. We did not proclaim the coming of the kingdom of God so much as institute the European model of church which we inherited from our homeland. We were more ecclesiastics than evangelisers.

With the passage of time there were changes, not least changes in attitudes. Sometimes there was resentment towards the missionaries on the part of local people. What missionaries saw as service, the people sometimes saw as domination. And this showed itself in negative aggression in such ways as non-cooperation, broken promises, lack of initiative, theft, vandalism, waste, and irresponsibility. That was not the whole picture, but it was part of it. It was a signal which we, for the most part, did not read. And we didn't read it because we didn't want to read it. It punctured our sense of importance, even of indispensability.

As missionaries steadily handed over mission institutions, such as schools and hospitals, to local control, there was—and still is, by general agreement—a marked decline in standards, one which has been openly acknowledged by almost everyone involved. To some missionaries, that fact serves to reinforce a sense of self-importance, even, in some cases, of arrogance.

It seems unlikely that we would have handed over our institutions to local control if we had had the personnel to maintain them ourselves. It was necessity rather than policy which brought about the transfer of control, and it is likely that the local people realised this.

Missionaries worked *for* people rather than *with* people; we were patrons rather than partners. We made the decisions and the people's role was to cooperate with us in them. It can be said that most of the decisions were good (not merely well-intentioned), but the fact remains that it was we, and not the people, who made them. There is a price to be paid for acting in that way. In some cases, it turned adults into children (calling a priest 'Father' accentuates that process), it turned honest people into liars and thieves, and independent people into scroungers. Fortunately, those were the exceptions, but such exceptions may serve as a warning of where an overall trend is pointing.

People tend to live up, or down, to the expectations that others have of them. If you make decisions *for* people, even good ones, without consultation, you are saying to them that you don't value their opinion, which is to say that you don't value them. Maybe you value the project more than the person, or getting the job done more than the relationship. That devalues them, and one has to accept that a practical consequence of such decision-making is that people will not commit themselves whole-heartedly to implementing those decisions. They become 'irresponsible' because they cannot have a sense of responsibility for decisions they had no part in making. You cannot buck human nature by separating power and responsibility. It doesn't work, and no amount of exhortation is going to make it work.

We missionaries sometimes patronised people without realising it. We thought we were being kind. To patronise people is a double vote of no confidence: in the people by its implication that they will not respond unless they are bribed; and in the message being communicated (in this case the Gospel), because it implies that the message by itself is not enough to attract people but must have a bait attached.

People do not become responsible for themselves by having responsibility removed from them by others, no matter how well-meaning. They become responsible by having responsibility for themselves placed on their shoulders, and being able to see that the success or failure of an enterprise rests with them. I think history shows that in such cases, more often than not, people rise to the challenge, deal with their problems, and become more fully human by doing so.

In the case of missionary work in western Zambia there is the example of an alternative approach. Twenty years after the Catholic church came on the scene, a small Protestant church known as the New Apostolic Church arrived. They have never to this day built a single institution for the service of the people, other than churches. From the beginning they created a local leadership with decision-making powers, and that has been their great strength. They have gone ahead very rapidly despite some serious internal problems. Their members, in general, have an adult attitude towards their faith; and they are vigorous in promoting it, and effective, too. One lesson to be learned from this example is that more will be gained by trusting people, letting them make their mistakes and correct them by themselves, than will ever be gained by fussy control and anxiety lest people take power into their hands. The situation is reminiscent of those over-protective parents who do not want to take the risk of letting their children grow up, but try to 'protect' them by keeping them at the level of children. Anyone with even a little experience of family life can see what problems that will lead to.

Experience by itself does not mean anything. What counts is what one learns from it by evaluating it critically. The experience described above might have something to offer to the church in other places, such as Europe or North America, though they differ widely from Africa in many ways.

This recalls what Pope Paul VI wrote: '[today] two aspirations persistently make themselves felt . . . the aspiration to equality and the aspiration to participation, and freedom', and he went on to emphasise how important it is to take these aspirations seriously.[14] Church leaders need to take such ideas seriously enough to put them into practise. All the members of the church are not equal, but all are equally members. The clericalisation and bureaucratisation of the church are products of its second millennium; they are not inherent in the christian faith itself. We need to combine a leadership from the bottom-up with the present top-down structure. To do so requires no more than applying our own teaching, such as, for example, the principle of subsidiarity first enunciated in Catholic teaching by Pope Pius XI in 1931 when he wrote that 'it is an injustice, a grave evil and a disturbance of right order, for a larger and higher association to arrogate to itself functions which can be performed efficiently by smaller and lower societies. This is a fundamental principle of social philosophy, unshaken and unchangeable.'[15]

Church leaders tend to respond to such statements of principle by saying, 'Yes, of course, but they were never meant to apply to the church itself, only to civil society.' Why? What *theological* reasons are there—there are plenty of other reasons, both good and bad—for maintaining that the principle of subsidiarity does not, indeed should not, apply to the church's own internal life? Are we still at the stage described as one where the lay apostolate is seen, not as the participation of the laity in the apostolate of the hierarchy (its standard pre-Vatican II definition), but as the interference of the laity in the lethargy of the hierarchy? Is full, conscious, and active participation by the ordinary Catholic reserved to the liturgy alone, or is liturgy not meant to be indicative of church life in general?[16]

At the moment we are in a logjam where the clergy say that lay-people don't respond and are not interested in getting involved, while lay people say that clergy are unwilling to share power. They are both right. What is required to break such a logjam is leadership. We need the kind of leadership that is prepared to trust people, and also to trust God. Do we believe it when we profess that God will protect and preserve his church, or do we act as if even God cannot be trusted to manage things without an occasional nudge from us? The present style of church leadership leaves the rank and file feeling like outsiders looking in, trying to find out what's going on, only to find the curtains being drawn.

I can anticipate that some clergy when they read the above may react by saying, 'What about doctrine? How far can you go in giving lay people decision-making power in the church?' The question betrays a false assumption, namely, that orthodoxy resides with the clergy while lay-people want to overturn everything. It is an assumption which does not stand up to the test of history. A few examples may illustrate that point:

1. In the fourth century, when the divinity of Jesus Christ was challenged by Arianism, it was lay-people who held firm to the orthodox position, while most bishops had gone over to the Arian view, often for political reasons.

2. In the sixteenth century, it was a lay-man, Thomas More, who stood firm in refusing to sign Henry VIII's Act of Supremacy, while the bishops, with rare exceptions, signed on the line, again for political reasons.

3. In this century, in Hitler's Germany, an outstanding Catholic example of conscientious resistance to Nazism was a lay-man, Franz Jägerstätter, who went to execution for his refusal to serve in a war he believed unjust. His bishop condemned him for disobedience to lawful authority, and maintained that stance even after the war when the full evil of Nazism had become known.

4. In the years after Vatican II, have lay-people, in many instances, not been the solid rock on which orthodoxy rested, while some clergy chased after every new idea as if it was the last word?

It was Chesterton who said that if you treat a man like a child, he'll behave like a child; treat him like a man, and he'll behave like a man; treat him like a god—and he'll behave like a devil.

3.6 RESPECT FOR THE PERSON

One of the closest links between the spirit of democracy and the christian faith is in their understanding of the essential role of the person. In christian tradition the person is made in the image and likeness of God (Gen. 1:27); and each person is endowed with an immortal soul which Christ came to redeem by his suffering, death and resurrection; and the person is called to share in God's glory in heaven. It is impossible to grasp even at a rudimentary level what the christian faith is about without understanding that respect for the inviolable dignity of every human being is central to it.

If democracy is government of the people, by the people, and for the people—using Abraham Lincoln's definition,[17] it is also clear that respect for the person is central to it. The purpose of democratic institutions is to enable people to achieve their humanity, to realise their potential, and to live in a truly human community.

On the matter of respect for the person there is a deep spiritual affinity between the spirit of democracy and the christian faith. The present world-wide trend towards the setting up of democratic institutions is one which christians everywhere should welcome as being a step in the direction of realising God's kingdom on earth. The more one becomes aware of the common ground between christianity and democracy the more one realises what a half-truth it is to say, as people in the church often do, that 'the church is not a democracy.' As a statement of fact, that is correct; the church is not a democracy. As a statement of how things ought to be in the church, it is just as much of a misrepresentation as if one said that 'the church is not a hierarchy.' It would be much nearer the truth to say that both democracy and hierarchy are elements of what the church ought to be since both are inherent in the christian faith.

One could justly say that God was the first democrat. God created people and endowed them with intelligence and free will. Throughout the Bible, God calls and motivates, but nowhere forces anyone to follow him. He respects human autonomy: 'Man fully alive is the glory of God' is how Saint Irenaeus expressed it.[18] Central to an understanding of God's relationship with the individual person is the role of conscience: conscience is a type of inner sanctuary where God and the person meet, where rights and responsibilities meet face to face in the presence of Truth. In the words of Cardinal Newman, 'Conscience is the aboriginal Vicar of Christ.'[19]

It is ordinary men and women who make the most basic and weighty decisions in life, such as whom to marry, and how to bring up a family and guide children on their way to the future. Those are the decisions that shape the kind of world we live in and the future it looks to. God has given that decision-making power into the hands of every man and woman on this planet.[20]

Social institutions, including the church, exist for the person, not the other way round. When this order is distorted, all sorts of evil consequences follow, especially lack of respect for the person, and the suppression of his or her humanity. 'The inversion of means and ends, which results in giving the value of ultimate end to what is only a means for attaining it, or in viewing persons as mere means to that end, engenders unjust structures which "make Christian conduct in keeping with the commandments of the divine Law-giver difficult and almost impossible."'[21]

It would seem to follow from the above that a system of government which wishes to be faithful to that tradition must be one which welcomes and gladly accepts the active participation of all members in sharing in the decision-making process. Democracy, far from being in some way inimical to the christian faith, would seem to be an appropriate element of church governance.

A further consideration is the life and example of Jesus of Nazareth. He claimed the greatest authority—for example, to forgive sin—but he always exercised that authority in service, not in domination, and he taught his followers to do likewise. If one compares a democratic system of government—where people have full access to information, are encouraged to participate in public debate of issues, have a share in decision-making, and can (no less importantly) correct mistaken decisions without the need of either a revolution or undue delay—with other forms of government— where decisions are made in a closed circle without public discussion, where information is restricted, and where correction of mistakes may take centuries—which form is the closer to authority as service, and which to authority as domination? Which of those two forms of government better describes the church as it is, and which of the two better describes the church as it ought to be in the light of christian teaching?

Furthermore, if the common good is the aim of society's institutions, and if the church likewise has the aim of promoting the common good, how can that be done without people in their totality? If the aim is to enable people to develop their full humanity (see Eph. 4:13), how can that be achieved by taking decision-making from them? The common good is always orientated towards the progress of persons, and it is necessary that all participate, each according to his or her position and role, in promoting the common good. This obligation is inherent in the dignity of the human person. And for the promotion of the common good, a balance of power is needed, with power distributed between various groups and individuals.[22]

Anyone who is even marginally familiar with the way in which the Catholic church is run knows very well that power is exercised and decision-making carried out in ways which are substantially at variance with the principles just stated. To put it plainly, the church is not practising what it preaches. Through its manner of government it is denying the principle of respect for the person which it proclaims in its teaching.

A few examples will help to illustrate this point:

1. It was not until the 1980s that the Vatican lifted its prohibition on membership of trades unions by its lay employees, and then only after the issue had become a matter of public controversy —and this was in an organisation which, since the encyclical letter *Rerum Novarum* of Pope Leo XIII in 1891, had proclaimed itself as the champion of workers' rights!

2. When I served on a diocesan marriage tribunal in the 1970s, one case was that of a man who had applied in 1947 for a declaration of nullity, giving his grounds for the application. His bishop replied to him in a letter of one sentence, dismissing the matter out of hand, and giving no reason. I am glad to say that when the tribunal looked at the case it was able to grant his request. But where was the respect for his humanity in a system which made him wait nearly thirty years for justice and left him without recourse to any appeal authority?

3. In the years after Vatican II, when lay-people were first allowed to read scripture passages at Mass, it was specified that women would be allowed to read only if they stood outside the sanctuary. It was alright for a woman to enter the sanctuary to scrub the floor, wash the linen, arrange the flowers, polish the brasses and so forth, but not to read the word of God to his people. The restriction was eventually dropped in the face of a public outcry.

The last point is worth noting: though they pretend otherwise, church authorities do respond to the pressure of public opinion when it is strong, organised and persistent. The case of Father Leonardo Boff, the Brazilian liberation theologian, also illustrates this point. Because of his views, he was banned from teaching for a specified period. Before the period had elapsed, the Vatican announced that the ban was to be lifted because of Father Boff's 'exemplary humility' in accepting it. This premature discovery of his exemplary humility coincided with a move by Brazilian human rights lawyers to bring the Vatican before the International Court of Justice on a charge of violating Leonardo Boff's human rights.

Where is the Good News (the Gospel) of Jesus Christ for people in such a situation? Have they any redress? In theory, they have; in practice, many Catholics who have experienced injustice at the hands of church officials know they might just as well expect redress from the man in the moon. It reminds me of an incident related by the director of students when I was a philosophy seminarian. A young couple, one Catholic and one Protestant, had applied to the parish priest for a dispensation allowing them to marry. He considered their case and refused it. They appealed to the bishop who replied that, having examined their case on its merits, he considered that they should have a dispensation. Despite that, he would not give it, because he felt that to do so would undermine the authority of the parish priest. The director of students cited this as an example of how the authority of the church must be upheld.

In order to give practical effect to our own teaching about respect for the person, we should have in the church a constitution which would embody basic principles such as those expressed in the Universal Declaration of Human Rights. (We already have such a statement—it is called the Gospel; but lawyers find it hard to get their teeth into that!) There should be effective channels which would enable people to seek and find redress for injustices done to them in and by the church. People are entitled to nothing less.[23]

If such an idea is ever to become a practical reality, it will involve a change in church structures requiring at least some degree of separation of powers into legislative, executive and judicial functions. People cannot have confidence in a system where the same people make the rules, apply them, and then sit in judgment on their own infractions of them.

In this field, others have led the way. As so often, the initiative has come from outside the church. But, if the church has not had the courage or the imagination to lead in the field of human rights, could it not at least follow, however belatedly?

4

DEMOCRACY IN THE STRUCTURES
OF THE CHURCH

4.1 BUILDING CHRISTIAN COMMUNITY
Community

The aim of democracy in the church is to build community. The christian vocation is itself a vocation to community, to a life of *communio* with God, with others, with oneself and with nature. Perhaps the greatest challenge of the next century will be to create a genuinely human community, a 'civilisation of love' (in the phrase of Pope Paul VI) where people will be enabled to reach their full potential. Faced with the problems of environmental degradation, the gap between the rich and the poor, world hunger, the arms race, and a technology which often lacks a human dimension, it is more than ever necessary for people to learn to respect and accept each other despite differences, to see pluriformity as a blessing to be welcomed, not a problem to be overcome by uniformity, and to learn the art of coping creatively with constant change. The success or failure of this future depends, substantially, on the quality of the human relationships we create in the present.

The radical individualism of the twentieth century western world does not meet such a challenge. It frequently degenerates into selfishness, into demands for rights without a corresponding recognition of responsibilities. And the imposed collectivism of Marxism, a parody of community, has been shown in the former Soviet Union to be no less a failure. What is needed is a different approach, not a half-way house, not a 'golden mean' between the above two, but a different re-orientation of human values. The challenge to the church is to provide a paradigm of such human relationships and values.

What is community? It could be described as a group of people who share a common vision, common goals and who have a common commitment, at least in the essentials, to the means of attaining them. The key word is 'share'. It calls for sharing information, ideas, commitment, responsibility and power. It also needs to be said that a strong community is built on strong individuals, not on weak ones. It is not by diminishing the distinctiveness or the initiative of the individual that one creates a healthy community, not by reducing all to a bland lowest common denominator that one develops human potential. But strong individuals, if they are not to take off centrifugally leaving a vacuum at the centre, need to learn to communicate at a deep personal level, and to commit themselves and their talents to the well-being of the community. And community is never a finished achievement; it is always a task to be worked on.

Likewise, community does not exist for itself, but for something, or someone, beyond itself. An inward-looking community becomes an incestuous club, as sterile as a dried-up leaf curled in on itself. And community is demanding: it requires sacrifice, personal effort, and renunciation of self. 'Community that is not mystical has no soul, but community that is not ascetic has no body.'[1]

Authority in community

Within this context, a question of central importance is that of the exercise of authority. If one sees community as a pyramid, then authority may be seen as trickling down to the ranks from the top. In such an understanding, authority resides at the summit. This is a widely prevalent view in the church at present. An alternative view is to see the principal task of authority as that of creating unity, bridge-building, healing divisions and fostering dialogue. The shift from the first view to the second is a substantial one, and it is not an easy transition to make.

The experience of many religious orders may illustrate what is at issue. In the recent past religious orders saw authority in terms of the pyramid. The role of the 'subject' was to keep the rules, ask permission, and conform to the pattern. 'Singularity' was the great deviation—it meant being an individual rather than one of the herd. More recently, authority has come to be seen as a community search for God's will through shared reflection on the Gospel, on the signs of the times, and on the particular character and mission of the religious order in question, taking into account the ideals of its founder, its traditions and charisms. In practice, the actual exercise of authority is carried out through community dialogue, shared responsibility, and the practice of the principle of subsidiarity.

The change has not come about easily. There are some who cannot see the second approach as having anything to do with obedience. For them, the obedience of following rules is the only real obedience and the new approach is simply the end of religious authority. In support of their position they refer to members of religious orders who have not had the maturity to adapt to the new approach, and who, reacting against the rigidity of the past, have scampered off 'doing their own thing', deluding themselves that such was a legitimate expression of obedience. But, as the Scholastics used to say, 'Abuse does not take away [legitimate] use.' The value of an ideal remains intact even if some individuals are unable to respond to it in an adult way.

Such experiences serve as useful prototypes or experimental models for the rest of the church, since the same challenge applies there no less than in religious orders. This is particularly the case in relation to what is called the *magisterium,* the teaching authority of the church.

Teaching authority

There has been substantial development, at least at the conceptual level, in our understanding of teaching authority, since the following statements were written and accepted as normal in the church:

1. 'Let not the laity dare to teach before the clergy do, unless the latter ask them to.'[2]

2. 'The Church is essentially an unequal society comprising two categories of persons, the pastors and the flock . . . Since the pastors alone possess authority, the one duty of the multitude is to allow themselves to be led, and, like a docile flock, to follow the pastors.'[3]

3. 'Let no private person take up the part of teacher in the Church. All know to whom the Church's teaching office was given. Let him [the pope], therefore, have an unimpaired right to speak as he chooses, when he wishes; the duty of the rest is to defer religiously when he speaks, and listen to what he says.'[4]

The theology expressed in those statements was summarised in the Latin phrase which categorised the church as the *ecclesia docens* (the teaching church) and the *ecclesia discens* (the learning church). One doesn't need a very long memory to recall the times when sermons along those lines were part and parcel of the education of the ordinary Catholic. The pope and bishops were the teachers; the rest of us were the learners, and that was it.

But there has been a development at the theological level since then, even if it has not yet been fully assimilated by the whole church. The authority of Jesus Christ derives from his being a teacher of truth (Jn. 14:6 and Mt. 7:29). That teaching authority is not transferable to any individual or group. The *magisterium* (from the Latin word *magister* meaning a teacher) means a teaching office. It is a function, not a person or group. Historically that function has been exercised by the whole church. The whole church is a teaching church and a learning church; the two are inseparable; both have their origins in discipleship, and are inseparable from living the faith and witnessing to it.

In the Old Testament, the prophets (who were lay-men) proclaimed God's word. The priests offered sacrifice and taught the law of God. There was often friction between the two, between the 'amateurs' and the 'professionals'. In the early centuries of the church's life, some of the greatest theologians were lay-men—even if, like Saint Athanasius, they later became priests. Similarly, the monastic movement began as a lay movement, though it too became clericalised. Saint Francis of Assisi, for example, was not a priest. And some at least of the Doctors of the church (the word *doctor* in Latin means a *teacher*) were also lay men and women.

It is the entire church which teaches, not just the pope and the bishops. There must be an enormous waste of talent and ability— God-given gifts—in a system which excludes the lay-people who constitute more than 99 per cent of church membership from an effective role in formulating its teaching. If the ecclesiastical system we now have reduces lay-people to passivity in that area of church life, clergy can hardly criticise them for being passive in other areas.

Where else, but in the Catholic church, would it be considered normal to have commissions on marriage and family life composed almost entirely of celibates? Such a situation is not only daft from a common sense point of view, but it also, more importantly, contradicts our own theology of marriage. We teach that it is the man and woman who are ministers to each other of the sacrament of matrimony—the priest is only a witness on behalf of the church;

and the man and woman together have experience of married life and love, yet decisions affecting their lives are made by celibates. It would be not only good sense but also good theology for celibates to stay quiet on such issues, and listen and learn with married people.

Reception

This consideration brings up the question of what theologians call *reception* of teaching, practices and decisions. The word *reception* is here used in a technical sense to mean that process by which the whole church through an exercise of discernment comes to accept, or not, as in keeping with apostolic faith, some matter presented to it. An example would be the way in which the early church came to receive some books, and to reject others, as being part of the revealed word of God in the Bible. It is a process which can take time. For instance, the decisions of the Council of Nicea in 325 on matters of basic doctrine took a long time to be accepted, while the teaching of Pope Boniface VIII on obedience to the pope as a requirement for salvation (more will be said of this in Chapter 8), though taught for several centuries, came not to be accepted by the church.

The process of reception involves the whole church. Vatican II expressed this as follows: 'The whole body of the faithful . . . cannot err in matters of belief. This characteristic is shown in the supernatural appreciation of the faith of the whole people, when, from the bishops to the last of the faithful, they manifest a universal consent in matters of faith and morals.'[5] This process, therefore, involves bishops and people together, not in a merely juridical decision, or in a public opinion poll, but in a common effort to articulate what is the christian faith, with confidence in God's abiding presence in his people.

The manner in which this process works itself out depends in large measure on how the church sees itself at any given period of history. In the first millennium, the universal church saw itself as a communion of churches, while in the second millennium, particularly in the post-Reformation period, as the church became more hierarchical, more centralised and more bureaucratic, the focus switched—when the idea was not lost sight of altogether—to seeing reception as a matter of the people's acceptance of a juridical declaration by the pope.

The idea of reception was revitalised in and after the second Vatican Council in association with the concept of collegiality—the concept that the entire college of bishops, with the pope at its head, has a corporate responsibility for *communio* in the christian community.

Both ideas are intensely practical ones for the life of the church. For example, if one takes the concept of reception, the question presents itself as to whether the teaching on birth control in the 1968 encyclical letter *Humanae Vitae* can be considered to have been received by the whole people, from the bishops to the last of the faithful, thus manifesting a universal consent? And how collegial was the decision-making process when the matter was taken from the consideration of the bishops in council, and decided upon, in the last analysis, by the pope alone?

In this context it is worth recalling what was said on the topic by the Anglican-Roman Catholic International Commission in the *Final Report* in 1981: 'although it is not through reception by the people of God that a definition first acquires authority, the assent of the faithful is the ultimate indication that the church's authoritative decision in a matter of faith has been truly preserved from error by the Holy Spirit.'[6] In its official *Response* to the *Final Report*, the Holy See made no specific comment on this point, only the general statement that nn.24–7 were 'a very positive presentation'.[7]

Church

What does the word 'church' mean? A recent commentator on Ireland wrote of what he called 'the longing for faith muted by resentment of the church'.[8] The writer is probably using the word 'church' to mean clergy; that is a very common use, or rather misuse, of the term. There is so much ambiguity and equivocation in the use of the word 'church' that it would probably be better if we could drop it altogether and replace it with a phrase such as the People of God. Language makes a difference to the way people think, and that in turn affects the way they live and act. The language of 'church' is a language that alienates many people: it suggests a cosy clerical club, an inward-looking bachelor caste, remote from and indifferent to ordinary people and their problems. I believe that is how many people perceive 'the church', even if the description is not accurate—and perceptions count for a lot.

What is more to the point is that the leadership of the church, by deliberately and effectively excluding lay-people from a decision-making role in the government of the church does, in fact

—regardless of 'good intentions'—belittle them. It does not give weight to their humanity, their adulthood, their maturity. They are expected to be and are mature in every area of life except in the church, where they are treated like children and not allowed to grow up. This is a denial of the mission that Christ gave his church. He said of himself, 'I came that they may have life, and have it abundantly.' (Jn. 10:10) And the church's task is to continue Christ's work.

There must be many people who have drifted away, not because they have lost faith in God, but because they have lost hope in the church. They see it as hopelessly reactionary, indifferent to public opinion, unwilling to admit to being wrong or to learn from mistakes, and seemingly impervious to all efforts at reform. Such people simply give up and go. They probably don't want to leave but they find it too hard to stay, not because the Gospel asks too much but because the church as it now functions is not a place where they can realistically expect to be enabled to 'have life and have it abundantly'. It is not that they have failed the church, but that the church has failed them. It might even be said that it is not they who have left the church but the church which has left them.

Many such people try to hold on to faith in God and to a life of prayer. Some succeed and some—perhaps many—do not, because it is extremely difficult to sustain faith and prayer on one's own in a secularised world. But many such people do not cease to struggle for justice, to do good, to speak the truth, and to help their neighbour. Wherever they stand in relation to the church, it might be said of them as Jesus said in the Gospel, 'You are not far from the kingdom of God.' (Mk. 12:28–34)

A heavy burden of responsibility rests with those who, while seeing people leave the church because they have given up hope for it, still insist on retaining those human elements in the life of the church which cause them to leave it. It is still worse when such insistence is presented as an example of courageous fidelity to the Gospel against the pressure of public opinion. One of those human elements is the exclusion of lay-people from an effective share in church government. The question that calls for an answer is not 'Ought we to have power-sharing in the church?', but rather 'Is there any theological basis for not having it?' If fear is the obstacle to change—and it almost certainly is—it is worth remembering that, 'Fear is nothing but a giving up of the helps that come from reason.' (Wisdom of Solomon, 17:12) If, on the other hand, the obstacle is not fear but a simple unwillingness to climb down from the pedestal and join the ranks of ordinary men and women, then it is a matter for confession.

All of this points to the need for substantial structural change in the church. One of the lessons to be learned from the experience of the post-Vatican II period is that good ideas, by themselves, are not enough—a lesson which has often been taught but rarely learned. If they are to make a difference, good ideas need to be expressed, underpinned, and reinforced in structural change. Otherwise, it will be a case of what the Gospel describes as putting new wine into old wineskins: the result is that the skins burst and the wine is spilled. (See Mt. 9:17)

What we see in the church today is a consistent movement towards centralisation, aided, unfortunately, by the power of modern technology: the fax, the phone and the computer. It should be said plainly that this process of centralisation has no evangelical mandate. It follows the role model of the multi-national corporation in which the Vatican is the management board, and the local church is reduced to the level of a mere agency to which certain functions are delegated. That model has no precedent in christian tradition. Under such a system there is no accountability at the top, and power ceases to be an instrument of service, but comes instead to be sought for its own sake. And greed for power is no less idolatrous than greed for money. (See Col. 3:5)

Liberty without equality leads to the power of might over right as, for example, in an unregulated free market economy; equality without liberty leads to collectivism and loss of human freedom, as was the case in the Soviet Union. A complementary force is needed and it is to be found in a sense of community. But one of the greatest enemies of community is a powerful, centralised bureaucracy backed up by the resources of technology and money. And such is the Vatican.

Alternatives are needed, and they can be found or created.

4.2 STARTING FROM THE BOTTOM UP

'God has not willed to reserve to himself all exercise of power. He entrusts to every creature the functions it is capable of performing, according to the capacities of its own nature. This model of governance ought to be followed in social life.'[9] And in the life of the church?

The individual

Changing the power structures of the church must start with the individual. It calls for a change of attitudes in many respects, some of which have already been discussed. Central to this must be respect for the conscience of the individual. Christian conscience is not something arbitrary; it is not a matter of 'doing your thing', and then applying to it the label of conscience—that is mere self-deception. Conscience needs to be informed by and to inform the faith and life of the christian community. It embraces a call to fidelity and responsibility; it looks more to attitudes than to actions; more to what a person can become than to what he or she is right now. It is motivated by the principle of charity; not the hand-out, but the hand-up, the charity which expresses itself in an active hope for what others can become with the help of my support.[10]

Family life

We need to give flesh and blood to the statement that the family is the domestic church. Christian marriage and family life are under threat today, and the church should devote its full resources to support them. That includes giving practical recognition to the ministerial role of husband and wife in the sacrament of matrimony. Married people need to become pastors to each other. Their unique contribution to a revitalised theology of marriage and human sexuality needs to be heard effectively; they are the ministers of the sacrament and they alone have experience of married life and love. We could learn a lot from the Jews about how to make the family the centre-piece, the lynch-pin, of religious life, one which all other structures exist to serve.

Small Christian communities

In an increasingly depersonalised world, where the individual risks becoming a mere cipher, small christian communities of many kinds, geographical or vocational or otherwise, can provide a human home, a place where people can relate to one another in a human way, as they face the challenges of relating the Gospel to life and life to the Gospel. They can take many forms and structures, but they are at their best when they seek to combine elements of prayer, Gospel-sharing, exchange of spiritual experience and mutual support. They can provide an opening for grass-roots ecumenism and evangelism, and for the development of lay spirituality and lay leadership. At a very practical level, they can motivate mutual help by neighbour to neighbour. If that sounds like too ambitious an agenda it must be said in reply that there are places in the world where it is happening. In these small groups of ten or twelve people, there is an opportunity for spiritual growth through self-help and mutual encouragement. These communities are not another rung on the hierarchical ladder, or even a new organisational structure. They can be a new way of being church.

Church councils

In order to give effect to the idea of participation and co-responsibility in church government, there needs to be a renewal of church councils. Here, I am using the term to cover all sorts of councils: whether in each church of a parish which has several, or councils at parish, deanery, or diocesan level. One major change that must be made is to give such councils decision-making authority. Without that they will never mature and act responsibly; they will be talking shops. The scope of decision-making authority vested in such councils can be a matter of experiment until a satisfactory balance is found, at which time it can be formulated in a constitution. The Anglicans would help us from their experience if we asked them.

Councils of this kind already exist and function effectively and responsibly. In some parts of Africa, it is not uncommon to find situations in which a parish of one or two priests has anything from twenty to sixty churches. In the diocese in which I serve in Zambia, the average rural parish is probably not less than 10,000 sq.km in area. In such a situation, active decision-making church councils have provided the only effective response to the challenge. Their members are chosen by election, and the responsibility of running the church in their area is in their hands. They lead the local christian community as it conducts Sunday services and funerals, they arrange for the preparation of candidates for the sacraments, and they look after the sick and needy. The care of the church building is in their hands, and when it is a question of building a new church they find the site and put up the building, using local materials which they supply. It is *their* church, not the priest's, and it gives meaning to the expression that the people are the church.

It must be admitted candidly that the shortage of priests is the principal reason for doing things this way. It would be good if it could truthfully be said that it arises out of a recognition of the legitimate role of lay-people in the church, but it doesn't. In this respect at least, the shortage of priests can be considered a blessing for the church, since it pushes us into doing what we should do anyway, even if for inadequate reasons. Since that same shortage is being felt in many other parts of the church also, perhaps it can be regarded as a providential way in which God is educating his clergy to accept lay-people as partners in collegial service. It is not something new for God to teach people through actions no less than words, and to turn human foolishness to good account.

Such church councils are regulated by a constitution which is the product of experimentation and experience over a period of some twenty years. It is interpreted flexibly in response to the needs of different situations, as no two communities are the same. Mistakes are made here as elsewhere, but they can be corrected. An essential element in such a system is mutual trust. People respond positively to being trusted, and when they see that they are genuinely responsible for the church in their area, that it sinks or swims with them, that their goodwill, intelligence and commitment constitute the difference between having a living church and having a dead one, then in most cases they take up the challenge, they work at it, and in doing so they build themselves up along with the community. The role of a priest in such a situation is not that of manager, organiser or controller, but that of motivator, trainer (as well as co-trainee) and guide. To paraphrase Walter Lippmann, his function is not to direct the affairs of the community, but to harmonise the direction which the community gives to its affairs.[11]

At a time when many people have lost confidence in institutions of all kinds—church, government, trades unions, the banks, or the criminal justice system—the empowerment by the church of its members at local level could set a precedent, provide a paradigm, for others to learn from—if we have the courage to grasp the opportunity.

4.3 SEPARATION OF POWERS

Pope John Paul II, writing in 1991 on the separation of legislative, executive, and judicial powers stated that 'it is preferable that each power be balanced by other powers and by other spheres of responsibility which keep it within its proper bounds. This is the principle of "the rule of law", in which the law is sovereign, and not the arbitrary will of individuals.'[12] The same principle could usefully be applied to the church.

There is a difference between the way the separation of powers operates in the USA and in most European constitutions, with the Americans opting for the more radical model. Europeans generally separate the judicial function while allowing for overlap between the legislature and the executive. The European model is probably a more appropriate one for the church. The church needs a separate judiciary. It could be called a court, an appeals tribunal, an ombudsman, even an apostolic signatura, or whatever—the name is not important. What matters is to have a structured institution not dependent on the 'arbitrary will of individuals' but on law which is sovereign.

Is there a need for such an institution? Consider the following examples:

1. A national church agency becomes involved in corrupt practices involving financial affairs on a sustained basis over a period of about ten years. The priests of the country concerned repeatedly draw the attention of the bishops to the problem, orally and in writing, specifying times and places, people and practices. For several years, nothing is done. In the face of renewed pressure, the bishops set up a commission of enquiry. It carries out its work, presents its report—and life goes on as before. Occasional press reports, and one or two court cases involving the small fry of the agency, do nothing to stop the wheeling and dealing. It is finally brought to a halt when international funding bodies, fed up with unfulfilled promises of reform, cut off the money that keeps the agency going.

The significant point about this example is that the church failed to clean up its own mess; it took secular organisations to do that for it. And secondly, it was money (or rather the cut-off of money) rather than morals which brought the corrupt practices to a halt.

2. A religious order fails to honour a contract with an individual. That person tries, over a period of seven years, using the church's internal structures, to sort the matter out amicably, but runs into a stone wall of resistance, a simple refusal to honour the signed and witnessed terms of the contract. Finally, the person threatens to take the order in question before a civil court. Immediately, the contract is honoured in full and a letter of apology sent.

3. A church organisation employs a person at a wage which is well below that required to enable him to sustain a family at even the most modest level. It responds to a request for an increase by

pointing out (truly) that there are many unemployed people who are willing to take the job, and that, besides, it does not have the money to pay more (not true). What can he do about it? At present, he can do nothing effective.

The examples quoted above make the point that an appeal tribunal in the church is a necessity demanded by simple justice. Readers could probably find similar examples from their own experience.

Defenders of the *status quo* might respond by saying that the church already has such a system, an informal one whereby any Catholic can write to his or her bishop with a complaint and ask for redress; a formal one as described in the church's civil code, the *Code of Canon Law,* and a 'supreme court' in the Vatican called the Apostolic Signatura.

But all of these procedures lack one essential element, namely, credibility. In the examples which I have given, the people in question used the church's internal procedures and got nowhere. Their cases were not unique. What happens is that church officials, perceiving themselves to be under attack—especially if the challenge comes from a lay-person—close ranks and back one another up, as do other professionals such as doctors, lawyers or journalists in analogous cases. They do this in order to 'avoid scandal', as if the denial of justice and the cover-up of injustice were not in themselves a scandal. In such cases there is a collective retreat into the fortress, the drawbridge is lifted, the moat filled with water, 'no comments' are shouted from the battlements, and scapegoats are sought for any resulting bad publicity.

This way of proceeding is wrong in principle and self-defeating in practice. Its end result is a spiritual loss for the church's members, by driving them to despair and cynicism, and a loss of credibility for the church as an institution.

The credibility of existing church structures and procedures in such matters is zero. They are beyond salvaging. Why? Because in the church we do not have a firm, unambiguous commitment to justice for its own sake. We have, in its place, long-standing practices of covering up, smoothing over, sweeping issues under the carpet, and keeping up appearances at all costs. In short, we are not ready to pay the price of justice. Loyalty to the perceived interests of the institution outweighs loyalty to truth and to justice. Our hierarchical mind-set inculcates deference to those in power which precludes any serious challenge to them, even when they are clearly in the wrong. Instead of the courage to opt for justice and truth unreservedly, what we have is political calculation of what will work for the moment.

In place of the present structures we need a judiciary which is independent, open, accountable to the whole church and to society, professional, lay and ecumenical. Such a system could win credibility for itself over a period of time.

A new system along those lines could adopt models other than those of the adversarial system of court procedure used in many English-speaking countries, and take instead an evangelical approach based on a commitment to justice, truth, respect for the person and a spirit of reconciliation. But no amount of procedural rearrangement will substitute for a firm commitment to justice, and that has to be the starting point for the church.

The church would benefit by having such a system. In the case of Archbishop Marcinkus and the Vatican Bank (the IOR), the Vatican accepted the recommendation of a panel of international lay bankers that it pay 250 million US dollars to those who lost out in the imbroglio with the Banco Ambrosiano, even though it denied having any moral or legal responsibility to do so. Despite this ambiguity, the Vatican's acceptance of the recommendation at least put the matter to rest. An independent judiciary in the church would win back lost moral standing. Its preaching of justice to others would carry weight because of the moral force of its example—the world listens to witnesses more than to teachers. And bad publicity can be turned into good publicity when it is clearly seen that people demonstrate the political will to clean up their affairs and to put their own house in order.

We have a long way to go before anything like that happens, but we can do it if we want to. It is not beyond human ingenuity to find a way through these problems. The test is whether we have the will to do it.

4.4 ELECTIONS TO CHURCH OFFICE
Why have elections?
'The case for representation as an intrinsic part of all good government was first elaborately stated in the conciliar theory of church government.'[13] The principle of holding elections to church office has been with us for a long time: at the very beginning of the church's life, Matthias was chosen as the successor to Judas by some sort of electoral process, even if its exact nature is unclear, (Acts 1:23–6); popes are elected, albeit by a very narrowly-

based electoral college; in the past, bishops were mostly chosen by cathedral chapters; and superiors of religious orders are elected. There is a good case to be made for extending this process and applying it across the whole range of church offices. It would also help if people were chosen for fixed terms, with an upper limit of perhaps two consecutive terms.

But why have elections at all? There are many good reasons for having them, such as that they give real participation to ordinary members of the church in the direction of its life; they are a practical expression of shared authority; they give life to the principle of subsidiarity because where people have a share in decision-making they normally have a greater sense of commitment to the implementation of those decisions; elections enhance accountability, and are likely to lead to an improvement in standards of service.

At present, bishops are not elected to office in the church. This means, for example, that if a man is appointed bishop at the age of fifty, and knows that he can expect to hold office for the next twenty-five years, he really does not have to be concerned about public opinion; he can ignore it if he wishes, since there is nothing in the constitutional structure of the church to stop a bishop from being a dictator if that is what he wishes to be. And a bishop does not need to shout to be a dictator. If there were to be elections, however, that would change things, and probably for the better.

There could be objections to the idea of having elections to church office on the grounds that it would politicise the church, and introduce some of the less desirable attributes of contemporary democratic processes, such as bribery, a readiness to compromise on issues of right and wrong, discussion of issues at the superficial level of TV sound-bites, and so on. But wherever there are people there are politics, since politics are about how people relate to each other in society. The process of selection for office, whether by election or by appointment is, in either case, a political one. The difference between the present system and one based on elections is not that one is political and the other isn't; rather it is that one is open and accountable, and the other is closed and without accountability. Without accountability trust is eroded. A system based on elections would be more in keeping with christian faith and tradition than the present system. It is no coincidence that democratic institutions came to be formed in recent centuries principally in countries whose cultural matrix was christian. There is a spiritual affinity between democracy and the christian faith which needs to find a home in the christian church. Instead of the cold shoulder, a warm welcome for democracy would be more in keeping with our heritage.

Terms of office

It would enhance the pastoral life of the church if, for example, parish priests were to hold office for a period of, say, five years, with the possibility of a second but not a third consecutive term. It would be better for them, for their curates, and also for their parishioners. No one is capable of giving his very best for twenty, thirty or more years. For shorter periods, with the knowledge that there is a break coming up, a person can try harder and do better. The experience of superiors of religious orders would seem to confirm this.

One of the advantages of the democratic ideal is that it is flexible, and capable of being adapted at the institutional level to the requirements of many different situations. Another is that on the whole it is a self-correcting system—if you mess things up, you can put them right more easily than in a tightly-controlled centralised bureaucracy where an error of judgment by those at the centre can jeopardise the entire system.

One way of doing it

In a democratic system there is room for a wide variety of direct or indirect methods of choosing people for office. For example, in the matter of choosing parish priests, would it not be for the good of the church for the choice to be made by a selection panel made up of the bishop, representatives of the priests and of lay men and women from the parish in question? Such a panel could involve all the parishioners in a process of consultation which would be more likely than the existing system to produce a more responsive type of church leadership, one more ready to listen to people, to work in partnership with them, and to share responsibility.

Would it not also benefit the church to have a similar process when it comes to the choice of bishop? 'He who has the trust of the clergy and the people should become bishop', said Pope Saint Leo the Great (440–61).[14] A bishop chosen in such a way would know that he had the solid support of the diocese with him. There would be a sense of *communio* bonding bishop, priests and people in a shared commitment arising out of a shared decision-making process. It would be better than the present system where a new bishop is 'parachuted' in out of the blue like an extra-terrestrial, often with minimal consultation—and, with such consultation as there is wrapped in the veil of 'papal' secrecy —with the result that it is not at all uncommon to find practising Catholics who do not know even the name of their bishop, much less anything about him, and do not have even the smallest sense of being a partner with him in a common mission.

Why is there such resistance on the part of the church's leadership, especially in the Vatican bureaucracy, to opening up church government to the democratic process? What *theological* reasons are there for this resistance? Of course there are excuses which are couched in theological language, but that is a different matter. As things now stand, the Vatican expends a great deal of time, energy, money and personnel in defending the *status quo*, as if in doing so it were defending the Gospel itself, though a democratic system of popular participation would seem to be more in keeping with the Gospel. If the obstacles to change are not theological, then what are they? If they originate from a love of power for its own sake, or merely for the sake of exercising control over others, then there is no place for them in the Gospel. 'The People of God includes a hierarchy but it is not a hierocracy.'[15]

4.5 CHOOSING BISHOPS

As an illustration of how power is exercised by the church's top leadership there are few examples that are more revealing than that of the manner in which bishops are chosen. Consider the following cases:

1. The archbishop of the capital city of a country died, and the nuncio began the process of finding a replacement. The priests of the diocese wanted the auxiliary bishop to succeed him, but there seemed to be no channels for making that known to the nuncio. Simply to contact him and say so was considered too risky—the nuncio might interpret it as mutiny from the ranks and turn against the auxiliary for precisely that reason.

   No one knows who was consulted—and the dean of the diocese stated publicly that he had not been. Finally, after a delay of about a year, a bishop was transferred from a neighbouring diocese. Before leaving his diocese for the capital he gave an assurance, published in the diocesan newspaper, that there would be full consultation with priests and people of the diocese about finding a replacement for him. He gave that assurance in an interview on Wednesday which was published on the following Sunday, while the nuncio had already announced his successor's name to the press on the Saturday. Clearly the consultative process undertaken by the nuncio did not leave room for consulting the bishop about his successor in the diocese that he had led for around ten years.

That took place in the early 1970s.

2. In another country consideration was being given to the division of a very large diocese. In one parish of that diocese the priests received a phone call from the nuncio's office at about 11 a.m. one day, asking them for their opinion on the matter. They were instructed to discuss the matter and to have their reply back in the nuncio's office by 2 p.m. that same day so that it could be sent to the Vatican, where it could be included for consideration at a meeting of the appropriate congregation at 3 p.m. on the same afternoon. That was the process of consultation in their case. But when people complain about long delays in the appointment of bishops—it recently took thirty-three months to find a new archbishop for Madrid—they are told that the process takes time because there is so much consultation involved, and the Vatican does not want to rush things.

3. In yet another country the question arose about appointing the first bishop of a new and very young diocese in a mission territory in the 1940s. All the priests and religious brothers of the diocese were asked to put forward the names of three candidates in order of preference. The man whom they clearly preferred by a large majority was not the man the apostolic delegate wanted. He had virtually promised the mitre to another. When the names were sent to the Vatican for a final decision the priests' choice was preferred over that of the apostolic delegate.

A number of points are worth noting about this case. One is that there was no consultation of lay-people, nor realistically could there have been any. The church was so young, and the number of Catholics so small, coupled with the fact that none of them had ever seen a bishop, and had little or no idea what a bishop was, that there could not have been any meaningful consultation with them.

Another point is that religious sisters were not consulted. However, in this particular case, they made their views known at the highest level in the Vatican through their own informal (but very effective) channels. They made it clear they did not want the apostolic delegate's choice. It is believed in that diocese that their intervention tipped the scales when it came to the final decision.

About twenty-five years later the bishop thus appointed retired and it became necessary to find a replacement for him. This time —now the mid 1970s—there was a new procedure. As before, neither lay-people nor religious sisters were consulted, but religious brothers were dropped from the process. The priests of the diocese were asked to state whether they had any objection to the appointment of Father so-and-so from another diocese as bishop. Since scarcely any priest in the diocese knew the man in question, they could hardly object to him, and so he was appointed. There was no opportunity of putting forward alternative names, or of raising questions, or proposing ideas about the special needs of that particular diocese—and to have complained about the lack of opportunity for doing so would have been seen as insubordinate.

Ten years later the bishop thus appointed was transferred to another diocese, so, once again, the process began. This time, now the mid 1980s, the process was narrower still. A few priests, perhaps half a dozen, were asked if they had objections to another priest from outside the diocese. Clearly they could not object to the man, since they did not know him. To have objected to the process would probably have evoked a homily on *communio* from the nuncio, so they remained silent, and the appointment went ahead.

Viewed over a period of forty years, from the first to the third bishop in that diocese, there was a steady narrowing of the process of consultation, despite the fact that, in the intervening years, Vatican II came with its theology of collegiality, and of priests and bishop together forming a *presbyterium*, a kind of fraternity. It seems as if consultation takes place in inverse proportion to the theological basis elaborated for it.

4. Recently, it was proposed that another large diocese be divided. It took the priests of the diocese eighteen months to get a clear statement as to what proposed re-structuring of the diocese the nuncio wished them to discuss. During that time there was a lack of basic information or communication; instead there was gossip and muddle. And will the consultation make any difference in the end?

What can priests do about all this? They know they are in a Catch 22 situation. If they object to the process they will be labelled insubordinate, and the Vatican will dig in its heels, saying that it will not be pressurised. If they do not object, the Vatican can say that it sees no reason to change a system that no one objects to.

But there is a price to be paid, as there always is, when people are treated in such a cavalier fashion. Partly it is a loss of morale as new episcopal appointments tend, more and more, to be greeted with weary resignation rather than enthusiasm by the priests with whom the new appointee must work. So *he* pays a price. Meanwhile, the Vatican, while treating priests and people so heedlessly, constantly calls them to greater *communio*. Such double-talk evokes cynicism rather than loyalty, and it undermines mutual respect.

It is not only the manner of making appointments that causes concern; it is the matter of the appointees. For a long time the Vatican has shown a preference for academics over pastors. It is common for new bishops to be chosen from the staff of seminaries, and some of them have little or no experience of ordinary pastoral work in a parish. By way of token gesture some are transferred to a parish for a few months before their appointment is announced. And there are some who, even after their appointment, show little interest in pastoral matters, preferring life at a desk in the office as executive bishops.

A long-standing anomaly of the system is that no training is provided for the office of bishop.[16] A man is trained to be a priest but it seems to be assumed that no training is required to be a bishop. It is as if it all comes with the mitre in a package. But if a man has neither pastoral experience nor training, what can be expected of him? It is not surprising if some bishops are seen by their priests as remote figures, talking up in the clouds, and best treated like the Mikado—honoured with all honours and troubled with no decisions. It is sometimes felt that the greatest favour a bishop could confer on his priests would be to keep out of their way and let them get on with the job.

One bishop I knew used to go to bed and stay there rather than make a decision. When I mentioned to another that in the teachers' training college where I was chaplain less than 1 per cent of the Catholic students attended Mass when it was available in the college, he thought that I was looking for consolation and sought to provide it by telling me that in pastoral matters one should never expect 100 per cent success. On another occasion I raised with a bishop the question of whether he thought the use of a condom could be morally justified in a situation where the husband was HIV positive and his wife was not. I pointed out that in such a case the purpose would not be to prevent life but to protect it. His reply was that we all had to carry our cross. To this day I still don't see what the reply had to do with the question. I think he did not know what to say and did not want to admit it, so he fell back on a platitude. But responses such as those do nothing to enhance the confidence of priests in their bishop. And what do they say of the bishops in question? They cannot be unaware of the ambiguity of their situation, so how do they live with it? I don't know.

There are better men available than those we are now getting, and a real consultative process involving the local church would bring them forward. But the Vatican's agenda seems to emphasise control of the local churches, even if that means stifling them, and so a 'safe pair of hands' becomes the priority. The Vatican commonly chooses as bishops men who are at the far end of the conservative scale, despite the tensions and alienation that such a factional policy generates. It seems to regard courage, imagination, and creativity as dangers to be avoided in bishops, opting instead for the type of leadership which finds safety in doing nothing—like the bishop who announced in the cathedral, on taking up his new appointment, 'I'm not afraid to say no.' It was a most unnecessary statement.

4.6 THE SYNOD OF BISHOPS

The synod was set up in 1965 by Pope Paul VI to provide an institutional structure for renewal of the church to continue on a systematic and permanent basis. Since then it has met about every two or three years, and has considered a wide variety of topics. It was meant to be an expression in practice of the doctrine of collegiality: that the bishops of the church share a collective responsibility for it in communion with the pope.

The process of holding a synod begins with a decision made by the pope about the time, the place, the topic to be discussed, and the cardinals who moderate the sessions. The practical implementation of these directives is entrusted to the synod secretariat which is answerable, not to the synod, but to the Vatican. It prepares a document called the *Lineamenta*, that is, an outline of points relating to the topic to be considered. This is sent to the bishops who are asked to consult others about the matter and report back their findings. These are then taken up by the synod secretariat and incorporated, or not, in a working paper (called the

Instrumentum Laboris) which is used in the synod's discussions.

Delegates to the synods are chosen by the conferences of bishops from among their own number . . . it is, after all, a synod of *bishops*. The synod secretariat chooses others, such as representatives of religious orders, and lay men and women who attend as auditors, that is, as listeners.

The synod itself begins with an address by the pope, following which are the addresses by the bishops in a plenary session. This is followed by discussion in language groups where numbers are smaller and a more open and easy exchange of views is possible. The plenary sessions have an attendance of about two hundred and fifty people, while the discussion groups vary in size according to the language in question. These groups are free to put forward propositions which are sent to the synod secretariat for inclusion, or not, in a post-synodal apostolic exhortation from the pope which follows after about one or two years. These propositions have no binding power, they are not 'votes' in the strict sense, but rather have a consultative value.

It is worth mentioning in passing that synods are a very old institution in the life of the church. For example, in north Africa, by the end of the fourth century, synods were a regular feature of the church's life, often being held as regularly as every year. The largest known such synod was in 418 and was attended by 223 bishops. One of the more significant ones was in 397 at Carthage in present-day Tunisia—where participating bishops agreed on the canon of scripture (that is, which books were and which were not to be considered part of the Bible). Such synods were also attended by priests and lay men, although only bishops voted and made decisions.

It will be clear from the above description of the synodal process that even when operating at its best it is a tightly controlled system, useful, perhaps, as a sounding-board, or a safety valve, or a public opinion tester, but not in the least—nor is it intended to be—a democratic decision-making process.

But the process does not always operate at its best. For example, the decision that the synod on Africa would take place not in Africa, but in Rome was a major disappointment to Africans. It meant that discussions would take place out of their context, without the value of active daily contact with the life situation that helps to bring theology down to earth. What the Germans call the *Sitz im Leben* was thrown out of joint.

On one occasion I was asked for comments on the *Lineamenta* of a synod. I did not know what to expect, but I had not anticipated receiving a document worked out in such detail. I asked myself if I was looking at something meant to be a set of proposals for a possible agenda, which is what the *Lineamenta* are meant to be. To me it looked somewhat like a set of minutes of a meeting that had already taken place. There was a great deal of detail under the headings, and the sub-headings and the sub-sub-headings. It was clear that, a year or more before the synod was to be held, the synod secretariat already had a clear and specific idea about what it wanted from the synod. And I believe it got it.

In regard to the choice of priests, religious and lay-people by episcopal conferences, the synod secretariat can and does exercise a veto, sometimes without informing the bishops concerned that it has done so. And in the group discussions the secretariat lays down ground rules about the order in which people are to speak: cardinals first, then archbishops, then bishops, then priests, then (if there is sufficient time) religious and lay-people. Some have been told not to speak, that they are there only to listen.

In the plenary sessions the bishops, it seems, practise some heavy self-censorship before they say a word. They have before them the example of Archbishop Quinn of San Francisco who asked during the 1980 synod for a fresh look at the teaching on contraception in *Humanae Vitae* and was subsequently sidelined—*pour décourager les autres*, presumably. Since many Third World bishops are financially dependent on the Vatican, they are unwilling to say anything that might offend the paymaster: he who pays the piper calls the tune. (What if it were the other way round, if those who support the Vatican financially started calling the tune? Such is the risk inherent in operating on such a principle.)

Perhaps some bishops also feel that there is nothing to be gained by saying anything other than what is expected, since it will be sifted out by the secretariat anyway. In the 1980 synod on the Role of the Christian Family in the Modern World, it was suggested by groups of conferences of bishops that they be allowed to determine some of the criteria for the validity of christian marriage in their areas, taking into account local custom and tradition. In the post-synodal document *Familiaris Consortio* the idea was simply ignored. Along with it were swept aside several ideas on which theologians had been working for a considerable time regarding the pastoral care of divorced and re-married Catholics. *Alia mens suadet.*

The essential organisational flaw in the synod of bishops is that every stage of the process is governed by a secretariat which is not accountable to the synod, but to the Vatican. The result of such a system is predictable: the synod has a serious credibility problem. In the words of the superior general of one large religious order of men, speaking of the synod on The Consecrated Life, 'It was a waste of time.' That conclusion was reached by other people, especially lay-people, long before that. In the 1960s, when the synods were new, there was hope that they would serve as the vehicle of ongoing renewal in the church, and they received widespread coverage in the mass media. I can clearly remember TV stations and the press devoting a lot of time to them. That hope is now only a memory, and the media largely ignore the synods, since they know that people no longer expect anything of them. The synods, it seems, must join the lengthening list of opportunities squandered by the church's leadership since Vatican II.

It is important to ask why, because it need not be so. There is no inherent reason why the synods could not live up to their hope. Lessons can be learned from experience, if people want to learn them—but I don't think that such is the case in this instance. Rather I believe that the synods have fallen victim to an ongoing power struggle in the church during and after Vatican II. Prior to that council, everything was centralised in Rome. Bishops, for example, had to ask every five years for faculties from Rome to do their job. In Vatican II there was a determined effort to decentralise power to national conferences of bishops, and in some instances to local bishops. The synods were seen as part of that process. But in the years since the council the Vatican bureaucracy has been exercising a preferential option for power, clawing back what it lost in the 1960s, waging a determined, politically astute, and—it must be said—successful battle to regain its power. We are back to the *status quo ante* Vatican II.

I'm reminded of Robert Southey's poem *After Blenheim* on the Duke of Marlborough's victory over the French and the Bavarians in 1704:

> 'And everybody praised the Duke
> who this great fight did win.'
> 'But what good came of it at last?'
> quoth little Peterkin:
> 'Why that I cannot tell', said he,
> 'but 'twas a famous victory.'

The Vatican has won the battle alright but it won it at the expense of the church. What good came of it at last? Why that I cannot tell, but 'twas a famous victory. The synods are Potemkin villages, all glittering façade, and nothing behind them.

If the aim of recentralisation of power was to strengthen unity, its result seems in fact to have been polarisation and alienation. The Vatican response to this is to intensify centralisation, thus accentuating the problem and probably ensuring that when the pendulum swings in the other direction, as it will sooner or later, it will take an extreme form, accompanied by excesses and irresponsible actions. This is the price to be paid for having an authority system whose dysfunctionality is the product of power games, mistrust, and lack of dialogue.

The dysfunctionality of the church's leadership is not only a matter of attitudes; it applies also to some of its major institutions, specifically, the Vatican City State, the Roman Curia, and the College of Cardinals, or simply 'the Vatican' considered collectively. These institutions are of ecclesiastical origin; they have no evangelical mandate. They have usurped the role of the bishops of the church, though *they* have a mandate from the Gospel. They constitute a top-heavy power structure which has shown itself, particularly since Vatican II, to be impervious to reform. They demand very large amounts of money, leading to financial scandals such as those in the 1980s involving the Banco Ambrosiano and the Vatican bank (the IOR). To support the Vatican there are also some dubious arrangements such as the *Kirchensteuer*, or church tax, in Germany, under which 9 per cent of income tax is paid to the churches, Protestant as well as Catholic, and a person who drifts away from the church is still levied taxes in its name by the state.[17] Christ and Caesar go hand in glove on that issue, not only in Germany but also in other countries which have a similar system. We would have a better church without the Vatican, while leaving intact the see of Peter, the bishop of Rome.

The recentralisation of power in the Vatican has almost certainly been carried out on the instructions and under the direction of Pope John Paul II. That does not for one moment take from the fact that it is a creeping *coup d'état* against the papal office. Popes come and go, while the Vatican, like the Tiber, flows on forever. It is highly paradoxical that, at a time when the pope—correctly— urges priests to keep out of politics, there have been few popes more intensely political than he, especially in the field of church politics. He probably has the force of character and the political skill to make the Vatican serve his will, but the same might not be true of his successors. By recentralising power in the hands of the bureaucrats he has tied a millstone around the necks of future popes—a millstone which will, unless it is jettisoned, drag down not just the papacy but the church itself, making it unable to fulfil the mission Christ gave it.

We need to reorientate our priorities in the church, with fidelity to the Gospel as the beginning, the middle, and the end of the process.

4.7 AN ALTERNATIVE SYSTEM

In looking for alternative systems of church government we need look no further than our own tradition, and commit ourselves seriously to adopting Gospel standards and priorities in the exercise of power. This is a challenge waiting to be taken up.

A change of structures is no less necessary than a change of spirit. Both-and, not either-or. And, as before, it is our own tradition which provides a pattern to follow.

In the first millennium of its life the christian church could have been described as a communion of churches. The focus was the local church—which is not the same thing as the local bishop. The local churches were in communion with one another and with the successor of Saint Peter. The papal office took its mandate from the Gospel commission to Peter; it was an adjudicator in disputes, seeking to bring peace where there had been division; the papal office was 'pontifical', that is, bridge-building, creating links between people. Through institutions such as general councils, doctrinal differences were resolved and common decisions reached which were regarded as validated when they were approved by the pope and received by the faithful.

Without attempting either to romanticise the past, or to follow it slavishly, such a model of church would be nearer to the Gospel than what we now have. Our present structures are too top-heavy, centralised, bureaucratised, clericalised, and too involved in financial affairs and political power. A move towards the model of the first millennium would let people breathe, the bishops could be bishops again, and the result would be a revitalisation of the church. Such a church would horrify tidy minds because it would have lots of ragged edges and loose strings; but it would have freedom and vitality, and the hope which springs from them.

Taking this a step further at the practical level, we could learn a lot from our Anglican brothers and sisters, while at the same time realistically acknowledging the limitations of their synodal system of government. Theirs is a communion of local churches which are relatively autonomous. There are synods in each diocese, in each ecclesiastical province (sometimes a group of dioceses, or a country), and in the world-wide Anglican communion. In each synod there is a 'house' of bishops, one of clergy, and one of lay-people. When it is a question of deciding something of special importance, a two-thirds majority is required in each of the three houses before it is accepted by the diocese as a whole. And for more important matters, such as basic doctrinal questions, nothing is decided until it has been agreed by all the provinces.

What the Anglicans lack is a pope, though it must be said that it is generally recognised by Catholics as well as Anglicans that the papal office, as it is now exercised in the Roman Catholic church, is probably the major obstacle to communion between the two. If the papal office were reformed to restore it to what it was in the first millennium, and if we adopted something similar to the Anglicans' synodal model of government, then it is likely that such a development would be faithful to the Gospel, to christian tradition, and be acceptable to Anglicans and also to Orthodox.

If instead of being elected by the College of Cardinals—which did not come into existence until about 1050—the pope were chosen by an electoral college made up of bishops, priests and lay-people drawn from the local churches, using any one of a variety of electoral systems, then the person chosen would be more likely to win the acceptance of christians across a wide spectrum of churches. It would not be beyond the ingenuity of the human mind to find ways and means of developing such structures.

A synodal system of government has checks and balances built into it to ensure that it does not succumb to the vagaries and fickleness of public opinion. Christians, indeed, ought to be particularly aware of how changeable public moods can be. Each year in the liturgy of Holy Week we recall that the people who cried out 'Hosanna' to Jesus on Palm Sunday were the same ones who shouted 'Crucify him', on the following Friday. And Jesus lost a 'referendum' to Barabbas (though it was the religious establishment of the time which rigged it—see Mk. 15:6–15). A synodal system of government does not open the way to democracy understood as 'the divine right of 51 per cent'.[18] It is an act of faith in the continuing presence of the Holy Spirit in the whole church (and not only its leaders), and in God's fidelity to his promise to be with his church until the end of time. And a synodal system with a pope exercising the papal office as it was for the first thousand years of the church's life would be copper-fastened against arbitrary change.

4.8 THE POSSIBILITY OF CHANGE

How likely is it that these changes will come about? Most unlikely, if the matter rests with the leadership of the church. But God has his own ways of creating new facts in the church and in the world, without asking for our permission. He works through people, events, and ideas. He is the God of surprises; he has his own agenda and will have his way despite our best efforts to frustrate him or to impose our agenda upon him. And he certainly has time on his side, which we don't. If God wants any, all, or none, of the above it will happen. We do not have to campaign for it, and a rearguard action fought against it will be equally futile. God works quietly, like the leaven in the loaf, bringing things to fulfilment in his own way and in his own time.

5

FROM INSTITUTION TO PERSON

5.1 THE DEVOURING INSTITUTION

'Individual human beings are the foundation, the cause, and the end of every social institution.'[1] This is one of those landmark statements which offer valuable service as guidelines in thinking about the relationship between the individual and the institution. It comes from the widely-acclaimed 1961 encyclical letter of Pope John XXIII, *Mater et Magistra*, a letter which, together with *Pacem in Terris* (1963), evoked a strong positive response, and helped to create an environment in which people outside the church began to look to it in the expectation that it had much to say to the world that was worth listening to.

The *Mater et Magistra* statement about individual human beings cannot be applied to the church without qualification. It would be more accurate to say that Jesus Christ is the foundation, the cause, and the end of the church. Nonetheless, the statement is still valid in the sense that the person is that for which the institution exists, not vice-versa—and by 'the person' we mean human beings, whether considered as individuals or in community.

It is worth recalling the teaching of Jesus Christ in this regard. When his disciples were criticised for plucking ears of corn on the sabbath, Jesus replied that 'The sabbath was made for humankind, and not humankind for the sabbath.' (Mk. 2:27) Jesus was reiterating what was already there in the Old Testament. For example, it was said of the Temple in Jerusalem that '. . . the Lord did not choose the nation for the sake of the holy place, but the place for the sake of the nation.' (2 Macc. 5:19) People come first in God's estimation, then institutions, even the holiest of them, such as the Temple.

The Catechism of the Catholic Church, in nos. 1877–1927, has much that is good to say on this point, though its authors may have had a *caveat* in mind when they were writing, namely, that this is a teaching to be applied in civil society rather than in the church. But civil society would listen more closely to what the church says if it—the church—were seen to apply its teaching fully in its own internal life.

Therein lies the problem. There is no doctrinal issue at stake: there is no disagreement about the centrality of the person in the christian view of life. The problem—and there is one—is in the application of the teaching; we must be so convinced of our own teaching that we apply it and live by it.

Ideals need institutions in order to have stability and continuity. But there is a constant risk that the institutions come, bit by bit, to give priority to their perceived interests, such as their preservation, promotion, and even status. The ideals can come to be lost sight of, can be gobbled up by the institution which was established to promote them. The institution can even subvert the ideals and can lead the way in undermining them. Structures, left to themselves, have a way of subverting the spirit they were designed to serve. This is an inversion of ends and means; the result is the diminution of the person, the loss of ideals, and confusion and lack of direction in the institution.

For example: the so-called 'public' schools in England are the most exclusively private schools in the country; in New Zealand, there is a college set up according to its charter for the education of 'indigent Maori boys', which is now the most exclusive school for the wealthiest of the wealthy in that country; and there are religious orders set up for the service of the poor which have become the servants of the rich.

It should be kept in mind that this takes place, less as a result of deviousness or cunning on the part of power-seeking individuals, than from ordinary human weaknesses, such as a lack of vigilance, an unwillingness to be self-critical and to stand back and take a hard look at how efforts are related to stated goals. To engage in such self-analysis is demanding and difficult; it takes courage and a willingness to rock the boat. It is not always well received: some see it as causing trouble, upsetting people, and raising questions best left alone. Whether they realise it or not, those who take that view are the ostriches with their heads in the sand who, more than anyone, help to bring the institution to stagnation and death, even while they see themselves as its defenders and most loyal supporters.

It is easy to find examples of the institution devouring the ideal, both in the world in general and also in the church. One thinks, for instance, of armies set up to defend the citizens of a country which then become their oppressors, or of the 'national security' regimes which torture, brutalise, and murder their own people.

The life of Saint Francis of Assisi provides an example of this in the church. Francis wanted to live a simple life, taking the Gospel as his rule, earning his food by manual work, living in a brotherhood among the poor. Yet, within a very few years of his death, work began on the construction of a basilica in his honour. It stands today in Assisi, dominating the Umbrian plain below, a massive symbol of power, money, and status, a denial of everything the saint stood for. It reminds one of the Potala palace of the Dalai Lama in Lhasa, the official residence of the Tibetan god-king. It represents a surrender to the temptation that Jesus resisted in the desert. (see Mat. 4:1–10) It reminds one of those people in the Gospels who were always asking Jesus for a sign; they wanted power symbols to reassure them. People are impressed by power symbols as, indeed, they are intended to be, even if those symbols flatly contradict the ideals they are meant to represent.

The Inquisition was set up to defend the truth of the Catholic faith. But it became corrupted by power so that, in the case of Galileo, to take a very mild example, it forced people to profess as true things which they did not, in fact, believe in. If one reads about the 'crusade' against the Albigensians in the south of France in the twelfth century while keeping in mind that it was carried out in the name of defending the truth, it shows how far one can go in subverting ends to means. The truth cannot be imposed by force; it 'imposes' itself on the mind only by virtue of its own truth. (As a matter of historical interest, it is worth recalling that Saint Dominic refused a direct request from the pope to send his friars to participate in the crusade against the Albigensians; he refused because of the coercive methods adopted.)

Another example from more recent times might be the way in which religious orders, called to live a community life following the pattern of the early christians in the *Acts of Apostles*, came instead to adopt the values of middle-class respectability, the 'upstairs-downstairs' model, and divided what should have been communities into very distinct groups of priests and brothers, or choir sisters and lay sisters. What should have been a community became instead a master-servant relationship. Vatican II, because of its readiness to look at the basics in a critical way, changed that and humanised community life in doing so.

In South Africa, the church had a good record in making clear its opposition to apartheid.[2] However, one wonders whether this witness to Gospel values might not have been more effective and persuasive if the church in South Africa had been willing to risk its institutions through a clear challenge to apartheid, by opening up those institutions to all races. To have done so would have resulted in a confrontation and, perhaps, the loss of the institutions, at least temporarily, but it would have been a striking affirmation of the primacy of the person over the prevailing ideology. Compromise and accommodation can help to ensure the survival of institutions but it may be that too much is compromised, that the legitimate rights of the person and fidelity to Gospel ideals are thereby diminished.

Are we afraid of the radicalness of the Gospel? Are we anxious to tame and domesticate it, afraid of the insecurity which results from challenging the conventions of a secularised society? Christ promised his church that it would last until the end of time; is our faith in this promise so weak that we feel that, if push comes to shove, it is best for the individual to be sacrificed for the sake of the institution? The church in its internal life needs to resist the temptation to manipulate, pressurise, or use the person, no matter what considerations of expediency might urge it to do so. And that is easier said than done.

But the church needs to go further than that and, in human terms, to build its life on the person by welcoming and respecting the individuality of every person, with all the diversity of gifts and talents that every person has. Building in this way calls for acceptance of diversity in theological opinion, the existence within the church of what might be called a 'loyal opposition', genuine freedom of expression, and a willingness to prune or eliminate those bureaucratic structures such as the Vatican which give so much priority to control that they stifle life in the church. Without this, the church's official profession of commitment to respecting individual freedom will ring hollow. More than anything else, respect for individual freedom calls for a readiness to trust people. In doing so, we show that we trust God who created them, redeemed them, lives in them through faith and the sacraments, and, through the Holy Spirit, continues to lead them through life to eternity.

Could the church not become more of a community and less of an institution, more concerned with developing people's full human potential and less concerned with adherence to rules? It is not so very difficult to do so if one begins at the level of spirit, of attitudes and motivation, by constantly reflecting on the person, life, and teaching of Jesus in the Gospel. He liberates us from a lot of unnecessary anxiety that stems from the 'control' mentality—Will things get out of hand? Will people go too far?—while at the same time challenging us in the most radical way. He shows us that to be faithful to the Gospel is to be radical, while 'playing it safe' and adopting a 'prudent' approach is often to sell the Gospel short and to succumb to conventional wisdom. We are like Peter being called to walk on the water, trying to summon up the courage to do something foolish, and being fearful and hesitant in doing so. But if we remember that Jesus is with us, the step is not so difficult.

Are we now at a point in the church where priorities have become transposed, where power and control are becoming less the servants than the masters of mission and ministry?

5.2 RESTORING DIALOGUE

The greatest single need in the church at the present time is for the restoration of the spirit and the structures of dialogue. We have many monologues, no dialogue. The church is like a dysfunctional family where everyone is talking, no one is listening and, consequently, tensions, problems and frustration multiply. Some of the children leave home because they can't take it any longer, but that does not solve their problem, because they take it with them. In short, we need to re-learn, again and again, the art of dialogue.

Revelation itself is a dialogue in which God takes the initiative. In the Incarnation it is God's Word, Jesus, who speaks to us. The Gospels record eighty-six dialogues with Jesus: thirty-seven with his disciples, twenty-seven with opponents, and twenty-two with others.[3] The initiative is with God, the response from us. In our relationship with the world we must be ready to ask for dialogue with others, without waiting passively to be called to it. Rather than merely waiting for opportunities, we need to create them. Such a dialogue should not depend on our assessment of the merits of those with whom we dialogue, nor on the expectation that specific results will follow. It should be accessible to all without distinction, relevant to all, and excluding no one except those who themselves reject it, or who only pretend to be willing to accept it. Dialogue is not about scoring points, or winning arguments; it is a common search for truth, in which all of us are learners.

Dialogue often begins with small things, and progresses on a step by step basis, taking account of people's differences, their sensitivities, their level of education and so forth. The common ground of our humanity constitutes a positive starting point for dialogue with non-believers. Such a dialogue is demanded by the dynamism of a rapidly-changing, multi-cultural and multi-religious society. We should be eager for the appropriate moment and sense the preciousness of time, so that each day sees a renewal of our dialogue.

Dialogue presupposes that we have something to say, that we believe in, respect, and live our own tradition. It is not a matter of trying to find the lowest common denominator with others, or seeking to neutralise differences by a process of reciprocal emasculation. Rather is it a matter of learning to respect and accept each other despite our differences, and being open to enrichment by the diversity of gifts, talents, and insights with which God has blessed all his people.

Dialogue requires clarity, and that may mean a reassessment of language so as to remove ambiguity and misunderstanding. (The Austrian philosopher Ludwig Wittgenstein wrote that the limits of our language are the limits of our world.) An example—even if not a strictly apposite one—from the life of the great English architect Christopher Wren illustrates this point. On one occasion he was showing the king of England through Saint Paul's Cathedral in London as it was under construction. The king commented that the building was 'amusing, artful, and aweful'. Wren was delighted by this, since what the king meant was 'amazing, artistic, and awe-inspiring'. But language may conceal instead of reveal, it may confuse instead of elucidating, unless an effort is made to develop clarity of thought and expression. One need only think, for example, of the multiple meanings of the words 'liberal', 'secular', and 'natural' in present-day usage to see this. Confucius is quoted as saying, 'If language is not correct, then what is said is not meant; if what is said is not meant, then what ought to be done remains undone.'[4]

The spirit of dialogue recognises that the only authority which counts is the authority of truth. And to that we are all equally subject. Dialogue uses only the methods of truth, rejecting sophistry, deviousness, and manipulation. It includes a willingness to learn from others, and an acknowledgment that no one has the final answer to any question. It is sparing of absolutes, living as we do in a contingent world. 'All is relative; that is the only absolute,' wrote the French philosopher, Maurice Merleau-Ponty—and there is a lot of truth in his observation. Dialogue also requires trust in both the intelligence and the goodwill of various parties even where profound differences exist between them.

Dialogue is flexible, undogmatic, and unideological. It recognises that there are many ways of coming to faith in God, just as a mountain although it has only one summit can be climbed by different paths. It encourages us to think in new ways and to be open to the discovery of truth in the opinions of others. It has many forms, chooses appropriate means, and is ready to adopt new forms of expression and communication in order to reach people at different levels.

And dialogue needs to operate at different levels: between God and us; within the church; and between the church and the world.[5]

5.3 OBSTACLES TO DIALOGUE

Such a spirit of dialogue does not exist in the church at the present time. We have dialogue by mime as a substitute. Why is this the case?

One reason is that instead of freedom of thought and expression in the church we have a mood of dogmatism and authoritarianism. It is as if we were being told by the church's leadership 'You're free to dialogue to your heart's content, provided that you arrive at the conclusions we have predetermined.' There can be no dialogue in such circumstances.

The following examples may help to show that where there is dictation instead of dialogue, ordinary men and women are not reduced to helplessness:

1. There is in the Irish midlands a small quiet town, indeed it is not much more than a village, whose population is made up of conservative middle-class shopkeepers and tradesmen, depending on the farmers in the surrounding area for business. It has never been a hotbed of radicalism, even in the 1960s when the story took place.

    The parish priest was a man well-respected and liked by his parishioners; he knew them and they knew him. But he had a weakness; he was an alcoholic. The people knew this and felt sorry for him, seeing it as his problem, his cross to carry. It did not diminish their respect for him. They supported him, covered up for him, and kept quiet about it.

    A new bishop came to the diocese, appointed, as is so often the case, from an academic background and without pastoral experience. Not long afterwards he heard of a somewhat spectacular episode involving the alcoholic parish priest, who had tumbled from the confessional onto the floor of the parish church, thoroughly drunk, one Saturday evening. The bishop was very disturbed by this news, though whether by sensitivity to the Gospel or outraged middle-class respectability is not known. Well, as the saying goes, the new broom sweeps clean, and the bishop decided to make a clean sweep of the parish priest. He made up his mind to remove him from office and appoint a replacement. The people of the parish who, needless to say, had not been consulted about any of this were stung and they reacted. They formed a delegation—there were no parish councils in those days—to see the bishop and to ask that the parish priest be left where he was. They put their case, pointing to the good relations that had always existed between priest and people while this man was in charge of the parish.

The bishop—the new mitre scarcely settled on his head—took this as a challenge to his authority and dug in his heels. He quoted canon law to the delegation about the rights of a bishop, and spoke of how necessary it was for the good of the church that priests set their people an example of upright conduct.

After more than one such meeting ended in stalemate, the bishop re-affirmed his decision and made it clear that he saw no room for compromise. The people, no less stubborn than he, said the same. They said they did not wish to challenge the bishop's authority to remove a parish priest but that if he did so in this case he need not trouble himself to send a replacement, because no one would go to Mass in the parish church, and the new priest would find himself saying Mass alone. They told the bishop that they would instead attend Mass in the church of a religious order which had a house in the same town, and, besides, most parishioners had cars and could without difficulty attend Mass in the surrounding parishes if the religious order made any difficulty about it.

The bishop had no answer to that, and the proposed change was dropped. Having learned a lesson about people power (long before the term was invented), he went on to much higher things in later years. And they all lived happily ever afterwards.

My source for this anecdote is a deceased relative of mine who was a companion in the spirit (the bottled variety, not the other) of the parish priest in question.

2. In another part of Ireland there was a supposedly ultra-

conservative archbishop who told me in a gentle and genial manner that every bishop in Ireland had a filing cabinet full of documents from Rome which he ignored.

3. In 1989, the Vatican tried to introduce an oath of loyalty for bishops, parish priests, and theologians and other office holders. It required them to swear on oath that, among other things, 'I adhere with religious submission of will and intellect to the doctrines which either the Roman Pontiff or the College of Bishops propose, when they exercise their authoritative teaching office, even though they do not intend to proclaim those doctrines by a definitive act.'

It will be noted that this requires religious submission (*religioso obsequio* in the Latin text) even to doctrines not being proclaimed by a definitive act.[6]

There was a strong reaction from all parts of the church. A not untypical example was that of an English bishop who stated publicly that he would not take the oath himself, nor would he ask any priest in his diocese to do so. After a good deal more of the same, the Vatican quietly let the matter drop—for how long?

4. Is it not also the case that, in more significant areas of the christian life than those mentioned above, ordinary Catholic lay men and women are quietly and without fuss, and for the most part without bitterness or rancour, making their own decisions about what they believe to be right, especially in those areas of life where they have particular skill, training, or experience, and are no longer afraid to take a different line from what church authorities say? That they are doing so is not an act of revolt on their part; rather is it a sign that they are beginning to act as adults should, that is, they are taking responsibility for themselves before God.

Dictation is only one obstacle to dialogue. Another is that there is in the church at many levels and in many places a mentality and a language of evasion. We do not examine issues on their merits, or face them squarely and honestly. We fudge, we prevaricate, we postpone, we twist and turn. Worst of all, we calculate who is most likely to be the winner of the 'political' side of the argument and we adjust our intellectual position accordingly. We trim our theological sails to the prevailing political winds in the church. We all want to be on the winning side; everybody loves a winner.

We live in an age of capitulation. Moral courage and intellectual honesty are rare. Instead we have the soft option, the line of least resistance, the lowest common denominator, what works for the moment rather than what is right, public relations in the form of sound bites, and photo opportunities in place of substantial discussion, elastic or economical truth as the occasion requires, and so on. Who could truthfully say that he or she has never indulged in it at some time?

By way of illustration—a very mild one—one may recall the years before Vatican II, when the topic of a vernacular liturgy cropped up from time to time in discussion. Heads would be shaken wisely, with an air of authority, profundity, and knowledge of the mind of Rome, saying that the church would never abandon the use of Latin in the liturgy. When the change came, we saw some of the same people do a mental flip, asserting that they had seen it coming all along and had been in favour of it. Something similar happened in the USA when Richard Nixon resigned the presidency in 1974—it appeared that no one had voted for him in 1972!

A more significant example of a similar process is what sometimes happens in regard to doctrine and its development. Some 'developments' would more accurately be described as 'changes'. But it is politically unacceptable in the church to speak of doctrine changing, even where it has changed, because to admit that a change has taken place is seen as undermining authority, and issues are decided on the basis of authority rather than on their merits, even though truth constitutes the only moral foundation of teaching authority. And so we see, at times, the unpleasant sight of professional seekers and teachers of truth engaged in intellectual acrobatics, trying to square circles, or pretending that a Yes which becomes a No, or vice-versa, is not really a change at all but only a development, and explaining such changes by explaining them away. *That* mode of behaviour, more than an honest admission that there has been a change, undermines teaching authority.[7]

From the perspective of a missionary working in a rural parish in Africa, the most striking example of the evasion of difficult issues has been the reaction, or rather the lack of reaction, in the church to the repeated massacres in Rwanda and Burundi in recent years. (It should not be forgotten that there have been several massacres in those countries in this century, though on a smaller scale—for example in 1959, 1963 and 1973.) Something more than 80 per cent of the population of both countries are Catholic, far and away the highest percentage on the continent of Africa. There is no reason to believe that Catholics were any less involved in slaughtering their neighbours than the 20 per cent who were not Catholic. As if that were not bad enough, there have been consistent reports from reliable sources that in some cases priests and religious joined directly in acts of murder, including the murder of their own confreres who belonged to the other ethnic community. And catechists drew up lists of victims who were offered sanctuary in churches, as had been done in the past, only to be slaughtered in the same churches where, one week before, those same catechists had led them in the Easter ceremonies.

It is also true that in both countries there were men and women who sacrificed their lives to save their enemies, and showed remarkable courage and also forgiveness in the face of incomprehensible savagery. But such cases were the exception to the rule.

If ever there was a situation which called for a radical reassessment by the church of its role in society, this is it. How could supposed Catholics do such things to each other? What did the Catholic faith mean to them? Was there any conversion before their baptism? What and how were they taught? Were overpopulation and competition for land in small countries involved? Why did the Vatican for so long choose bishops from only one faction, the ruling Tutsi minority who for so long had lorded it over the 85 per cent who were Hutu, in the most arrogant and contemptuous manner? These are only a few of the questions which need to be addressed.

But, as yet, there is very little evidence that any of the above questions are being seriously asked, much less answered, by the church in those countries or elsewhere in Africa. (And what of Bosnia and Northern Ireland?) How far are we prepared to go in evading difficult questions? Are we afraid to ask those questions lest the answers disturb us? In contrast to the church's failure to look at such issues, we have seen the German people facing up to the evils in their recent past with an intellectual honesty which is as admirable as it is rare. They have looked facts in the face and called them by name. They have acknowledged their guilt and asked for pardon.

By contrast, when difficult issues such as Rwanda and Burundi are raised in the church, we have at hand a rag-bag of clichés which we use to evade them. We say: 'Rome wasn't built in a day;' 'We live in an imperfect world;' 'Let sleeping dogs lie;' 'Don't cross your bridges until you come to them' and so on. Like every other cliché, there is a truth in them. However, we use them as a way of doing nothing and making that sound like an act of virtue. If even the death of about a million people is not enough to waken us from the slumbers of complacency and fatalism, then it will rightly be said of us that we stood for nothing.

We have a long way to go before we achieve the practice of dialogue so that the church becomes what Christ called it to be, a community of disciples. Dialogue is indispensable to community. If we recognise the obstacles to dialogue that are to be found among us, call them by name, confront them, and have courage and perseverance in tackling them, there are solid grounds for believing that we can overcome those obstacles. Then the latent energy of that great disenfranchised majority, the Catholic laity, would be released, and the church would have life. There is nothing to lose and everything to gain by trying.

The future of the church lies in the hands of its laity. If we want to make progress we must start from the bottom up, in contrast to the top-down approach that has been dominant since Vatican II, and which by now has shown itself to be a blind alley. A renewed papacy may indeed be necessary for a genuine renewal of the church, but it is not as indispensable as the re-creation of the spirit and structures of dialogue so that lay-people will find an effective voice in the church.

The ninth-century Irish poet, Sedulius Scotus, also seems to have had some doubts about the value of looking to the top for solutions. He wrote:

> To go to Rome
> is much trouble, little profit.
> The King whom you seek there,
> unless you bring Him with you,
> you will not find.[8]

5.4 LETTING ADULTS BE ADULTS

In any society or organisation there is always some tension between the demands, the needs, and the rights of the institution and those of the person. Such tensions can be creative rather than divisive. For this to happen, certain conditions need to exist or to be brought into existence where they are absent. Among them are some of those already referred to in this book.

In the church at present, there is an imbalance in the relationship between the institution and the person—it is heavily in favour of the institution. Such an imbalance is unhealthy for the person, who is diminished by it; it is also unhealthy for the institution, which is likely to succumb to the danger of self-aggrandisement and as a result to lose sight of its goals and ideals, so that its members lose hope in it and gradually drift away.

One step which is both necessary and possible for the correction of this imbalance in the church is for adults to be treated like adults. We treat them like big children. The traditional 'pray, pay, and obey' role of lay-people belittles them. The 'simple faithful' are not so simple; they know a lot more about many things than the clergy do. When they are treated like adults they will behave like adults; they will be more ready to accept responsibility, to acknowledge the fact that they are the church, to take decisions maturely in the name of the church, and to work actively in implementing them.

I learned those lessons when I was working in the area around Shangombo.[9] I gradually woke up to see and accept something that had been staring me in the face for a long time, though I had failed to recognise and acknowledge it: the most active and committed churches were those that I visited least often. This was a consistent pattern during the years I served that area. The conclusion I drew from this experience was that I had been spoon-feeding the people and keeping them at an immature level. When I was unable to go there they got on better without me, as they were able to take charge of affairs for themselves. Other missionaries report similar experiences, for instance in Mozambique during seventeen years of civil war.

A major mistake being made in the church is that we underestimate our own people. We ask too little of them, and when they give little we accept it, giving them the impression that we will settle for anything, even the most nominal gesture of goodwill. Would the story of Rwanda and Burundi have been different if more had been asked of people before they were admitted to baptism, if a catechumenate requiring clear signs of conversion had been insisted on before adults were baptised? Such an approach is sometimes described as being too hard on people, but is it so in fact, or is it not treating them like adults? In the Catholic church we could learn a lot from other christian churches about the extent to which people are prepared to commit themselves in service when they are challenged to it. But we are often afraid to challenge people in case we lose numbers.

The next century will be either the century of the laity, or it will be the one in which the church fizzles out like a damp squib, though a remnant will remain. And the decisions that will shape the outcome are being made now by the church's leadership, including those who make no decisions. This development is already taking place, helped—unwittingly—by insistence on the maintenance, without change, of the present ecclesiastical discipline on clerical celibacy.

A change is taking place among the ordinary members of the church. It is long overdue, very welcome, and full of promise for the future. Many lay men and women are moving away from being passive spectators to being active participants in the life of God's kingdom. They are ceasing to hide behind formulae, systems, and institutions and are making the church their own. Instead of being pressurised into doing what is right, they are motivating themselves to choose what is right. They are moving from a passive obedience based on fear, or group pressure, or conformism to intelligent choice and individual responsibility.

An example from the world of adult education may illustrate the change that is taking place before our eyes. In the relatively recent past, adult education in the church (where it existed at all) often took the form of lectures in a parish hall, where the participants sat passively on rows of tubular steel chairs while someone poured information into their heads. They were allowed to ask questions of the speaker to make sure they had got it right. Then they went home, and, for the most part, life went on as before. For many people this is no longer acceptable.

There has been a shift of emphasis from teaching, regulating, controlling and organising people to enabling, motivating, and enthusing them. Instead of being taught, people are becoming involved in the process of discovery. Instead of being fed answers they are learning what questions to ask. They are undertaking the new venture of learning how to think critically, to evaluate perceptively, to challenge the *status quo*, to situate their faith in life, and their life in faith. There is a shift from teaching to learning, from the status of a child to that of a mature adult.

This change is most noticeable in the so-called 'under-developed' world, where the blessing of a shortage of vocations to the priesthood is most evident, and as a result lay-people have been able to come into their own. That shortage is a mixed blessing, but it has had the positive benefit—given the dominance of clerical culture in the church—of making it possible for lay men and women to come to the fore.

5.5 WOMEN: DO WE BELIEVE OUR OWN TEACHING?

Among lay-people in the church women are without doubt the most patronised, belittled, and under-appreciated. One need only look at some basic facts to see that this is so. Women make up half of humanity, but a good deal more than half of the church's membership—an observation which can be verified by a glance around a church in almost any place at any time. Among members of religious orders, women constitute more than 75 per cent.[10] Yet official attitudes towards them are moving only slowly away from the idea that women should be seen and not heard. They have been formally excluded from virtually all decision-making in the life of the institutional church, and the church has lost much because of this. Experience in development work suggests that if you want to get a project off the ground, the people most likely to do so effectively are women: women find remedies while men seek excuses. It could be the same in church affairs if women moved into decision-making at all levels.

There is no serious theological reason why this should not be the case. Leaving aside for the moment the question of the admission of women to priestly ordination, there is no reason why women could not be cardinals, as was suggested by an African bishop, Ernest Kombo, from the Congo, at the synod on religious life in October 1994. The matter of the role of women has an urgency that seems to be unrecognised in the church. In Africa, for example, should Islam make a concerted effort to take the continent from the Sahara to the south, as some Islamic leaders have stated as their intention (and they have oil money and political clout to back them), women could be in the front line against such a threat. However, if they are consistently marginalised, their effectiveness in such a situation would be greatly lessened. The status of women in Islamic countries is generally lower, sometimes much lower, than in countries of christian tradition, and it is very much in the interests of African women to see that the christian faith is not overcome by Islam south of the Sahara as it was a millennium ago north of it.

The same principle applies to the rest of the church. If the nineteenth century was the one in which the church lost the working classes, the twentieth century may be the one in which it loses women, unless it gives them real recognition. If that were to happen, there would not be much of a church left.

The christian *faith*, as distinct from the christian *church*, has a very positive attitude towards women and (as a matter of historical record) has had a beneficial effect on women's position in society. Christian opposition to polygamy and divorce has liberated women in many societies, such as Africa today, from the tyranny of male egotism and selfishness. The work of christian missionaries, especially women, has produced a quiet revolution in the education of women, liberating them from many of the limitations which traditional life imposed on them.

But christian church leaders have often failed to accept the implications of christian teaching about the dignity of women. The record is not good. Consider the following quotations:

1. Saint Clement of Alexandria (died 220): 'A woman should cover her head with shame at the thought that she is a woman.'

2. Tertullian (died 220): 'The judgment of God upon the female sex endures to this day and with it inevitably endures their position of criminal at the bar of justice. Women are the gateway of the devil.'

3. Saint John Chrysostom (died 407): 'Woman is a foe to friendship, an inescapable punishment, a necessary evil . . . Among all savage beasts none is found so harmful as woman.'

4. Saint Jerome (died 420): 'Women are the gate of hell.'

5. Saint Augustine (died 430): 'Women are not made in the image of God.'

6. Pope Saint Gregory the Great (died 604): 'Woman is slow in understanding, and her unstable and naive mind renders her by way of natural weakness to the necessity of a strong hand in her husband. Her use is two-fold: animal sex and motherhood.'

7. Saint John Damascene (died about 750): 'Woman is a sick she-ass . . . a hideous tape-worm . . . the advance-post of hell.'

8. Saint Bernard of Clairvaux (died 1153): 'There are two things which defile and ruin religious: familiarity with women and daintiness with food.'

9. Saint Thomas Aquinas (died 1274): 'Woman is an . . . incomplete being . . . a misbegotten male. It is unchallengeable that woman is destined to live under man's influence and has no authority . . .'

10. Pope John XXII (died 1334): 'Woman is more bitter than death.'

11. Constitutions of a male religious order, 1945: 'What straw gains by fire is what a male religious gains by conversation with women.'[11]

Apart from individual statements such as the above, it may be added that, for almost all of its history, the church offered no challenge or alternative to the prevailing mentality of male superiority. It was 'natural' and therefore not challenged.

Most, but not all, contemporary churchmen would reject those sentiments unambiguously. The knowledge that we have come so far in our thinking should alert us to the possibility that we may still have far to go before accepting women as the equals of men in theory and in practice. It is neither comfort nor excuse to point to the prevalence of similar attitudes among non-christian writers and among Protestant theologians, such as the following small sample indicates:

1. Euripides (died about 406 B.C.): 'There is no evil so terrible as woman.'

2. Aristophanes (died about 184 B.C.): 'There is nothing in the world worse than a woman save another woman.'

3. Plautus (died about 184 B.C.): 'There is no such thing as picking out the best woman; it is only a question of comparative badness.'

4. Friedrich Nietzsche (died 1900): 'When a woman is inclined to learning there is usually something wrong with her sex apparatus.'

5. Karl Barth (died 1968): 'Woman is ontologically subordinate to man.'[12]

The hatred and contempt for women expressed by these writers, both christian and non-christian, should caution us against assuming too readily that such attitudes are now a thing of the past. Do attitudes and people really change so quickly?

In the church we have some of the best ideas where this issue is concerned, but we are slow to apply them. We have not moved from equality of right to equality in fact. For example, the Vatican has intervened on a number of occasions to block the appointment of women as professors of theology, even when they were better qualified than the male candidates despite many official church statements acknowledging the just ce of womens' claim to equal access to such positions.[13] It seems to be a characteristic of the church in our time that while we have the finest of ideals we are the slowest to live up to them. Other people, with lesser motivation than ours, take the lead while we drag our feet, make excuses, and speak the language of evasion.

If the rights of women in the church were given real recognition, the church would be a better place for all, both men and women. In general terms, women are probably more person-centred than institution-centred, and men are probably more institution-centred than person-centred. The integration of the feminine into the life of a male-dominated church would give it a completeness which it lacks.

Think, for instance, of the difference it would make if our understanding, and our image, of God went beyond seeing him (!) as male, and incorporated a feminine dimension. There is every reason why we should. Since all theology is ultimately about God and proclaims a particular vision of the divine, the inclusion of a feminine view of God would open up dimensions not appreciated at present. That, in turn, would broaden and deepen our understanding of what it is to be human. There is a whole new vision of God, the person and society, as well as of nature, waiting to be developed in that area.

However slowly, reluctantly, hesitantly or ambiguously, this process is taking place. One significant step, even if an isolated one, was the declaration by Pope Paul VI in 1970 that Saint Catherine of Siena and Saint Teresa of Avila were doctors of the church, recognised as outstanding teachers in the church and for their contribution to christian spirituality.[14]

Women have been taking their full place in professional life over the last century. The church is often seen as one of the last bastions of resistance to this movement. But within the church there are many capable and determined women who have what it takes to change that situation, though it is also true that there are others who lose hope, give up and go elsewhere. We can respond constructively to such a challenge, or we can dig in our heels and refuse to budge. The choice is in our hands.

6

FROM LAW TO LOVE

6.1 IMMORAL THEOLOGY

We have come a long way in moral theology in the last forty years, but we still have a long way to go. Perhaps a few examples will illustrate the point:

1. A handbook of moral theology commonly used by seminarians in the post-war period had this to say about the fast prescribed before receiving the Eucharist:

    'Communion is forbidden under grave sin even though one has taken only the *smallest amount* of food or drink, e.g. a few drops of medicine.'

    'Swallowing blood from bleeding gums does not break the fast. However, if one swallowed the blood sucked from a bleeding finger the fast would be broken.'

    'That which is taken must, according to the common opinion, be digestible. Hence, the fast is not broken by smoking, swallowing a hair, a few grains of sand, a piece of chalk, glass, iron, wood, and probably not by swallowing pieces of fingernails, paper, wax or straw.'

    The fast was not broken by chewing tobacco unless one swallowed the juice, nor by inhaling dust, steam, raindrops or an insect, nor by a priest who swallowed a piece of cork from the wine bottle in the split second before drinking from the chalice.

    The same section of the book goes on to deal with the problem of particles of food stuck between the teeth, and sucking cough-drops or lozenges before midnight the night before receiving the Eucharist.[1]

    That handbook was popular in seminaries because, unlike

most moral theology texts, it was available in English instead of Latin— which seminarians were supposed to be (but in fact were not) able to read. However, for that reason, seminary staff cast a cold eye on it, and warned students that it was also somewhat liberal.

2. Until the introduction of the new Roman Missal in 1969, the instructions for the priest printed in the early pages of the old missal warned about the importance of fidelity to the rubrics, stating '*A quibus non declinet sacerdos, etiam in minimis, sine peccato*' ('from which the priest may not deviate, even in the smallest matters, without sin'). An example of such deviation would be to deliberately wear the wrong colour vestment. Thus, if an Irish priest, for example, wore a green vestment on Saint Patrick's day instead of the prescribed white, that would be a sin.

   If a sacristan, through carelessness, allowed the sanctuary lamp to remain unlit for twenty-four hours, that was also a sin.

   Someone once made a study of the potential sins that could be committed by a priest while saying Mass and came up with a list of some two hundred and sixty!

3. When the Eucharistic fast was reduced to one hour only, during the mid-1960s, one of the staff of the then Holy Office (now the Congregation for the Doctrine of the Faith), Father Sebastian Tromp, a Dutch Jesuit, explained carefully that every hour had sixty minutes, and every minute sixty seconds, and therefore every hour had 3,600 seconds, not 3,599 or less.

4. The common opinion of theologians was that 'offences against the sixth commandment do not admit of parvity of matter.' What that theological jargon meant when translated into English was that any and every sexual sin was mortal.

What is one to make of all that? Firstly, it needs to be said that most people had the sense not to take it seriously, except for the ʼ point which was taken very seriously indeed. But some people ᴉke it seriously and tied themselves in a knot of scrupulosity ᵊrminable worry over the intricacies and minutiae of these laws. Any priest who heard confessions during that ᵛe had experience of penitents who drove themselves ᵓr) to distraction with unending worry and anxiety

What would the Pharisees have made of it? They surely would have appreciated it greatly and added it to their deliberations on whether a hen should be stoned for laying an egg on the sabbath.

But it inflicted much suffering on good people who wanted to be faithful to God, like the woman whose four stillborn babies were buried in unmarked graves at the back of her farmhouse because —since they were stillborn and therefore unbaptised—they could not be buried in consecrated ground. Her question was, 'Is there any chance that they will get to heaven, or are they all in limbo?' That was when the farce turned to cruel tragedy.

It was also, to say the least, a deviation from the Gospel. What is astonishing, with the benefit of hindsight, is how anyone who read the Gospel, and especially the strictures of Jesus against the Pharisees, in Matthew 23 for example, ever took any of it seriously. And yet it was the official teaching used in seminaries for most of the post-Reformation period, that is, for more than four hundred years.

The credit for ridding the church of that mentality goes to Vatican II, and to those who had the courage and the vision to re-work moral theology by being radical, going to the roots, and not being content with a few minor adjustments here and there. Prominent among those was the German Redemptorist, Bernard Häring. A more cautious approach than his would have failed the Gospel and squandered the opportunity for badly-needed change. But it took his courage, and that of others, to create the opportunity in the first place.[2]

If the church is able to change, as it clearly has done, in relation to the above and to much else besides, then there are real grounds for hope that it may continue to change in other no less significant areas of moral theology. Foremost among them is sexual morality, which badly needs a re-working, starting from the basics. In the present repressive climate of intellectual debate in the church, are there people of courage and vision to do that, to publish *and* perish?

6.2 MORAL PERSPECTIVES

Some years ago I undertook a study of moral attitudes and processes among the people where I live in Zambia. I asked myself about the relative influence of two factors: the christian faith which most Zambians profess, and traditional attitudes, values, and assumptions deriving from tribal custom. It took me some time to realise that I had posed the question wrongly and therefore would not get a 'right' answer. It had not occurred to me that there was another, no less important, element at work in the process of moral thinking, and that was what might be called the morals of survival.

As I write, there is an investigation going on in a bank branch not far from me into alleged dishonest practices among the staff. I ask myself how honest I would be if I were handling the equivalent of thousands of dollars a day, while expected to support a family on about fifty dollars a month in a country where most prices are at European levels. Or how about a lady employed by a district council in a situation where she handles large amounts of cash, while she herself has not received any salary for eight months, nor her husband either in his job? When people are very hard pressed simply to find food for one meal a day, or one every second day in some families, it alters perspectives on priorities. Moral probity is much less difficult on a full stomach. How about the woman who sells herself at night for a bag of salt which she will divide into smaller packets and then sell in the market? Her survival and that of her children is at stake. She can die now of malnutrition or the diseases it brings, or prostitute herself and die later from AIDS, leaving her children orphans. What are the choices for her?

It is not only circumstances that alter cases; perspectives do also. There is, for example, the view that what matters is not to get caught. Or the idea that it doesn't matter what sort of crookery or manipulation you get involved in as long as it turns out alright in the end. Or the identification in the minds of some between christian morals and middle-class respectability, or even just simply keeping up appearances.

Another moral perspective is that of the Pharisees. The Pharisees are popularly seen as hypocrites, but that is an oversimplification. First and foremost they were systematisers. For every problem they had a solution, for every dilemma a formula. One thing they did not have was doubts. Over a period of centuries they had constructed a system which, as they saw it, was a form of comprehensive insurance against error. If you accepted the system and lived by it, it would save you. The individual was relieved of the responsibility of having to think matters out for himself; all he had to do was to accept and obey.

There was the arrogance of the perfectionist about their system; it made God virtually redundant. It could be said, without much exaggeration, that as long as you believed in their theology you did not need to believe in their God. They had it all worked out.

There are always well-meaning people who want to do others'

thinking for them, forgetting that one person cannot substitute for another in the love of God, which is the essence of what morals are about. Morals are about relationships, commitment, sacrifice and effort, more than about answering the question 'What should I do now?' There is no *system* which can answer the question 'What kind of person am I called to be?' The heart of christian morality is a personal relationship with God. In that alone lies the motivation which gives moral significance to particular actions.

The search for a moral system which will answer all the questions is not merely futile; it is worse than that. It is a distraction from the real focus, a diversion from what matters. That begins with conversion, and continues with faithful searching for all that is good, true and beautiful—in God. The intellectual towers of Babel which systematisers build are attempts to master what is a mystery, whereas a christian is called to surrender to the mystery and to be mastered by it.

What is moral theology? What is any theology? Some of what is called theology is merely semantics and word-games, and has nothing to say. There is also the theology which develops into an attempt to encapsulate, to define, to limit God, to reduce him to the level of a puppet on our string. When that happens, theology has moved to ideology, and from there to idolatry, re-making God in its own image and likeness. That type of 'theology' makes itself a substitute for God. And the church which embraces it also makes itself a substitute for God. Such a church is no longer a road-sign pointing the way to God but a road-block denying access to him. It is a perennial danger.

Some theology, especially moral theology, has fallen back into the veneration of the law from which Jesus came to save people. 'We begin in acknowledging God as our ruler, and end in making rules for God. We begin with a sense of wonder and end stifled in bureaucracy.'[3] Saint Paul, especially in his letters to the Romans and the Galatians, goes to great lengths to point out that a person is made right in the eyes of God, not by observance of the Law (that is, the Old Testament), but by faith in Christ. The law, he said, can point out right and wrong but it cannot motivate anyone to observe it. Salvation is not an achievement brought about by clearing a moral obstacle course, but a gift from God in Christ through faith.

Christ came to free people from the impossible burden of the law. Much of our theology has been an exercise in re-creating and re-imposing that burden. Have we ever really understood or accepted what Saint Paul taught? Or do we think that law, and its observance through our effort, is the means of salvation?

Those who wish to systematise the faith, the perfectionists who are not satisfied until they have dotted every *i* and crossed every *t*, are unwittingly casting a vote of no confidence in the cross of Christ. Whether they realise it or not, they preach a do-it-yourself salvation which makes Christ's death and resurrection redundant. Theology in their hands becomes not the servant of faith but an occupied territory in the mind.

When Jesus condemned the Pharisees as hypocrites, he may have meant that in more than one sense. Of course, some of them were simply insincere and devious, prepared to use the truth as a bargaining chip aimed at scoring points in a one-upmanship contest. But there were others who were not insincere in that sense. Rather they tried in good faith to impose on themselves by sheer will-power a *persona*, an image of what they thought they ought to be, instead of allowing themselves to be led by God into what he wanted them to be. They were not true to themselves, perhaps because they were afraid to let go and let God lead them.

And then again there are people—one sees them in positions of leadership in the church—who act out a role, adopt an official persona, become the spokesperson for God, though one suspects (and hopes) their inner self is different. In doing so, they may be motivated by a spirit of loyalty to the institution they represent, but they are not true to themselves, they have lost their souls. (What the Bible means by the word 'soul' is what we mean today by the word 'self'.) Shakespeare wrote,

> This above all: to thine own self be true,
> and it must follow, as the night the day,
> thou canst not then be false to any man.[4]

He could have added 'or to God either.'

God does not need PR men; he needs witnesses to truth. Crucifixion is only one way of killing the Word of God: another is to strangle the faith by forcing it into a conceptual strait-jacket; another is to make morals a control mechanism; perhaps the worst is to play games of political calculation with the truth. Not all contemporary moral theology has avoided these pitfalls; some of it has embraced them.

I recall again some of the teachers of moral theology I had when I was a student for the priesthood, and I realise that I was blessed in them. One was an elderly man who did not live long after his appointment. He made an impression by his understanding, his liberality and, above all, his compassion. He used to describe the standard textbooks of the time as books on immoral rather than moral theology because they were so concerned with sin. They were, he said, the ethics of Aristotle sprinkled with quotations from canon law. Without explicitly saying so, he gave us to understand that we should not take them too seriously. Above all, he gave us students a sense of the primary importance of compassion, forgiveness, and reconciliation.

6.3 AUTHORITY THE SERVANT OF TRUTH

The 'Magisterium is not superior to the Word of God, but is its servant. It teaches only what has been handed on to it.'[5] It is good that the church, at the highest level of its teaching authority, a general council, affirms that its role is to be the servant, not the superior, of the word of God. It is one of those basic principles which is sometimes stated more emphatically than it is applied. It is not uncommon to hear church leaders make statements about papal authority which have a strongly 'absolutist' character, open to the interpretation that a pope may act, one might say arbitrarily, independently of scripture, tradition, sacraments, or the college of bishops. Such a notion is a form of papolatry and should be emphatically rejected; it is not the tradition of the church. A church teaching is not true because it has been proclaimed, even by the pope; rather one should say that it is proclaimed because it is true.

It was Saint Augustine who wrote that a crisis of obedience is, in the first place, a crisis of authority. It is not the principle of authority in the church which is more and more being called into question, but the way in which it is being exercised, and the goals it serves. The problem is not so much the theory as the practice, not so much the theology as the politics. Everyone agrees that authority is meant to be an instrument of service and that teaching authority, in particular, is meant to be the servant of truth. Similarly, it is agreed that authority is meant to be exercised collegially—for example, that the pope, while in no sense being merely a mouthpiece for a majority, should not teach as if above or apart from the college of bishops. Autocratic domination is not christian authority, and it has no claim on the allegiance of a christian.

There is a problem about authority and obedience in the church, especially at the practical level. However much the concept of authority may be formulated in the language of service and *communio*, it seems in practice to be not infrequently exercised by the Vatican in the form of assertive power not far removed from dictatorship. The unspoken, but nonetheless clear, message of many Vatican documents is, 'Don't forget who's in charge; *we* are the church.' Probably the best known example of this is the question of the appointment of bishops, which has become such a divisive issue in many parts of the church. But there are other examples as well. Some church officials are quick to see every question, problem, or issue as one of authority. Instead of examining issues on their merits in the light of the Gospel, they see discussion and debate as an implicit challenge to authority (usually *their* authority as they see it), and seek to stifle such discussion. This is to forget that authority is a means to an end, not an end in itself. The end is *communio*, and that is enhanced by authority as service, and diminished by authority as dictation. The latter form of authority is divisive and should be recognised as an error. It needs to be said again that if church authority is sacred—and we are reminded often enough that it is—then the corollary is that its abuse is sacrilegious.

When a person in authority seeks to stifle discussion of an issue by a unilateral *fiat*, discussion does not come to an end. Instead the focus of discussion shifts from the issue in question to the authority of the person who issues the order, and to his manner of exercising authority. The end result is usually a loss of respect for the person in question and for the office which he holds.

The way in which some of the ecumenical debate is conducted is an example of the misuse of authority in the church. It is repeatedly stated in official documents that ecumenism is a task for the whole church. Yet when, in 1981, the first Anglican-Roman Catholic International Commission produced its report and presented it to the respective churches for assessment, the Vatican, not long afterwards, instructed episcopal conferences not to publish their responses to that report. They were to submit them privately to the Vatican. As in many other cases, a soundly-based theological principle is undermined in practice by what appears to be the political power-games going on within the Vatican. It is not too difficult to see in the official Vatican response to the report echoes of ongoing turf battles between the Congregation for the Doctrine of the Faith, the Pontifical Council for the Promotion of the Unity of Christians, and episcopal conferences.[6] Is ecumenical theology a form of ecclesiastical politics by proxy?

Similarly, anyone who has had experience of the inner workings of ecclesiastical circles knows that it is not unusual to find that what is called consultation takes place *after* decisions have already been made in private by a closed circle of people who can be depended upon to give their assent to whatever is proposed by those in power. (The word 'power' is deliberately chosen; it is more to the point than 'authority'. Authority presupposes moral limits, goals, and methods; power does not always do so.)

All of this is a long way from Gospel authority. On one occasion, recorded in Mk. 9:33–5, Jesus asked his disciples what they had been quarrelling about on the road as they walked along. They said nothing because they had been arguing about which of them was the more important. He told them that anyone who wants to be first must make himself the last of all and the servant of all. And elsewhere he said that he had not come to be served but to serve and to give his life as a ransom for many. (See Mt. 20:28) The context of christian authority is *communio* (*koinonia*, or fellowship); and the method of exercising authority should be in harmony with the message of Jesus in whose name it is exercised. Nowhere does the Gospel sanction arbitrary or autocratic use of power.

Why is it, in fact, frequently exercised in that way? I think Bertrand Russell may have had a point when he said that 'Religions which condemn the pleasures of sense drive men to seek the pleasures of power. Throughout history, power has been the vice of the ascetic.'[7]

We hear a lot about *magisterium*; the other side of the same coin is *ministerium*, and it is no less necessary. We hear much of the teaching authority of the pope and the bishops; the other side of that coin is reception of doctrine by the church. It is not either-or but both-and. We hear much of the words of Jesus to Peter in Mt. 16:19 that 'whatever you bind on earth will be bound in heaven, and whatever you loose on earth will be loosed in heaven.' We don't often hear that Jesus said the same thing to any or all of his disciples in Mt. 18:18. A scripture scholar comments, 'The power and authority which Peter exercises in his own person are the power and authority given by Christ to his community.'[8] We hear much of authority located at the top, as if Jesus had never said that 'where two or three are gathered in my name, I am there among them.' (Mt. 18:20)

One imbalance evokes another; one extreme evokes another. The kind of 'creeping infallibility' noticeable in some Vatican documents[9] tends to evoke a response of dismissal or a shrug of the shoulders. It is a variant of *qui nimis probat nihil probat* (the person who proves too much proves nothing). Likewise the person who claims too much authority undermines himself and the authority which he legitimately holds. The Vatican's increasing tendency to want to run the affairs of local churches, reducing the bishop to the level of a local agent carrying out instructions from the head office, has begun to defeat itself. The law of diminishing returns has come into play so that the more insistent the demand for control, the more people switch off and don't listen. However understandable that reaction may be, it does not help in the long run to promote the dialogue that builds *communio*.

A constant tradition in the christian community is that of maintaining, often with difficulty, a creative balance between the external, visible sign of God's presence manifested in the *magisterium*, and the internal, invisible working of the Holy Spirit 'who blows where it chooses' (Jn. 3:8), and who continues to breathe life into dry bones, raising up people in unexpected places and times to respond to the needs of God's people. A *magisterium* nervous about its prerogatives is uneasy about that which it does not control. But, like it or not, it has to live with it unless it wishes to incur the censure of the apostle Stephen to the Sanhedrin, 'You stiff-necked people . . . you are forever opposing the Holy Spirit, just as your ancestors used to do.' (Acts 7:51) The Holy Spirit is the spirit of truth who leads people to the complete truth. (See Jn. 16:13) Have we, in the church, the courage to believe that 'the truth will make you free?' (Jn. 8:32)

6.4 MORALS: FROM PASSIVE ACCEPTANCE TO CRITICAL DISCERNMENT
In January 1994 a survey conducted among the French population showed that only 1 per cent look to the teaching of the Catholic church for guidance in moral matters.[10] In the same survey, 64 per cent declared themselves to be Catholics.

What is one to make of such a result? One has to be careful about reaching conclusions in religious matters on the basis of statistical surveys, but one thing can be said with certainty: right and wrong do not depend on numbers. However, while making full allowance for that fact, there is reason to be disturbed at the tiny percentage of people in a traditionally Catholic country who look to the church's teaching for guidance, even though nearly two-thirds still consider themselves Catholic. The figures strongly suggest that the church is not getting its message through. Could this be due to the way in which the message is presented or perhaps to the process by which it is arrived at in the first place?

Law

For a long time the church's moral teaching has been presented in terms of law, rules and regulations. One such example is found in the 1992 *Catechism of the Catholic Church*. It states 'the faithful are obliged to participate in the Eucharist on [Sunday and] days of obligation unless excused for a serious reason.' And it goes on, 'Those who deliberately fail in this obligation commit a grave sin.'[11] The catechism ignores distinctions between grave and mortal sin which theologians have worked on for the last thirty years or so. Elsewhere it states that 'Mortal sin . . . if it is not redeemed by repentance and God's forgiveness . . . causes exclusion from Christ's kingdom and the eternal death of hell . . .'[12] It follows from this that to miss Mass deliberately, for example through simple laziness, causes the eternal death of hell unless one repents of it.

This raises many questions of different sorts. One which comes to my mind is how the church can teach this while also saying that 'the Church addresses people with full respect for their freedom. Her mission does not restrict freedom but rather promotes it. The church proposes; she imposes nothing.'[13] To threaten a person with hell unless he or she obeys a given rule is indeed to impose, unless one re-defines the word 'impose' in such a way as to empty it of meaning. And what kind of freedom is promoted by such a threat? One can read and re-read the Gospels without finding any example of Jesus pressurising or even urging people to go to the synagogue on the sabbath. Was that because it was unnecessary? Maybe. Yet the Gospels tell us only that Jesus himself usually went to the synagogue on the sabbath. (Lk. 4:16). The almost frantic concern with fidelity to Sunday Mass attendance is a feature only of the post-Reformation church, and especially of the twentieth century. It is unbalanced.

We can and should do better than take such an approach to moral teaching. The sources of a renewed approach are already there within our own tradition.

In the Old Testament, law is didactic rather than regulatory, that is, it is concerned with teaching more than with control. For example, the laws about jubilee celebrations in Leviticus 25, involving the freeing of slaves and the remission of debts, were almost certainly never adhered to, yet they still served the useful function of offering a prototype of social justice. In the New Testament, the attitude of Jesus towards the law made it clear that the law is not salvific; people are not saved by its observance. It is faith which saves. It is no wonder that the lawyers and the scribes found it so difficult to accept what Jesus was saying: he was doing them out of a job!

We need a great deal of mental adjustment in the church before we are able to grasp what Jesus was saying and doing. The moment one begins to assert that law is not primary, there are many who see this as an invitation to irresponsibility and anarchy. They cannot grasp that there is only one source of security for a christian, and that is faith in Christ; he alone is the way, the truth, and the life. (Jn. 14:6) Systems are no substitute; on the contrary they may become an obstacle to union with him, especially when they are imposed in a way which takes away human freedom. We need order and discipline as 'occasional crutches to our weakness' but not as dominant values. When they dominate, we have reduced religion to 'a handy form of social organisation'.[14]

Responsibility

In the church we have reduced morality to obedience. The message that people have caught is that to be a good Catholic you should go to Mass on Sundays, receive the sacraments, and obey the rules. If you do that, the institution will carry you along, it will do your thinking for you, and you will be saved by being a member. We have encouraged passive acceptance more than critical discernment. In short, we have not taught people to be responsible for themselves; indeed, we discouraged it as being too risky an idea which might lead people to go off the rails. We are afraid to trust our own people. Instead of trusting people, we have inculcated an attitude of deference to authority to the extent that it amounts, at times, to an abdication of personal responsibility.

The effect of this is to diminish the individual, despite the message of Jesus who said, 'I have come that they may have life, and have it abundantly.' (Jn. 10:10) By contrast, the Lutheran tradition has strongly emphasised the responsibility of the individual before God, one which cannot either be shrugged off or subsumed under some collective church responsibility. Do the differing emphases in Lutheran and Catholic theologies of the individual account, in part at least, for the very large differences between traditionally Lutheran countries such as those in Scandinavia, and traditionally Catholic ones such as those in Latin America, in the matter of human rights, individual freedom, and social justice? Does the lack of emphasis in Catholic pastoral practice on individual responsibility (which necessarily presupposes the right to think and to decide freely) help to account for the fact (and it is a fact, though we often try to deny it) that Catholics form a disproportionately large percentage of the prison population in many countries of different confessional groups, such as Britain or New Zealand?

As in so many other cases we need to combine the individual and the group in our thinking, not choose one at the expense of the other. Individual conversion and commitment are indispensable, and a sense of group responsibility is also indispensable.

In view of what has been said above, it is paradoxical that Catholic moral theology in the post-Reformation period had little to say about matters of social responsibility. For instance, the textbooks used in the seminaries had little or nothing to say on topics such as human rights, individual freedom, or social justice. Papal teaching on such matters in the social encyclicals was almost totally ignored. The focus was so narrowly on the acts of the individual that wider issues were passed over. Sometimes it was 'the world' which opened the eyes of the church to them.

We need to reorientate our thinking with a substantial shift of emphasis in our moral framework of reference. At the risk of some repetition, it could be summarised as involving:

> human freedom more than conformity to law;
> responsibility more than obedience;
> growth more than control;
> attitudes more than individual actions;
> processes more than specific rules;
> love more than law, fear, or guilt;
> future potential more than present limitations;
> critical discernment more than passive acceptance.

What is involved is a shift of emphasis; it is not a matter of discarding one in favour of the other. It is not a matter of saying 'I make my own laws'; rather it would be nearer the truth to say that it means 'I make the laws my own.'

Relationships

An essential part of this process of widening our framework of reference would be to see moral theology in terms of relationships: with God, with other people, with oneself, and with the physical world of nature in which we live and of which we are a part. In retrospect, it is astonishing how little the moral theology manuals had to say about God and our relationship with him. They might be described accurately as texts of ethical philosophy rather than of moral theology.[15] Links with scripture, with what used to be called dogmatic theology, and with spirituality were tenuous at best. Moral theology lived in its own isolated semi-Aristotelian world, piling up burdens on people's shoulders and not lifting a finger to help them. There is a need to go back to the drawing-boards and to re-establish the links with God.

God is the necessary foundation of moral obligation. This does not mean that atheists cannot have a moral sense; it means that, for the great majority of people, a morality which does not look beyond purely rational motives, such as enlightened self-interest, lacks the dynamism for commitment in extent and in depth in those areas of life where reason fails to motivate. Another way of looking at this is to ask the questions: Why should I care about you? Why should I bother about anyone other than myself? Why should I sacrifice myself for another, or commit myself beyond what I am required to do by law or social convention? In brief, why care? Reason takes a person part of the way in answering those questions; faith goes further and deeper. God is the foundation, the motivator, the giver of life, the enabler. Belief in God personalises morality, lifting it beyond a philosophical system or a personal ideology to the level of a human relationship.

The somewhat arid concepts of God in the textbooks are given flesh and brought to life in spirituality, and especially in the practice and experience of prayer. Morals need to be interwoven with a theology of God, with spirituality, and with prayer if they are not to be simply a burden, sometimes one which is too heavy to bear. Seen in that wider context, moral theology becomes a map, and personal prayer the compass pointing out the way. Morals then become a force of human liberation, freeing a person from the preoccupation with self which is inherent in human nature. They do not impose except in the important sense that the truth imposes itself on the human mind because it is true, and love impels beyond the frontiers of reason.

It is sometimes said that what's moral isn't practical and what's practical isn't moral. It would be nearer the truth to say that good morals make for good relationships, good conscience, good praxis, and—in the context of AIDS—good health also. For example, good morals and good medicine go together. Nonetheless there is something to be learned from the above criticism: it is a reminder that orthodoxy and orthopraxy are two sides of one coin. They go together and interact on each other, a point often made in another context by liberation theologians. A renewed moral theology will be interdisciplinary, taking into account the experience of psychology, sociology, anthropology and specialised subjects, as for instance in the medical field where genetic engineering and neurology are making remarkable advances.

Ecumenical

We need to open our ecumenical horizons. Catholic clergy could learn a lot about pastoral theology from Anglicans. And looking wider still, we can see many movements for good which started outside the church—sometimes indeed with opposition from the church—from which we could learn if we were willing to do so. Among such examples could be cited the movements against slavery, apartheid and colonialism, civil and human rights organisations, the trade union movement, conscientious objection to military service, women's liberation, the care of the environment, disarmament, the Red Cross, Amnesty International, and so on. They are a reminder that God's Kingdom is wider than the church, that God gives gifts freely where he wills and that if we wish to have a moral theology which is catholic as well as Catholic, we need to look over the fence at what others are doing. The lesson from Mk. 9:38–40—'whoever is not against us is for us'—applies to moral theology also.

Communitarian

Some of these considerations point to another area of Catholic moral theology which needs development, namely, that it should have a communitarian character as well as focusing on the individual. An example of this is found in the encyclical letter *Quas Primas*, issued by Pope Pius XI in 1925, in which he pointed out that the first world war had been conducted mostly by men who were pious christians in their private lives, but failed to apply christian principles in public affairs.[16] (Perhaps they were 'keeping religion out of politics'?) They were mostly praying, Mass-attending, Bible-reading christians who either could not or would not see that faith is meant to be lived no less in politics than in personal life. However trite or pedantic it may sound, it still needs to be said that morals are not just about sex but also about war and peace, government, economics, and social policy, in short, about anything that affects the way people relate to one another in society.

Furthermore, morals need to relate to the culture of a people: to what makes them tick; to what makes them to be the kind of people that they are; to their priorities, values, attitudes, assumptions and unconscious reflexes. They need to penetrate the culture, moving beyond narrow individualism with its prissy 'I don't want to impose my values on others', to get involved, to be committed, and to contribute to the ferment of ideas that shape a people's lives. And why? Because the christian faith has much to say that is of value to society, and it would be an injustice to society if we failed to speak to it of the message we have.

Our moral theology will be enhanced, and its impact on society the greater, if we do not seek to give absolute or definitive answers to questions which are relative or provisional, and if we also recognise that one of the functions of such theology is not only to suggest answers to questions but to suggest questions to answer, such as 'What kind of person am I, a christian, called to be?' 'What kind of person am I, in fact, becoming?' 'What could this or that person become with the help of my human solidarity?' (A useful New Testament study would be to look at the questions Jesus put to people: for instance, 'Who do you say that I am?')

To think intelligently, and to act responsibly with law as a guide and God as the motivator, while continuing, however inadequately, to maintain a life of prayer will carry the average person a long way. Conscience is the place where all this comes together.

6.5 CHRISTIAN CONSCIENCE THE SUPREME MORAL DECISION-MAKER
Conscience is the practical decision-making faculty in moral matters. To look at conscience in a christian perspective presupposes that the person has an overall moral vision formed in a christian mould, and that the person in question is trying to live a life of christian discipleship, including prayer and penance. If that is the case, then the person is likely to be free of the aberrations of either an arbitrary individualism where 'doing one's thing' becomes the practical rule of life, or at the other extreme where a rigid legalism minimises the individual's personal evaluation of an issue to the point where his or her conscience counts for little.

In making moral decisions the person needs to identify clearly what the problem is. Is it one problem or several? Is there sufficient information to enable an informed judgment to be made? If a person believes that the facts and relevant information are available, it is then necessary to proceed to an evaluation by asking such questions as the following:

What are the likely long-term and short-term consequences of any given course of action in this situation?

What are my motives in this matter? Self-seeking or not? Am I acting in truth, in justice, in love?

Have I examined this issue from the viewpoint of the other person(s) involved?

Am I proposing to do to others as I would wish them to do to me?

What do the Gospels have to say about the issues involved?

What does the church have to say about the issues?

The church's teaching proposes principles for reflection, criteria for judgment and guidelines for action. Conscience needs to be informed by and in turn to inform the faith and life of the christian community. In doing so it will seek to be faithful to specific precepts such as those in the Ten Commandments.

In many cases it will happen that a person will find it difficult, maybe impossible, to work through all the above processes. Life can sometimes be complicated and with all the good will in the world practical decision-making is fraught with the possibility of error. For a christian, the knowledge that God forgives should help to remove some anxiety from decision-making. On an ordinary day-to-day basis a person will find it useful to follow the sayings, 'If you can't do the best, do the best you can,' and also 'Do what you can, and don't worry about what you can't.'

I believe that there is much sorting out that needs to be done in the church in our attitudes to conscience. On the one hand there are some strong, emphatic statements about the primacy of conscience, statements which speak eloquently of the right and responsibility of the person to follow conscience, even one which is mistaken in good faith. There is the landmark statement of Cardinal Newman that 'conscience is the aboriginal vicar of Christ.'[17] This view is endorsed by Pope John Paul II when he states that 'If Newman places conscience above authority, he is not proclaiming anything new with respect to the constant teaching of the Church.'[18] And elsewhere he states that the church honours what he calls the 'sanctuary of conscience'.[19]

On the other hand there are also official church statements which appear to state that authority is above conscience. For example, the Congregation for the Doctrine of the Faith states that 'argumentation appealing to the obligation to follow one's conscience cannot legitimate dissent.'[20] That would appear to leave little room for dissent. If that is the case, what room is there for conscience, unless conscience is reducible to obedience? If that is what is meant, it would have been better to say it unambiguously. This is one of those situations where we proclaim a principle (in this case the inviolability of conscience), and then go on to explain it by explaining it away; it is another example of the 'Yes, of course, but . . .' type of affirmation, where everything hinges on what follows the word *but*.

For example, it is common to hear Catholics, in a discussion on conscience, say 'Yes, of course we must follow our conscience, but conscience must be informed by the teaching of the church,' and since the church has something to say on everything, sometimes in absolutist terms, then you are back to square one, and conscience means simply 'Do as you're told.'

We could preserve the element of truth in that attitude while including other necessary truths which it omits by saying that conscience needs to be informed by, and in turn to inform, the faith and life of the christian community. There is a reciprocal interaction between the individual and the community. It is not only the community which has the grace of God at work in it; it is not only the community which teaches. So does the individual.

Teaching and learning are inseparable in christian discipleship, and if the church shows that it is willing to learn from the individual, its teaching is more likely to meet with a receptive hearing. Furthermore, it is not only the faith of the community but also its life which serves as a guide for conscience. The Holy Spirit is in the community, not alone in its teaching but also in its life. Indeed, people are more likely to learn from the life of a community than from its formal teaching. And finally, it is better to speak of the christian community than to speak of the church. The former is a more inclusive term. The latter is often reduced by Catholics to mean the pope, or the pope and bishops, or even the Vatican bureaucracy. But it is the whole church which teaches, not just part of it, no matter how important that part may be. (Pope John Paul II quietly gave the *coup de grâce* to the distinction between the *ecclesia discens* (the learning church) and the *ecclesia docens* (the teaching church).[21]

In addition, there is much that we can learn, if we want to, from our christian brothers and sisters of other churches. Those who think we know it all are those who have never tried to learn from others.

There is an ambiguity in the life of the church about conscience. It is as if we think conscience is a great idea until we realise that people are taking us seriously enough to actually do something with that idea without necessarily deferring to church leadership. Then we become frightened and start to backtrack, and to introduce qualifications and limitations and sub-clauses which have the effect of reducing to nothing the practical impact of the idea. It is not too much of a simplification to say that our real—as opposed to our official—attitude to conscience could be stated in this way: 'Conscience is a great idea, marvellous, wonderful; of course you must follow it; but really, you mustn't take that so literally that you actually start to do it—heavens, no! We never meant that! Just do what the church tells you; that's much safer, and you won't get into any trouble that way.'

We are afraid to trust our own people: 'give them an inch and they'll take a mile' is our unstated fear. And so we sometimes fall back on the scare tactics which were common in the old-style parish missions. They were nothing less than an abuse of religion. By frightening people into conformity they helped to destroy a moral sense, because to be moral one must be free. To think of scaring a person into being moral is a contradiction in terms. Not to trust people is worse than not loving them; it is the ultimate vote of no confidence in them, and in God who created them and who daily entrusts himself to them.

For many Catholics the mainspring of their moral life is not love, nor even law, but fear and guilt. Those are not the ways that Jesus Christ showed us. In fact, fear is one of the things from which he sought to free us; as Saint John wrote, 'Perfect love casts out fear.' (1 Jn. 4:18) And also, 'if our hearts do not condemn us, we have boldness before God.' (1 Jn. 3:21) Fear as a motive for morality is the short-cut, the quick fix that provides instant compliance—at the expense of freedom and growth.

We need to move from a norm-centred to a person-centred morality. That means, among other things, that we should drop the penal approach to morals which we still retain in some areas of life, such as attaching the penalty of hell to deliberately missing Sunday Mass. If we spent time, effort, and money on trying to enthuse people with the ideals of the Gospel, it would be better and more productive all round.

Furthermore, we still retain in some ways the tendency to reduce ideals to laws, thereby diminishing them. An example of this was that while we upheld the Gospel call to repentance as an essential part of the christian life, we diminished its value by moving from there to the imposition of the most exquisitely detailed rules about

Lenten fasting. Doing so diminished both the Gospel ideal and the people bound to the observance of the rules. Pope Paul VI changed that in 1966, pointing out that the call to repentance is constant, while dropping the rules about fasting. However, we do the same today in insisting on the present law on clerical celibacy as our response to the Gospel ideal in Mt. 19:12.

Are we afraid that if we do not impose something by law then people will just drop the ideal altogether? That may indeed be part of our thinking. To the extent that there is some force in it, it is substantially a by-product of our own tradition of reducing ideals to laws, of looking to external compliance more than inner motivation, and of being afraid to trust people.

Take a particular case as an example. Catholics are required to attend Mass on Sundays. And all over the world Catholics arrive late for Mass. It is such a universal and long-standing practice that it might almost be called one of the marks of the church! By contrast, no such *obligation* rests on Protestants; they are invited and encouraged to attend a service but there is no penalty for not doing so. Protestants generally attend church less often than Catholics, but habitual late-coming is almost unknown among them. Why? Could it be that Catholics are registering a protest against the compulsion attached to Sunday Mass, while Protestants have no similar reason to protest?

And what of the effect of compulsion on the quality of Mass attendance? One need only take a place near the back of a Catholic church on Sunday morning to see that the quality of attendance is less than ideal.

We diminish the Mass and belittle ourselves by such foolishness. Are we really serious in saying that those many Catholics who miss Mass through their own fault, and do not repent of it, will go to Hell? We would do better to educate people to the value of prayer in general and the Mass in particular and drop all talk of penalties—much less hell—for non-attendance. We could learn something from mission countries. In many of them nothing at all is said about an obligation to attend Sunday Mass, for the simple reason that it is not possible for a priest to reach anything more than a fraction of his churches on a Sunday. In the diocese where I work in Zambia there are, on average, fifteen churches for every priest. What happens is that, for the most part, people conduct a service themselves. On the few occasions when a priest comes for Mass, they appreciate it, it is valued and welcomed.

It is better by far to motivate people to choose what is right than to pressurise them into doing what is right. It is better to take one step freely than to take many as a result of fear or the threat of punishment. We would do well in the church not to pressurise people, and by the same token not to patronise or spoon-feed them either. Rather we should encourage people to think, to pray, to read the scriptures, to act responsibly and take the consequences in terms of praise or blame. We should aim at educating people on their right and responsibility to form and follow a christian conscience. The task before us is one of persuasion and motivation.

6.6 FROM LAW TO LOVE—IN MARRIAGE

Just two or three years ago, a bishop who works in a Vatican office put forward the case for a 'Catholic' condom. It was one which would have in it a microscopically small hole which would allow a minuscule drop of sperm into the vagina. The chances of a pregnancy resulting from this would be tiny but the good news for Catholics, as he saw it, was that the marital act would be complete, it would not be contraceptive, but would be a 'natural' act because it was open to the transmission of life.

At about the same time another official in a senior teaching position offered his insights into the problems arising from a situation where one partner in a marriage is HIV positive while the other is not.[22] He illustrated his point by an example. Let us suppose that the husband is HIV positive while his wife is not. What are they to do? They should not use a condom, he said; its use is everywhere and always mortally sinful. Neither should they stop having sexual intercourse since that might tempt the husband to go to a prostitute. So what should they do? He said they should continue to have sexual relations as before. But what about the risk of transmitting the AIDS virus to the wife? He acknowledged that this was highly likely, but he saw it as the lesser of several evils in the case. By what reasoning did he reach that conclusion? He argued that a man needs to have sexual intercourse with his wife; otherwise he will be tempted to promiscuity, and that would endanger his soul. By contrast, if he continues to have sex with his wife, the danger is to her body. But since souls are more important than bodies, it is the lesser evil that she lose her body through physical death than that he lose his soul through spiritual death. The wife who consents to this is a shining example of the sacrificial character of Christian motherhood. The official said nothing about the orphans that such an arrangement would leave behind.[23]

What is one to make of such thinking? In my view the first

example indicates thinking which is simply daft. The second is criminal.

I think it is clear, and not only because of thinking like that just illustrated, that we need to go back to the basics and start again from the beginning in sexual morality. Nothing less than a radical reorientation will restore credibility to our teaching. Among other things we need to overcome our suspicion of the body and our unspoken but real fear of sexuality. There are people in the church who have begun to do some of that re-thinking, but we have a very long way to go.

One foundational idea for such-rethinking, in addition to those already mentioned, would be to focus on relationships rather than on individual acts, and especially on relationships as a whole rather than on each and every individual act considered in isolation.

Another principle would be to recognise that values, even when they have an absolute character, should not necessarily lead to absolute rules. Nor does it necessarily follow, where there is agreement on values, that this should or will necessarily point to agreed conclusions deriving from them.

Furthermore, our moral teaching, and not simply our pastoral practice, should take account of the fact that what is desirable is not always possible. The best possible solution is not always the best solution possible. As Immanuel Kant taught, no number of *shoulds* makes an *is*.

In any re-examination of our moral theology a key consideration must be the methodology we adopt. It should be human and flexible rather than legal and mechanical.

If our teaching is to be true to the realities of life some flexibility should be built into it. At present we proclaim teaching in an absolutist way, while making all sorts of accommodation at the pastoral level. This creates a dichotomy between theory and practice, the objective and the subjective, the official teaching and the pastoral practice. We could overcome this dichotomy by building flexibility into the teaching itself. And it is desirable that we do so in the interests of intellectual honesty, for example by getting away from the present situation where people in search of some flexible pastoral guidance have to shop around and build up clerical contacts, while the person who is unable to do that is left alone to cope with a rigid teaching which may act as a strait-jacket.

If any of this is to come about there needs to be an overhaul in the way we do our theology and formulate official church statements on morals. We should not repeat what was done in the case of *Humanae Vitae*, the encyclical letter of Pope Paul VI which dealt with contraception, among other things. Consideration of the question was removed by the pope from the second Vatican Council, then in session. The bishops, as a body, were not consulted about it, nor did they even receive an advance copy of the text. They read about it in the newspapers, and found themselves put on the spot, trying to defend a document which they had not seen. Apart from anything else, this showed that the church's leadership had not assimilated the then recently re-discovered doctrine of collegiality which had been formally stated at the council just a few years earlier.

The development and formulation of teaching should involve the whole church. Where sexual morality is concerned, and especially where the teaching is one that has a bearing on marriage and family life, it should be axiomatic that married people would have a central role, not only at the level of providing information, or in some merely consultative capacity, but at the decision-making level in conjunction with the pope and bishops. Married men and women are the ministers to each other of the sacrament of matrimony, and they alone have experience of married life and love.

In addition, we should watch our language. Much of what we say in theology is incomprehensible jargon to ordinary people. Jargon inflates the ego of the specialist and it reminds the lay-person of who's boss, as indeed it is intended to do, but it limits communication. It is noticeable that *The Catechism of the Catholic Church* has recourse to the language of metaphysics when it has a weak case to make in human terms.[24] But without communication there is neither dialogue nor *communio*. It reminds me of the clerical gathering where the chairman, in his opening remarks, stated 'We are now approaching the area of appropriateness of methodology.' There was a pause for a moment; then the silence was broken by a voice saying 'We're trying to figure out how to do the job.' The translation was appreciated by a burst of laughter all round. There is something to be learned from this: if we cannot speak of morals in language which is comprehensible to ordinary people, that fact itself should serve as a warning signal that we are going off the rails. It is a pity that theologians who do use ordinary language, and are able to communicate, are sometimes dismissed as mere popularisers by peers who regard their own obscurity as evidence of depth.

Looking in particular at the question of marriage, there is a great need to find room in our thinking and practice for compassion, understanding and forgiveness when marriages fail. I have no difficulty in accepting fully the Gospel teaching on the permanence of marriage, and I have no wish to 'dilute' it—I hope that a plea for compassion towards those who have failed in some way in their marriage will not be seen as such.

People differ; sexual acts differ; marriages differ; and divorces differ. Out of the 5.5 billion people on this planet, not even two are the same. There is a difference in the significance of sexual intercourse when it takes place, for instance, between an engaged couple and when it takes place in casual sex or promiscuity. (The *act* may be the same; the significance is not.) Marriages differ, for example, as between a contract arranged for a couple by their parents and which may never get beyond the level of a family alliance, and one in which there is real communication, sharing, and love between husband and wife as equal partners. Divorces differ, as, for instance, when a couple grow apart or learn that they made a mistake by marrying each other in the first place, or, at a different level, when one person, for example, has a concept of personal freedom which includes no hesitation about infidelity, indifference, or exploitation towards the other.

And there are differences in people's understanding of christian marriage. Some people may have an adequate *conceptual* understanding of marriage, that is to say that at the intellectual level they have the right ideas. They could, if invited, give a good talk on christian marriage. But perhaps as human beings they cannot go much further. A higher level of understanding might be called *evaluative*, where a person grasps and appreciates why the christian faith teaches what it does about christian marriage. This understanding goes beyond the merely intellectual level and engages the person in a more comprehensive way. A still higher level is one which involves real *commitment* on the part of the whole person at all levels, the intellectual, the emotional, and the physical.

The point being made here is that if we wish to take account of the realities of life, we should not treat all marriages and all divorces as if they were the same, as if a single system or rule could cover them all.

It is worthwhile asking some questions about the link between love and marriage. For instance, if love has come to an end in a marriage, does a sacramental bond still exist? (Indifference rather than hatred is the opposite of love; hatred is love which is sick or perverted, and it can be healed.) Does the phrase 'till death do us part' apply only to the people concerned, or does it also include the death of love? If a marriage is dead as a human relationship where, for example, a new marriage has been entered into and the original couple have not seen each other for years, does their marriage still live as a sacrament when the sacrament itself is defined in terms of interpersonal communion? But it also needs to be recognised that there are times when love may seem to be dead, when, instead, it is maturing, developing, and deepening at a different level from earlier stages.

'What God has joined together, let no one separate.' (Mk. 10:9) What if it has come asunder simply because people made a mistake? What can or should be done about it? This is where compassion is called for. In the Catholic church we have a long tradition of compassion towards sinners. Indeed, the church has sometimes been accused, usually unjustly, of being so compassionate towards sinners that it implicitly condones sin. But if we are to err, it would be better to err on the side of compassion than on the side of severity. The church is a church of sinners, and a church for sinners. It could be said that the forgiveness of sin is what the church is about, it's what it's for.

In the church we have compassion on everyone who fails—the murderer, the liar, the thief, the drunkard—to almost any extent, but not when it comes to those who divorce and re-marry. Then it is as if we believe that fidelity to the Gospel requires severity towards the person who falls short of it, and anything less than severity is seen as a betrayal of the Gospel. An example of such severity is found in the *Catechism of the Catholic Church* where it is stated that 'the remarried spouse is . . . in a situation of public and permanent adultery.'[25] That language betrays a guillotine mentality: you're in or you're out; you're a success or a failure, and there's no room for anyone in between.

It is no answer to say that the church has marriage tribunals to which a person may apply for a declaration that a marriage was null and void from the beginning. Having served on one such tribunal —and it was a good one, run professionally—I know that even at its best a tribunal cannot help more than a minority of cases. Firstly, a man or woman may have a case, but be unable to prove it before the tribunal. And secondly, there are many cases where the marriage was genuine and worked alright for years before things started to go wrong. It cannot be declared null and wrong from the beginning because quite simply it was not null and void but full and happy until something, or someone, brought it to an end.

It is worth asking (I don't know the answer) what was done about these matters for the first millennium of the church's life. Marriage was not recognised as a sacrament either by Catholics or by Orthodox until about the twelfth century, and that partly in response to problems about the inheritance of property, so what did they do when a marriage broke down?

Living as I do in a country with a massive rate of marital breakdown, and a bewildering and constantly changing pattern of marriages and divorces, with one divorce begetting another, and seeing the disastrous effect of this on family life and on the happiness of children, I do not want to encourage anything which might open the way to yet more divorce. One of the effects of frequent divorce on children is that they learn early not to trust people; that is for them the way to hurt and disappointment. But how can you have community or development of any sort without trust? Nonetheless the 'appalling vista' argument, that to make any concession will lead to the undermining of marriage, should not be the last word either. Law is neat and tidy, human beings are not. Law can say a firm *No* and leave it at that, but human beings and their problems remain and they continue to call for help. Compassion and understanding must be part of the answer to that call. There are no 'right' answers, but entrusting the individual person and his or her conscience to the compassion of Christ must be part of avoiding the wrong answer.

6.7 GOD IS LOVE

God is.
God is here.
God is here now.
God is within me.
God is within you.
God is love.
God loves me.
God loves you.
What more do we need to know?

7

RISING TO THE CHALLENGE OF CHANGE: FROM THE STATIC TO THE DYNAMIC

'You never step into the same river once.'
(the Greek philosopher Heraclitus, c. 540–480 B.C.)

7.1 IMAGES

Some years ago I celebrated Mass for the jubilees of three missionary sisters who, between them, were completing 170 years in their congregation. One was 'only' fifty years a member, each of the other two had been a member for sixty years. During the procession in which gifts were brought to the altar, a young Zambian sister carried on her head, unsupported by her hands, a saucer-shaped basket of rice, about half a metre in diameter. As she came forward she danced to the rhythm of the drums which beat out the music. I watched the basket with some anxiety, wondering if it was going to stay put or go careening off, spun like a flying saucer with the centrifugal force of the swaying and swinging of the dance. 'If it takes off', I thought, 'this is going to look more like a wedding than a jubilee of religious profession.' Then for a moment, my attention was distracted by the ululating of the sisters as more of them joined the procession. When I looked back I saw something I had missed before. There was a second basket sitting in the rice, and it was full of eggs, some of which occasionally wobbled in the dance. I began to see myself with raw egg streaming down the front of the vestment. At last she reached the edge of the sanctuary where I stood, and I sighed with relief. 'She's made it,' I thought, and I reached out to take the baskets. But as I did so she went into reverse gear and started dancing backwards down the nave. Then forward again and she swung past me like a satellite in an elliptical orbit, gathering speed for the next loop. Three times she swung past until finally she came in to land with eggs and rice intact, the basket within the basket still sitting safely in place. I have a feeling that she knew what I had been thinking, as her smile when she handed me the basket seemed to say, 'You didn't think I'd make it, did you?'

Another image of the static and the dynamic that comes to my mind from Africa is of the river which flows near one of the missions I have lived in. Standing on the bank watching the river flow past, you sometimes see a piece of wood carried along by the current, drifting this way and that, at the mercy of every whirl and eddy of the stream. Whatever way the water flows, the wood flows too, powerless to resist or to determine its direction in any way.

Elsewhere, a tree has fallen across the river. Its dead weight seems to defy the current; it is as if the tree wants to block the path of the river. But it does no more than restrict it; the river flows around, and under, and over the tree. Gradually a build-up of debris against the fallen trunk creates a wall of resistance, with water building up against it, until the point is reached when the weight of water is greater than the passive inertia of the tree. The tree begins to move little by little until it is dislodged. Once the initial resistance is overcome it gathers speed, pushed quickly downstream by the accumulated weight of water until it is swept onto a sandbank, there to be bleached dry by the sun, while the river, having shed the obstruction, flows on calmly, its battle for freedom won, serene in its victory, the struggle forgotten.

And then again, in another place, you might see a canoe paddled by a man standing upright, using the paddle, the currents, and his skill and experience to get the best value for his effort. When the river flows strongly in the rainy season there is at either bank a strong reverse current which flows against the direction of the main stream. A skilful paddler will not waste energy trying to go upstream against the flow of the current. He stays close to the bank and lets the reverse current do the work for him. Riding the currents he is able to direct the canoe, using skill more than strength, to bring it safely home.

Change is the great constant. How to respond to it is the challenge. One can dance to the rhythm of life and keep a sense of balance, like the sister at Mass. One can be carried along any and every way like driftwood. One can resist stubbornly like the log, and be swept aside. One can ride the waves and the currents, and, as it were, walk on the waters. It's risky, you'll get your feet wet, maybe fall in and have to swim for the shore, but it's better than the alternatives, and it certainly makes for a more interesting, challenging, and human life.

7.2 THE CHALLENGE OF CHANGE

The church has a problem with change. And it does not cope with
it very well. There are many in the church's leadership who see
change as a threat, a danger, a source of instability, disruption and
tension. They feel their security undermined by the speed of
change in the contemporary world. Their feelings might be
expressed in the words of J. F. Lyte's *Abide with me*:

> Change and decay in all around I see . . .[1]

Lumping change and decay together in one breath reveals a lot
about how a person sees life.

It is not surprising that in the church there are deeply
entrenched negative attitudes towards change. For a long time we
boasted that the Catholic church would never change, even if
everyone else did. Our image of the church was not that of the
barque of Peter riding the waves, but of a castle built on a hill
standing firm against the assaults of its enemies. There are people
who respond to the challenge of change by putting their heads in
the sand and saying, in effect, 'I don't want to know about it; tell
me when it's over!' In addition, we have evolved a wonderful
vocabulary of waffle to pretend that we are not changing even
when we are in fact changing.

We change in spasms and convulsions interspersed with long
periods of inertia and stone-walling. For example, the period of the
counter-Reformation from the Council of Trent to the death of
Pope Pius XII in 1958 was one in which the church dug itself
deeper into the trenches, emerging from time to time to take a pot-
shot at its perceived enemies. To have raised, during that period,
the possibility of change in the church would at least have raised
eyebrows, and created the suspicion in some minds that one's
loyalty was in doubt. Then came Vatican II with a great flurry of
excitement, though when the dust had settled it could be seen that
a lot of the change was superficial, more a matter of style than
substance, and life continued much as before. With the death of
Pope Paul VI in 1978, the brakes were firmly applied and gears put
in reverse.

My own country, Ireland, offers one example among many—
some of them worse—of deeply-ingrained resistance to change, of
a theologically baseless identification of the *status quo* with God's
will. Consider the following:

1. In the 1820s Daniel O'Connell launched a campaign for the repeal of a series of laws which seriously limited the civil rights of Catholics. The campaign, which came to be called Catholic Emancipation, was based on peaceful mass protests, perhaps the first of their kind in Europe. It was viewed with deep suspicion by the bishops who preferred to present addresses of loyalty to the kings of England, assuring them of the devotion of their Irish subjects, and petitioning for redress of grievances. However, when it became clear that the Catholic Emancipation campaign was likely to succeed, not least because of the sympathy of liberal public opinion in Britain, the bishops changed course and authorised church collections in support of it. When Daniel O'Connell won, he was the favourite of the bishops, some of whom had previously considered that his views were dangerously close to those of the revolutionaries of France.[2]

2. Some decades later a movement for land reform began under the name of the Land League. Tenant farmers called for fair rent, fixity of tenure, and free sale. Their methods of protest were peaceful, their usual weapon being a boycott of their opponents. A significant difference from the protests which led to Catholic Emancipation was that the people concerned were no longer being led, as it were passively, by a distant leadership, but were themselves active agents of change. What accounted, in part at least, for the difference was that in the meantime people had become literate and were avidly reading a local press which responded to their needs.

   The bishops opposed the Land League, seeing it as a threat to social order, and as inherently hostile to the Catholic faith because it involved the taking of a secret oath. What may also have influenced them was the fact that one of the early actions of the League was undertaken against a parish priest who had been rack-renting his tenants. The Land League chose to take action against the priest so that the struggle for land reform would not take on a sectarian character in a situation where the great majority of landlords were Protestant and the great majority of tenants Catholic. Pope Leo XIII became involved and sent an emissary to investigate the League, who reported back positively on it. Despite this, the pope condemned the Land League in 1888, going against the recommendation of his own emissary because he valued more highly the contrary advice received from Queen Victoria of England, a lady whose views on land reform in Ireland were unlikely to have been radically progressive. However, the papal condemnation was widely ignored, and the League went on to succeed in its objective: the restoration of land to those who worked on it.[3]

3. In the early part of the twentieth century the trade union movement began to gather strength in urban areas. It came under suspicion because of the fear that it might be communist in its outlook. In 1913, a full twenty-two years after the encyclical letter *Rerum Novarum* which taught that workers had a right to form trades unions, some Irish clergy supported employers in locking out and trying to starve into submission workers who had gone on strike for just that right. And for many years afterwards policies with even a mildly social democratic flavour were smeared with the suspicion, or even outright condemnation, of being communist.

4. A little later a movement for political independence developed. In this case the response was mixed: many bishops favoured independence but did not accept that the use of force was either a moral or a practical way of achieving it; some bishops excommunicated leaders of the independence movement; others sat on the fence, waited to see who would win and then declared their support for them. Independence came in 1922.

Thus, in the century between 1820 and 1920, four significant movements for reform met with success despite episcopal opposition. When they succeeded, the bishops gave them their blessing.

But why were the bishops so reactionary or opportunistic in the first place? There are many reasons, of which the following are particularly important:

a) The bishops were largely chosen from an unrepresentative section of Irish society. They did not represent the people so much as a class. Many were what the Irish called 'Castle Catholics', that is those Catholics who for reasons of political expediency allied themselves with the dominant power, which was British, residing in Dublin Castle.

b) The four reform movements spoken of above were all mass

movements in one degree or another, and such movements among the 'lower orders' of society always cause unease in the 'upper orders' who see them as a threat to their position.

c) The Irish bishops had accepted an offer by the British government in 1795 to build a national seminary for Ireland at Maynooth. Coming at the end of a long period of persecution, when any formal theological training for future priests was difficult, the offer was a tempting one. But, as always in such cases, there was a price tag: the immediate one was that the bishops would not oppose the Act of Union between Britain and Ireland in 1800; and the long-term one was that clergy trained in Maynooth would support the existing political and social order.

d) The spirituality in which Irish priests were formed, and in turn sought to form the people, was one which in effect turned a theology of the Cross into a sanction for passivity and fatalism in the face of suffering. There was much preaching on the theme of accepting suffering, that God would right wrongs in his own good time. It was as if whatever happened was God's will because, if it was not God's will it would not have happened in the first place. Such a theology is closer to the Islamic *inshallah* than to the christian faith; the Incarnation is nothing if not interventionist.

One might well wonder how it was that the Irish people remained Catholic at all in the face of such leadership. One reason is that there were many ordinary clergy, especially the parish priests and curates, who were close to the people and took their side against the positions adopted by the bishops. And there were a few individual bishops who had the moral courage to stand against the official positions of the church establishment.

There was also a more basic reason, namely, that the Irish people were able to distinguish between clergy and church, and between church and christianity. So when they rejected what the church leadership was telling them they did not reject the christian faith along with it. That took considerable maturity on the part of the 'simple' faithful. In other countries with similar experiences people dropped out of the faith altogether, often with rancour and bitterness that still lingers.

The Irish example is only one of many which illustrate how not to manage the process of change. No one will blame church leadership for being cautious in the face of new ideas; that is not what is at stake. But people may well blame that leadership for being reactionary, for having an almost reflexive hostility to change —for reasons which do not have an evangelical foundation though they may borrow the language of theology for their formulation, but for reasons which are closer to the conventional wisdom of not rocking the boat, not challenging the *status quo*. That may be safe politics but it is not what the Gospel calls us to.

If the church is to respond to the challenge of change better than it has done in the past, it needs to find an organic model of change so that we can get away from the stop-go, on-off model. It also needs leaders with moral courage, especially the courage to challenge structures and attitudes within the church when they no longer serve the Gospel or God's people.

7.3 OBSTACLES TO CHANGE

Many factors help to account for the negative and hostile attitude towards change in the church. Among them:

1. There is a good deal of smugness and self-satisfaction in the church. In some of its official documents the church calls itself the 'mother and teacher of all nations', and 'an expert in humanity'. This sounds like complacency and even arrogance rather than indicating a willingness to learn from others, recognising that God gives his gifts to whomsoever he wishes. If we were more willing to listen to others and to learn from them it would be a step forward.

2. A lot of resistance to change comes simply from laziness and inertia. That is true of all human beings and institutions. But there is a difference in regard to this problem in the church: we seem at times, and in a way that is entirely uncritical and unexamined, to identify the *status quo* and the will of God, as if proposals for change were almost inherently subversive of the Gospel. But if the *status quo* changes in any case, regardless of our efforts—as for example by the creation of new facts beyond our control—then the new *status* becomes mysteriously invested with the aura of immutable tradition.

3. Resistance to change is sometimes the product of fear, fear of what is new and unknown, and especially the fear of losing

control. But the church, of all bodies, should be least troubled by such fear since it alone has Christ's promise that it will not ultimately fail: 'And remember, I am with you always, to the end of the age.' (Mt. 28:20) The church, secure because of its faith in Christ, should be a pathfinder, a trail-blazer, instead of, as is often the case, lagging behind everyone else only to catch up eventually and reluctantly, but having lost the opportunity of leading humanity forward or giving direction to a movement. This means that, despite many official statements about the primacy of mission in the life of the church, our real priority is maintenance.

4. Another obstacle to change in the church is mistrust and cynicism. There is a widespread perception in the church that the process of consultation is often mere window-dressing for public relations purposes, and is sometimes invited *after* decisions have been reached. This leads people to conclude that there is no point in trying to change the church, and that efforts to do so are simply an exercise in frustration. Two examples may illustrate this point:

a) In 1959, Pope John XXIII called for the revision of the code of canon law. Over the next twenty-four years the canonists went to work, spending much time, energy, and hope in the task of creating a new code, or codes, in the spirit of Vatican II. But the process was short-circuited at the end, when the final edition was drawn up by a small unrepresentative group working alone and forbidden to discuss their work with others. The text published in 1983 ignored much of the work of the previous twenty-four years. For example, the new canon law on marriage was simply the old canon law with some cosmetic changes. In short, it was an opportunity thrown away.

b) In the 1960s and 1970s moral theologians put a lot of care and effort into looking at questions such as a distinction between serious and mortal sin, social sin, a fundamental option for or against God, and, along with pastoral theologians, a new look at the pastoral care of divorced and re-married couples. These matters were discussed at the Synods of Bishops. The post-synodal documents, *Familiaris Consortio* of 1981 and *Reconciliatio et Penitentia* of 1984, elbowed these ideas out of the way, sometimes misrepresenting and belittling them in the process.

One consequence of this is an enormous wastage of human potential within the church. There are many people who care about the church, love it, want to make it a more human place, one which reflects the compassion of Christ to the less-than-perfect, but who give up and go because they see it as an impossible task to create in the church an environment conducive to creative change. To the world outside the church, it comes to be seen either as irrelevant or as an obstacle to human progress.

What is more damaging still is that, among those who remain in the church, some cope with their frustration by accommodating themselves to the prevailing inertia, give up hope, regard enthusiam as evidence of foolish naïveté, while coming to regard cynicism, that most corrosive of spiritual cancers, as a sign of maturity and experience.

But the future lies with those who can offer hope.

5. The church does not give an effective voice to public opinion within its own membership. Catholic mass media institutions are widely seen as clericalised; this may be one reason why an independent lay journal like the English *Tablet* is widely read and respected, while many other church journals are regarded as little better than propaganda sheets. The renewal of censorship, and the dismissal of assertive editors by church authorities undermines the credibility of church periodicals. Without a vigorous public opinion in the church there can be no discussion of issues on their merits, and decision-making necessarily becomes distorted by other considerations such as those of ecclesiastical politics.[4]

If we really value people and the gifts that God has given them we will find ways and means of giving them an effective voice in the church. If lay-people believed that they were truly being listened to, then they would become committed on a large scale, and the present inertia of the church would be transformed.

6. Moral courage and intellectual honesty are in short supply in the church. There can be no creative change without them.

It is worth noting that the six obstacles to change listed above are all psychological, and without a theological basis. That is all the more reason why they should be challenged, not accepted passively. The most effective challenge is not to be found in argument, however persuasive, but in creating new facts.

There is another obstacle to change which may have a theological basis, although it is possible that in reality it is another psychological obstacle dressed up in the guise of theology. I am thinking of our ideas of God. Traditionally, God has been seen as unchanged and unchanging. Lyte's hymn again expresses it well:

> Change and decay in all around I see;
> O thou who changest not, abide with me.[5]

Is it necessarily a part of the Christian faith that God must be unchanging? It has been seen as such, with the argument that if God was not unchanging then there was no solid foundation or security in anything; truth itself would be undermined. But does this necessarily follow, or is it a matter of projecting our inner insecurities onto our theology of God?

Is there anything inherently contradictory or impossible about a God who is dynamic rather than static, who is open to change rather than unchanging? Is an unchanging God a foundational element of the christian faith or a pre-Copernican theology which has become hardened by repetition into immutable certainty? One thing that all of the sciences have made clear to us is that we live in a dynamic, evolving, changing universe. If creation is such, does not that of itself constitute a case for saying that its creator may be dynamic, evolving and changing? The book of Wisdom says that 'from the greatness and beauty of created things comes a corresponding perception of their Creator.' (Wis. 13:5)

In insisting that God is, must be, and cannot be other than unchanging, is there not a risk of the idolatry of making a god to suit ourselves, if not in our own image and likeness, then in the image and likeness of what we might wish to be? A static God will lead to a static church and a static view of truth. This could lead to our identifying our theology of God with the reality of God itself. It was Saint Augustine who pointed out that if you think you have grasped the mystery of God, then whatever it was that you grasped, it was not God. God remains a mystery never amenable to human explanation. If we can live happily with the idea of a God who is open to change, then the prospect of an evolving understanding of truth, of a church which is less of a solid institution that a people on pilgrimage, then we can lift the institutional log-jam and begin to navigate in freedom.

7.4 THE CHURCH HAS CHANGED

A great deal of time, energy and ink has been spent in trying to persuade people that the church does not and has not changed. Yet the church's position has changed in many areas. Consider the following:

1. The third general Council of Constantinople (680–81) censured Pope Honorius I for the ambiguity of his teaching on the nature of Christ. It seems that, for the sake of peace, he had compromised an essential point of doctrine, and the council condemned him for this. Pope Leo II also condemned Honorius, saying that he had 'allowed the immaculate faith of this apostolic church to be stained by an unholy betrayal.'[6]

2. Pope Innocent IV urged that heretics be hunted down and executed by burning. He also urged Saint Louis, King of France, to expel the Jews from his country for disobeying the directives of the Holy See. Pope Clement V ordered King Edward II of England to use torture to extract confessions in criminal cases, and threatened him with punishment if he did not do so.

3. The doctrine of purgatory was not mentioned in any official church documents until the second Council of Lyons in 1274.

4. Slavery was allowed, condoned, and even ordered by several popes.

5. The church taught that it was morally wrong to take interest on loans and condemned as a heretic anyone who taught otherwise.[7]

6. Until the eighteenth century choirboys who sang in Roman churches were sometimes castrated so that their voices would not break.

7. The encyclical letter *Mortalium Animos* of Pope Pius XI, published in 1928, declared it unlawful for Catholics to take part in ecumenical gatherings; Vatican II (1962–5) welcomed such participation.

8. In the 1950s the church condemned organ transplants and conscientious objection to military service. Both were accepted a decade later.

9. The *Catechism of the Catholic Church*, published in 1992, upheld capital punishment (see n.2266–7); Pope John Paul II rejected it in the encyclical letter *Evangelium Vitae* in 1995 (see n.56).

It would be a useful lesson in humility for the church if someone were to compile a comprehensive list of official teachings and statements by church authorities which were later changed, contradicted, or simply abandoned.

One very clear-cut case of a doctrinal change is in regard to the teaching on salvation outside the church. In 1215, Pope Innocent III, in the fourth Lateran Council, declared that 'There is but one universal Church of the faithful, outside which no one at all is saved.'[8] In 1302 the same teaching was reiterated more forcefully by Pope Boniface VIII in the bull *Unam Sanctam*: 'There is only one, holy Catholic, and apostolic Church . . . outside of whom there is neither salvation nor remission of sins . . . We declare, state and define that it is absolutely necessary for the salvation of all men that they submit to the Roman Pontiff.'[9] In 1442 Pope Eugene IV, in the bull *Cantate Domino* stated:

> The most Holy Roman Church firmly believes, professes, and preaches that none of those existing outside the Catholic Church, not only pagans, but also Jews and heretics and schismatics, can have a share in life eternal; but that they will go into the eternal fire which was prepared for the devil and his angels, unless before death they are joined with Her; and that so important is the unity of this ecclesiastical body that only those remaining within this unity can profit by the sacraments of the Church unto salvation, and they alone can receive an eternal recompense for their fasts, their almsgiving, their other works of Christian piety and the duties of a Christian soldier. No one, let his almsgiving be as great as it may, no one, even if he pour out his blood for the name of Christ, can be saved, unless he remain within the bosom and the unity of the Catholic Church.[10]

For many centuries this was the official teaching of the church. It was repeated, albeit in less aggressive fashion, in 1950 by Pope Pius XII in the encyclical letter *Humani Generis*.[11] However, it was a teaching which was not received by the general body of the faithful, thereby providing a good example of reception, or rather non-reception, of an official teaching. It was gradually changed so that Vatican II could state that 'Those who, through no fault of their own, do not know the Gospel of Christ or his Church, but who nevertheless seek God with a sincere heart, and, moved by grace, try in their actions to do his will as they know it through the dictates of their conscience—those too may achieve salvation.'[12]

There remains the problem—for some—of trying to reconcile one set of statements with the other, of trying to convince us that what Vatican II said is no more than a development of what the earlier popes and councils said. One way of attempting this is to explain the anomaly by explaining it away, to 'interpret' it in a way that would be unrecognisable and unacceptable to the original authors of those statements.[13]

This seems dishonest. It would be better to say without ambiguity, 'We have changed our teaching.' Would such an admission destroy people's faith in the church's teaching authority? I believe it would strengthen it. People are more concerned for authenticity than for consistency (wasn't it Saint Thomas Aquinas who said that only the devil is truly consistent?). The church's credibility would be enhanced rather than diminished by a simple acknowledgment of what can be recognised by a study of the question: that what has taken place is not merely a development but a change. When an acorn becomes an oak, that is a development; if it becomes an ash it is a change. What does diminish credibility is the suspicion that slippery semantics are pressed into the service of theology, and that we are sacrificing the truth rather than admitting to having been wrong.

There is another point as well: if we play games of semantic sleight of hand so that the statement of Pope Eugene IV becomes compatible with the above quotation from Vatican II, then the same process can be applied to the statements of any pope, including the incumbent, and they can then be read to mean whatever one wants them to mean. And that would tear credibility to shreds. Those who try to square the circle by means of theological revisionism fool no one but themselves; the 'simple faithful' may be faithful but they are not simple, and they do not like being treated as if they were. In everyone's interests, and on grounds of practicality no less than principle, it would be better all round to acknowledge that church teaching can change, not merely in style or emphasis, but in substance. And it has so changed.

7.5 A TALE OF TWO CITIES

Jerusalem

Jesus of Nazareth was born and reared a Jew. As a child he was circumcised and presented in the Temple in accordance with the requirements of the law of Moses. His parents observed Jewish custom and tradition. As a grown man, Jesus also observed the law of Moses. He said of himself that he had not come to abolish the law but to fulfil it. (Mt. 5:17–19) He taught his disciples to follow it. (Mt. 23:1–3)

After the death, resurrection and ascension of Jesus, the early christian community, which was made up of Jews, began to spread the Gospel to other Jewish communities. This brought them into contact with gentiles (non-Jews) who wished to become followers of Jesus. After some initial uncertainty it was agreed that they could join the community. Peter said, 'I truly understand that God shows no partiality, but in every nation anyone who fears him and does what is right is acceptable to him.' (Acts 10: 34–5) But after this had been agreed a new question arose. On what basis should gentiles be admitted to the christian community? Should gentile converts be required to observe the law of Moses—including, for example, circumcision—or not? This seemingly arcane question was one of deep significance. It touched on a foundational question: is a person saved, that is, redeemed from sin and death, through the observance of the law of Moses or through faith in Christ? There were some, associated with the apostle James, who insisted that circumcision with its associated commitment to Jewish observances was necessary. We do not know what arguments they used, but they could have said that this was what Jesus himself had done and taught, and his church could not do other than he did. But after the apostles, the elders and the assembly had discussed the matter for a long time, Peter addressed them saying that the law had been an impossible burden and 'We believe that we will be saved through the grace of the Lord Jesus.' (Acts 15:11)

Had the early church insisted on circumcision and Jewish observances, christianity would have remained a sect within Judaism. By deciding that faith in Jesus was the basis of salvation they opened the way to becoming a universal church. It is clear from the context in Acts 15 and Galatians 2 that the motive for this change was mission, that is, bringing the Good News to all humanity. The entire matter from beginning to end took roughly six years, from about A.D. 43 TO 49.

Rome

In the late 1960s the question began to be raised in the church as to whether girls, and not only boys, should be allowed to become Mass servers. The question was not insignificant.

In 1970, the Vatican ruled out altar girls in the document *Liturgicae Instaurationes* (n.7). This was repeated in the face of continuing discussion in another document in 1980, *Inaestimabile Donum* (n.18). Discussion continued, however, and the prohibition was repeated on other occasions. It was also widely ignored.

One common argument against altar girls was they were the slippery slope to women priests. Arguments in their favour were usually around the idea of inclusion and equality. Discussion went on for another decade until in 1992 Pope John Paul II confirmed a decision by the Congregation for Divine Worship and the Sacraments allowing altar girls, and ordered its promulgation. The promulgation took two more years, finally appearing in 1994.

Just how the decision was reached, and who the decision-makers were is not known. The process had taken almost twenty-five years.

7.6 What happens if you're not open to change?

There is a price to be paid for closing one's mind to change. Simply to dig in one's heels and refuse to budge is a decision with consequences as real as any other. And trying to put back the hands of the clock and return to some imagined golden age in the past, when the sky was always blue and the grass was always green, is not a realistic option. But there are powerful leaders in the church who openly advocate a policy of 'restoration'. They want to go back to the past, and they react to proposals for change with a degree of caution which cripples initiative and dispirits those who do not see a return to the past as a viable agenda for the future. When the avenues to change are blocked, opportunities are lost or thrown away. For example:

1. I believe history will see *Vatican II* as a lost opportunity. The bishops were so naïve as to imagine that good ideas by themselves were enough, and that it was unnecessary or perhaps even unworthy to consider the politics of the process of change. But where there are humans there are politics, and in the years after the council a struggle developed between the centralised bureaucracy in the Vatican and the bishops for control of the church and of the process of change within it. The bureaucrats won, while the bishops seemed unable to grasp what was

happening. They know now what happened, but it is too late for them. They are reduced to the role of carrying out orders as mere delegates of the Vatican.

In addition, little attention was given to the need for structural change to accompany and reinforce changes of attitude. The post-Vatican II church poured new wine into old wineskins and both were lost. (See Mt. 9:17) Where new structures were introduced, as in the Synod of Bishops, they were controlled so tightly that they have suffocated. And that situation is paralleled at local level in many church councils.

2. *The ecumenical movement* is in danger of becoming another lost opportunity. It is being driven with one foot on the accelerator and the other on the brake. As a result, it has stalled, and in doing so it has lost a vital element, the interest of the faithful, many of whom now see it with something like indifference. The enthusiasm of thirty years ago is gone.

3. *The charismatic movement*, with all its oddities and eccentricities, was a welcome breath of fresh air in the church. I can remember a senior bishop, whose initial attitude to it was one of intense hostility, being won over when he saw that the charismatics were prepared not only to sing 'Alleluia, Jesus' for an hour or two but also to roll up their sleeves and willingly undertake thankless work like feeding dropouts and drifters in a relief centre. But, with the very clear exceptions of Pope Paul VI, Cardinal Suenens and a few others, church leadership did not welcome the opportunity created by the charismatic movement. Enthusiasm, that freshest and rarest of gifts, was allowed to die of indifference.

4. In the area of *human rights*, the church had a lot of catching up to do at both the practical and the doctrinal levels. There was a significant body of opinion in the church which viewed the very concept of human rights with suspicion, because they saw it as a by-product of the French Revolution—Pope Saint Pius X is one example. Despite this the church did catch up through the influence of people like the late Cardinal Pavan. Pope John Paul II has made the promotion of human rights a constant theme of his pastoral visits. But the effectiveness of this witness is undermined by the church's denial of human rights in suppressing dissenters within its own ranks.

How deep is our commitment to the right of church employees to receive a living wage? In this area it sometimes seems that we have excuses for the past, promises for the future, but no remedies for the present.

5. *The womens' movement* is yet another opportunity lost as a result of lack of imagination, excessive caution, and the fear of taking risks. Can the ground be recovered? Probably, with the right leadership, but not without it.

6. The church and *the ecological movement* have become embroiled over one issue: birth control. But there is a much wider field than that to be examined. There is the relationship between the person and nature, and the person in nature, to take only one example. There is scope for developing a vigorous and positive theology of conservation which goes beyond the concept of stewardship and into areas of human participation in God's continuing work of creation and conservation. For instance, the encyclical letter *Humanae Vitae* is often understood as a single-issue document; but another reading of it opens up a challenge to the ecological movement to re-examine itself as to whether it really believes what it says about the person working in a harmonious partnership with nature, especially in that part of nature most intimate to the person, namely, the human body.

7. *The world-wide movement towards democracy* is something which the church should welcome, and there are signs that it has begun to do so, moving from the scepticism, if not outright hostility, expressed by popes at the turn of the century to the more positive approach of Pope John Paul II who stated simply that 'The Church values the democratic system.'[14] But the welcome stops at the church door. It is radiantly clear that the Vatican does not want any democratisation of the church, even though the best paradigm of a christian democracy is the Trinity, where persons, distinct but equal, live in a community of shared love.

8. The *decline in 'vocations'* to the priesthood and religious orders in many parts of the world provides an opportunity for a fresh look at all aspects of ministry, at the balance between mission and maintenance, at priorities and structures in the church. But that has not happened. Instead we have the massaging of statistics, exhortations to try harder with old methods, and a refusal to

examine the problem realistically. The 1990 synod on the formation of priests, and the document *Pastores Dabo Vobis* which followed it, are examples of looking at a wide problem while wearing blinkers.

When the avenues to creative change are blocked, all sorts of results may follow, and some of these are evident in the church at present. We have stagnation and we call it stability. Initiative is crippled, people grow demoralised, give up, and quietly walk away, sometimes hurt, sometimes struggling to keep alive the flame of hope, and sometimes bitter. The longer this problem remains unaddressed, the more likely it is that there will follow either an explosion or an implosion: an explosion, such as happened at the Reformation when the long unresolved problem of the failure to reform the church despite several centuries of effort—as in the Lateran councils of the thirteenth century—led to a division in the church; or an implosion, a quiet collapse of support, where people weigh up the pros and cons of staying in the church and decide that staying is not worth it, so they try to live a human life elsewhere. The implosion is already taking place, not only in the First World,[15] but also in the Third World where there is a steady loss of youth to sects and to a practical atheism. Responsibility for this situation rests in part with those whose policies have killed hope in the lives of so many of the faithful. There is a problem there and it needs to be faced. It is not being faced with an open mind and there will not be any solution until the church is ready to change. Sticking-plaster solutions will not work; fidelity requires approaches which are radical, which go to the roots.

I'm reminded in this context of what was written by one Petronius Arbiter, a wise old pagan who lived in the time of Nero: 'I was to learn late in life that we tend to meet any new situation by reorganising; and a wonderful method it can be for creating the illusion of progress while producing confusion, inefficiency and demoralisation.' That is a good description of what went on in the church after Vatican II. The council did not fail the church; it was the church which failed the council. We tamed and domesticated its impulse, drew the teeth of its radicalism, and suffocated it with caution.

A good illustration of this is what happened to religious orders. While some of them have experienced a genuine renewal in the spirit of their founder and have recovered a sense of their collective vocation, others have substantially remained at square one, with a few cosmetic changes to sustain the illusion of having responded to the call of Vatican II. The latter are not seen as places to look for a radical evangelical alternative to contemporary life. They have become conventional, reflecting rather than challenging the value-system of the world around them. This is not the way to attract the best of the young people.

It is said that vocations are growing in the Third World,[16] and that is certainly true of some countries, though it does not keep pace with population growth. But look at motivation, consider quality, abandon the numbers game. Ask also whether we are not introducing into the church of the Third World a form of religious life and of priesthood which is in terminal decline elsewhere, and introducing structures which are non-viable without an indefinite level of dependence, especially financial dependence, on external aid. Are we grafting on something which may indeed survive, but may not thrive?

The church at present is like a human body suffering from a contraction of the arteries. The flow that gives life is being slowly choked off; we are becoming rigid and sclerotic; we are staggering our way into decline. We need to open up new channels, to let the streams flow, to ride the currents and the waves with all the risks which that entails.

If an organisation refuses to adapt to changing situations, it will find itself left behind like a log thrown up on a sand-bank. To cling to outmoded positions, attitudes and structures when there is no Gospel mandate for doing so is an act of infidelity. One example of unyielding resistance to overdue change is the insistence of maintaining the present ecclesiastical law on clerical celibacy, even though in many places the right of the baptised to receive the sacraments is negated by doing so. If an ecclesiastical law undermines the life and growth of God's kingdom, then there is a moral imperative to change it.

If the arguments for openness to change which are based on principle are not weighty enough, it is worth looking at one based on considerations of practicality or political expediency. It is possible to learn something from the example of the Soviet Union. For decades it seemed to be as solid as a rock. During the 1960s and 1970s, when the western world was often in the throes of political and social turmoil the Soviet Union seemed, to outsiders, to be immune from all such difficulties. In fact, all it was doing was postponing the day when they would have to be faced while, at the same time, narrowing the range of available options in facing them because of its rigid inflexibility. What happened? When Gorbachev opened the windows of the Kremlin to let in some fresh air, the Soviet Union evaporated like dew in the morning sun. The same thing could happen in the church, and we should confront any complacency on the matter with the fact that it did happen before. It happened some twelve centuries ago to the church in north Africa which, from being one of the strongest centres of the christian faith, was swept out of existence by a combination of its own internal weaknesses, such as its lack of inculturation and localisation, and the military action of an aggressive Islamic movement.

How long does it take to learn and apply the lessons of history?

7.7 DEVELOPMENT AND RECEPTION

In this context the word 'development' refers not only to development of doctrine but also to the development of the life and experience of the christian community, its liturgy, its structures, attitudes and practices. The other side of the same coin, and inseparably linked to development, is reception, the process by which the christian community, from the bishops to the last of the faithful, guided by God, shows a spiritual sensitivity in matters of faith, enabling them to hold fast to what is true while rejecting what is false. Development implies a deeper understanding of what is already there; it assumes an essential continuity between the old and the new, not a different conclusion. It builds on the past, and does not contradict it.

Many examples could be cited of development in matters of doctrine. In Mt. 5:21–42 when he deepened existing teachings Jesus himself used the words: 'You have heard that it was said . . . but I say to you . . .' There is also in the New Testament a clear development in the understanding of who Jesus was, from the confusion of the early disciples to the hymn to Jesus' divinity in Paul's letter to the Philippians (2:6–11). It was not Jesus who changed, but his disciples' understanding of him. Similarly, the early centuries of the church were characterised by intense discussion at all levels of the church on the nature of the Trinity, resulting in a richer and deeper grasp of the inner life of God.

The doctrine of papal primacy has developed very substantially from the church's early years: the roles of Peter in the New Testament and of the popes in the twentieth century are different to the extent that there are elements of the present-day papacy which were neither present nor foreseen in the early church. For example, the word 'infallibility' did not enter the vocabulary of theology until the thirteenth century. The understanding of priesthood in today's church is very different from that of its early days,[17] and the present-day faith of the church regarding Mary the mother of Jesus is also a long way from its early antecedents. In some of these cases, while there is no contradiction between the old and the new, there are elements in the new which are so different from the old that one could legitimately ask whether it might not be more accurate to describe what has taken place as a change rather than a simple development.

The how and the why of development may be as important as the what, the content. It is a process where both-and, not either-or, should be the rule. It should be experiential as well as theoretical, inductive as well as deductive, secular as well as sacred in its influences. One example of the latter is the experience of the United States which led the way for others in its constitutional separation of church and state, a development in the understanding of the church vis-à-vis civil society which was substantially secular in its origins but which is now widely accepted within the church, after much initial hostility.

An indispensable precondition for development is free and open discussion, and room for initiative and experiment, and the recognition of a right to dissent. This applies to theology no less than to other matters: doctrine may be stated in propositions but it is lived by people and is subject to a process in people of what might be called 'organic' growth—and this includes the freedom to make mistakes and to learn from them. The context in which development takes place is *communio*, not power politics.

Development takes place because people learn from mistakes; they learn from history, the teacher of life. They become aware of the limitations of language, and consequently of any doctrinal formulae, since these are necessarily conditioned by the language, the hermeneutics, and the culture of their place and time. People learn from the world around them, including the non-christian world, because the Spirit breathes where it wills. Development is also the result of popular pressure, however much ecclesiastical authorities may resent this or try to pretend that they are not influenced by it.

The other side of development is *reception*. This is a process involving the whole church which, while it does not create a truth, nor legitimise a decision, is the final indication that such a decision has fulfilled the necessary conditions for it to be a true expression of the faith.[18] The role of church leadership is, through a process of discernment and response, to articulate what is the faith of the church.

The history of theology provides examples of situations where doctrinal positions were sometimes received, sometimes not. In the first four centuries of the church's life there was prolonged discussion as to what religious writings were to be considered part of the Bible, and what were not. For example, were the 'gospels' of Thomas and Peter to be held by the church as those of Matthew, Mark, Luke and John? The matter was not resolved until the fourth century, when the books of the present Bible were agreed upon. That was an example of the *sensus fidei* (the sensitivity to faith of the baptised) at work.

That same *sensus fidei* can reject something even when it comes from a general council of the church. For instance, the decision of the council of Constance (1414–17) that a council was superior in authority to a pope was not accepted by the church.[19] The council of Basel-Ferrara-Florence (1431–45) declared union between Catholics and Greek Orthodox, but this came to nothing, perhaps because the process of re-union did not involve the lay-people of either church but was imposed as a decision from the top down, motivated in part at least by political considerations, and on the basis of acceptance of the doctrine of no salvation outside the church.[20] The short cut, quick-fix approach of trying to impose something on people does not work; they will not accept it.

From the beginning of the church up to the time of the Reformation, *reception* both as an idea and as a practice was widely accepted in the church; it was part of its normal life. During the counter-Reformation, and in the centuries which followed it, there were strong centralising tendencies, with an over-emphasis on the role of the hierarchy at the expense of the laity. Vatican II re-discovered the doctrine of reception, but it is now in danger of being lost again. Many Catholic theological dictionaries, encyclopaedias, and theological textbooks omit any reference to it, and it is not well understood in the church. It raises many eyebrows, arouses suspicions of unorthodoxy, and is considered by some of those who are aware of it (and many are not) to be best left to die a natural death due to inertia. It is strange that a doctrine and practice which was normal in the church for fifteen of its twenty centuries should now be left to gather dust on library shelves.[21] Yet it was to this that Pope Gregory VII appealed when he called on christian lay-people to reform the church when his appeals to the clergy to reform themselves met with indifference. Those who wish *reception* to die a quiet death may themselves come to regret its passing and their part in its death.

Suppose for a moment that *reception* had been as alive in the church after the Reformation as before it, what might have happened? Would it have taken the church 350 years to say to Galileo, as Pope John Paul II did, 'Sorry, we were wrong,' or more than nine hundred years for the excommunication against the Orthodox to be lifted? And there are other similar questions. The questions can be ignored but the consequences of doing so have to be lived with.

7.8 ENABLING IT TO HAPPEN: SPIRIT AND STRUCTURES

The greatest need of the church today is the re-creation of the spirit and practice of dialogue. One requisite for bringing that about is to express theology in language which is comprehensible to ordinary people. Much of it is incomprehensible, and maybe it is intended to be so in order to keep theology within the preserve of specialists and to keep lay-people at a distance. Professionals as a rule do not like amateurs, especially enthusiastic ones, grazing on their patch of grass. Language is meant to be a bridge, not a barrier, and theologians should speak about God in language that can be widely understood.

In order to cope with the challenge of change we also need to re-learn to trust one another. The world is not full of enemies of the church, and even those who are enemies could be potential allies, while the indifferent may be stimulated to interest by a call to open dialogue. We live in a sharply divided world, but it is also one which probably has never before been so aware of sharing a common humanity. Experience is teaching people that the pursuit of individual selfishness does not add up to the common good of all. The church has much to offer the world and much to receive from the world. Dialogue is the way forward for both.

When an institution is gripped by stagnation, leadership is needed. Jesus Christ was a superb leader. He encouraged, enabled, and enthused. He accepted and respected people despite differences, welcomed a two-way flow of communication, a dialogue, and worked to create unity on a foundation of truth. The church today needs leaders with an unambiguous commitment to intellectual honesty and moral courage, who will tackle what is wrong in the church itself, and be prepared to take the criticism that this will inevitably bring, the misrepresentation, and the imputation of disloyalty. We need leaders who can differentiate between the essentials and the non-essentials, who can calmly let go the latter while holding on to the former with firmness. We need leaders who can live with the spiritual poverty of uncertainty, and be sparing of absolutes, while having enough trust in God to take risks.

Another quality of leadership is vision—and the ability to articulate and communicate it. A church leader needs a vision of the church, formulated by and with the church, and which is for the church and the world, because the church does not exist for itself but for others. Such a vision requires that it be communicated through ideas, images, gestures, structures, and new facts. It recognises that anything we do is provisional, limited, inadequate and stumbling, but it still goes forward, ready to change, adapt, and try again and again.

Structural change is a necessary accompaniment to a change of attitudes. Both are needed.

One structural change needed is for us to lighten the load of institutional baggage we carry around. There is a sort of institutional reflex in the church whereby we smother every idea under a structural load. We could learn from the evangelical churches who, as it were, travel light. We put vast resources of time, energy, personnel and money into maintaining structures, and relatively little into mission, though mission is nearer to the central role and definition of the church. Fortunately, the situation is changing, even though it is doing so despite our efforts rather than because of them. Because of the personnel crisis in the church the shedding of much of our institutional burden becomes unavoidable. This creates a situation of freedom from maintenance in order to be free for mission.

A second structural change needed is to decentralise, and to make the local church the foundation, the centre, the heart of the church's life. The universal church would be a communion of local churches delegating whatever functions, if any, they considered required delegation to a bureaucracy which would be their servant. The heart of the local church would be the family, not the school or the parish, however important they might be.

8

A Vision of the Future

8.1 Getting one's bearings

> It is not easy to remember
> that in the fading light of day
> the shadows always point toward the dawn.[1]

There is a lot more right with the church than wrong with it. For instance, the church has committed itself strongly, and sometimes alone, to the defence of the life of the unborn; that is an act of courage and solidarity with humanity which deserves more credit than it gets.

Having said that, it is necessary to point out what is wrong with the church—and to do so is not being negative. Needs must be admitted before they can be addressed. And they need to be addressed with realism: optimism is not hope, nor is wishful thinking positive thinking.

8.2 A church open to self-examination

At the risk of some repetition, it may be worth listing briefly some essential points which need to be addressed:

1. There is a power battle going on in the church. Much of the present disharmony is about power, the goals it serves and the manner in which it is exercised. The Vatican has progressively re-centralised power over the past twenty-five years or so; we have an over-centralised, top-heavy, bureaucratic power monopoly in the Vatican.

2. We have fallen into ecclesiolatry: we have made the church an end in itself, instead of a means to the End, which is, and can

only be, God. But God will never be reduced to a means to the achievement of our ends, and any attempt to do this can only lead to confusion, demoralisation and loss of direction.

3. We do not trust our own people. There is increasing mistrust in the church and, with it, a tendency to write off those who fail to conform to the party line as not being 'real' Catholics. Orthodoxy, defined in terms of one theology, is being used as a stick to beat people with, and to drive them from the church.

4. In place of dialogue, without which there is neither communication nor *communio*, there are monologues, dictation and the pursuit of hidden agendas.

5. The signs of the times are being misread. For example, one hears it said that people no longer accept authority. The truth is that people don't accept dictation any more; they will accept authority in which they participate. They will not accept a power structure which equates authority with its view of its own power, and which is without accountability or clearly defined and operative moral goals and limits.

What results flow from this situation? Here is a sample:

a) There is a silent schism in the church. People are alienated and some are in despair; others have given up and have simply gone away, perhaps for good. An African priest said to me some years ago, 'I feel like a stranger in my father's house.'

b) There is fear in the church. As evidence of this, one can see the clear contrast between the private and the public statements of clergy on issues ranging from contraception to celibacy to women's ordination.

c) There is a loss of identity in the church. We are in a state of drift, without direction, and this is accentuated by efforts to restore the ecclesiastical *ancien régime*.

d) There is a loss of morale among Catholics, including some—perhaps many—clergy. With this there is sometimes a sense that it is futile even to attempt to reform the church, that it is simply effort wasted.

There are people who, on reading the above, will dismiss it as a series of exaggerations and generalisations. To those I would say, 'Have you listened? If you think you have, try again, listening not only with your ears, but with your head and your heart.' Others will say that it is all negative, and want to know why I haven't looked on the bright side of things. I have a parable for such people. If your house is on fire and I run and tell you about it, would you respond to me by saying, 'I was alright until you came along bringing me bad news. Go away, I don't want to hear any more about it.'

I remember listening some thirty-five years ago to a lecture given by a university professor of history in which he said something similar to what I have written above—but in milder form, because the problem wasn't so serious then. What happened? His ideas were dismissed and he was written off as an 'enemy of the church'.

It needs to be said again and again that things need not be like this; they can be better, and they will be better, if we begin with an acknowledgement of what is wrong.

8.3 A CHURCH WHICH DOES PENANCE

Confession is good for the soul, and that is true for the church no less than for the individual. It would be good to see the church rid itself of smugness and self-satisfaction, complacency, triumphalism, or pretentiousness. We are a church of sinners. Let us get away once and for all from the mentality which allows us to say, for example, that 'The world was created for the sake of the church' or 'The church is the goal of all things.'[2] Is it not rather that the church was created for the sake of the world, and God alone is the goal of all things, and the church is a means to God?

Recent years have provided us with two examples of public communal repentance. One is in Germany (West more than East) where the German people and the German state have openly faced the crimes committed during the second world war, and have asked pardon for them, as well as doing whatever was humanly possible to make up in some way, however inadequately, for those crimes. This has enabled the German people to stand up again and look the world in the face; it has been a cleansing and purifying process which has won them world-wide respect. (Japan, for the most part, tries to pretend it has no crimes to confess—and the wartime Allies likewise.) The second example is that of the Dutch Reformed church in South Africa which provided the moral underpinning and motivation for apartheid through some bizarre interpretations of scriptural texts. It has acknowledged in recent years, for instance in the Kairos document of 1986, that it was wrong, that apartheid was in fact sinful, and the church has asked pardon of the victims of apartheid.

Is it shameful, humiliating, or degrading for an institution to acknowledge its wrongs publicly? Some people would think so, but a christian shouldn't. Let us not fall into the trap of thinking that the church cannot be wrong; it can be and has been many times. Let us recognise for what it is—pride and arrogance—the mind-set that seems to say the church is always right, even when it is demonstrably wrong.

For what should the church apologise? It needs to apologise to those people who suffered because the church condoned, sometimes practised, sometimes even ordered slavery, torture, colonialism and anti-semitism. It should apologise to women for their long-standing relegation to an inferior status in the church. To his credit, Pope John Paul II has acknowledged all of those things, and has apologised for them at different places and times.[3] But it has not gone far enough; the whole church needs to be involved. Think of what it would mean if the men of the church were publicly to make a collective act of repentance for the crimes committed by men against women, for the rapes, beatings, enforced prostitution, mutilation, and multiple acts, attitudes and systems of discrimination against women, and at the same time commit themselves to fighting against those in the future. Sincerely entered into, it would make a real difference; if not genuine, it would be better left undone.

And what of repentance for the ways in which religion has been abused to force people to toe the line? It is an abuse of religion to use people's fear of God, or fear of hell, to pressurise them into doing what is right; it is simply wrong and without moral justification. This repentance would best be expressed by re-orientating our moral theology away from a framework of punishment and reward to one which looks at issues instead, in a framework of wounding and healing, falling and rising, division and unity. The best way for the church to repent for its frequent suppression of the human right to freedom of thought and expression would be to recognise that right willingly and without ambiguity in its internal life. That will require a change.

And it would be good if the church moved away from politically timed (and motivated?) canonisations.

Lastly, under this heading, when there are scandals in the church—and Jesus has told us that we will always have them—let us clean up, not cover up. Let us face issues, not fudge them. Let us have the courage to apply our own teaching. Let us set the record straight. And while on the subject of setting records straight, let us open up our archives to students of history. This would lift from Catholic historians of the church the suspicion that their symbol is the white-wash brush. Jesus has taught us that the truth will make us free. (Jn. 8:32) Have we the courage to take him at his word?

8.4 A CHURCH WHICH WELCOMES ALL OF GOD'S GIFTS
Priests and Priesthood: Women Priests?
When the question of the ordination of women to the priesthood first came to be discussed at a significant level in the church some twenty years ago, the context in which it arose was that of the womens' liberation movement with its demand for equality of rights and opportunity. The same question is now being discussed in a different context, that of ministry to God's people. This is a substantial step forward, and helps to situate discussion of the question in a more positive and constructive framework.

In the document *Inter Insigniores* of 15 October 1976[4] the Sacred Congregation for the Doctrine of the Faith defended the church's discipline in this matter,[5] by saying that Christ chose only men and the church could not do otherwise. It went onto say that priests must be male since they act *in persona Christi*, and Christ was a man.[6] It acknowledged that this was not a demonstrative argument but was profoundly fitting in view of the analogy of faith.[7]

Nearly twenty years later, Pope John Paul II, in his letter *Ordinatio Sacerdotalis* of 22 May 1994, drew substantially on the earlier document, and concluded, 'I declare that the church has no authority whatsoever to confer priestly ordination on women and that this judgment is to be definitively held by all the church's faithful.'[8]

More recently, on 18 November 1995, the Congregation for the Doctrine of the Faith published a letter it had earlier sent to episcopal conferences on the same subject. It stated that the teaching contained in *Ordinatio Sacerdotalis* 'requires definitive assent, since, founded on the written Word of God, and from the beginning constantly preserved and applied in the tradition of the church, it has been set forth infallibly by the ordinary and universal magisterium.' It went on to state that the pope, 'exercising his proper office of confirming the brethren, has handed on this same teaching by a formal declaration, explicitly stating what is to be held always, everywhere, and by all, as belonging to the deposit of faith.'[9] It concluded by saying that the pope approved the CDF letter and ordered its publication.

What is the scriptural basis for this teaching? None of the three texts listed above cites any scriptural texts in its support. The Pontifical Biblical Commission reported to Pope Paul VI before *Inter Insigniores* was written that there was no solid biblical basis for the exclusion of women from the ministerial priesthood, and that texts adduced in support of their exclusion were not strong enough to bear the burden of argument being placed upon them.[10] If the Pontifical Biblical Commission is right, it is difficult to see how Cardinal Ratzinger's statement stands: that the exclusion of women from priesthood is a teaching founded on the written Word of God.

It may be said that there is an argument from scripture in that Christ was a man, and a woman cannot be an 'icon' of Christ for that very reason, and that being such an 'icon' is what priesthood is about. This raises the question of what exactly the 'iconic' character of priesthood is about. Is it about masculinity or is it about holiness? What confers it? If it is the sacrament of order which does so, then is it not begging the question to say that a woman cannot be an 'icon' of Christ because she is a woman.

Furthermore, does a woman not represent Christ when she baptises, as women have done since the earliest days of the church? She baptises in the name of the Father, and of the Son, and of the Holy Spirit. It seems to load the 'iconic' character of the priesthood with too heavy a burden of theological significance to rule out priesthood for women simply because they are of a different sex to Christ. But if one insists that this is legitimate then one opens up the question of how a male priest can be an icon of our holy mother the church who is the bride of Christ.

Arguments for the exclusion of women from priesthood based on tradition need to be used with caution. It is certainly true that, as a matter of fact, women have not been ordained to the priesthood (the diaconate is another matter). Historically, their exclusion was based on the assumption that they were inferior to men. To the extent that the question was examined at all—and it was more often dismissed out of hand—it was said that since women were inferior to men, they could therefore not exercise the leadership role over them which priesthood implies. A textbook in use in seminaries until the 1960s summarises this position well: 'The reason why a woman cannot receive holy orders is because the clerical state demands a certain superiority since it involves ruling the faithful; whereas a woman by her very nature is inferior to man and subject to him, even though at a personal level she can excel a man in her natural and graced giftedness.'[11]

Those who argue against priesthood for women on the grounds of tradition need to consider whether they do so despite the fact that there are many recent statements of church authority about the equality of male and female.

Church leaders sometimes say that it is their duty to reject in feminism whatever is contrary to the Gospel. That is certainly true. But if that position is truly motivated by fidelity to the Gospel, and not an excuse for anti-feminism, then it needs to be accompanied by an equally firm rejection of anything in the life and teaching of the church which is contrary to the status and dignity of women as taught by the Gospel. And that poses a problem for the argument from tradition.

The letter of the Congregation for the Doctrine of the Faith states that the teaching in *Ordinatio Sacerdotalis* 'has been set forth infallibly by the ordinary and universal magisterium'. Vatican II teaches that the 'Magisterium is not superior to the Word of God, but is its servant.'[12] And it goes on, 'sacred Tradition, sacred Scripture and the Magisterium of the church are so connected and associated that one of them cannot stand without the others.'[13] Clearly, then, the magisterium cannot offer a teaching which does not have a solid basis in scripture or tradition and say that it is part of the deposit of faith because it says so. 'All teaching in the church is ultimately exposition of scripture,' wrote Cardinal Ratzinger.[14]

The infallibility of the ordinary and universal magisterium referred to in the letter is described in the Code of Canon Law as follows:

> The College of Bishops also possesses infallibility in its teaching when the Bishops, gathered together in an Ecumenical Council and exercising their *magisterium* as teachers and judges of faith and morals, definitively declare for the universal church a doctrine to be held concerning faith or morals; likewise, when the Bishops, dispersed throughout the world but maintaining the bond of union among themselves and with the successor of Peter, together with the same Roman Pontiff authentically teach matters of faith or morals, and are agreed that a particular teaching is definitively to be held.
>
> No doctrine is understood to be infallibly defined unless this is manifestly demonstrated.[15]

What is in question in the CDF letter therefore is not *papal* infallibility, but that of the college of bishops in union with the pope. This may be exercised either in an ecumenical council, though that does not apply in this case, or when the bishops, although dispersed throughout the world, are agreed that a particular teaching is to be definitively held.

One may well ask how the bishops exercised their collegial infallibility in this latter sense since they neither met to discuss the question, nor were they asked for their opinion about it. In view of this consideration, can it honestly be said that infallibility has been manifestly demonstrated? In the encyclical letter *Evangelium Vitae*, Pope John Paul II stated that he had written a personal letter to each bishop asking for his co-operation in preparing it, and that he had received replies from bishops in every country of the world.[16] That represents a greater level of consultation than with the CDF letter, yet no one claims that *Evangelium Vitae* is infallible.

Is there some significance in the fact that Pope John Paul II has not, as yet anyway, said that the statement is infallible? The CDF says it is, and the pope approved the CDF letter which said it. Those two are not quite the same thing. Is that a legal loophole being left for future generations of theologians to reverse through should some backtracking be required? It is open to question whether the teaching, as formulated by the CDF, meets the criteria spelled out in canon law for infallibility.

What case is there *for* the ordination of women? Perhaps the best argument proposed so far is that a priesthood drawn from both sexes is necessarily better able to reflect the fullness of the humanity of Christ, who is true God and true man, that is, fully divine and fully human, than a priesthood drawn from only one sex. This point, (though without this conclusion) was made by Pope John Paul II when he wrote, 'It is only through the duality of the "masculine" and the "feminine" that the "human" finds full realisation.'[17] If the present situation were one in which only women were admitted to priesthood and the debate was about the admission of men, the same argument would hold equally well.

A point worth reflecting on, though it does not constitute an argument as such, is that the first witnesses to the resurrection of Jesus were women, and being a witness to that event was a requisite for being an apostle. (Acts 1:22)

It is sometimes said, arguing against the ordination of women, that the church cannot do other than Christ did, and since he ordained only men, then the church likewise should ordain only

men. But, as we have seen already,[18] the early church did other
than Christ did in admitting gentiles to the christian community
without the need of either circumcision or a commitment to the
observance of the law of Moses, and has continued to follow that
practice ever since. Furthermore, Christ ordained married men,
so, using the same logic, the church should ordain only married
men. Yet not only does the church not ordain married men, but it
prohibits their ordination, even though Peter and the apostles were
married.

It is also said that, in view of ecumenical relations with the
Orthodox, the question of the ordination of women should be set
aside for the present. Such a viewpoint raises important questions
about ecumenical methodology, but it is also based on a
misunderstanding of the position of many Orthodox. The
Orthodox churches have already indicated a willingness to admit
(strictly speaking, to re-admit) women to the diaconate, and one of
them, the Armenian Apostolic Church, has already done so. So
who is waiting for whom?[19]

What has been written above is about theological arguments for
and against women's ordination. I have not heard any arguments
against their ordination which I find convincing. That is not to say
that they do not exist.

The burden of proof rests with those who wish to introduce
women's ordination, since they are proposing to change a practice
of twenty centuries. The case for women's ordination needs to be
better developed, going beyond the 'why not' argument, and
received by the church, before it can be considered to have fully
met the requirements for change.

Those who argue against it need to watch carefully the
implications of the bases of their arguments. In particular, there
will be an enormous loss to the teaching authority of the church if
it appears that infallibility is being invoked without adequate
theological support; if without solid support in scripture, tradition,
or consultation among the college of bishops it is being presented
like a *deus ex machina* to short-circuit dialogue and discernment,
and to beat opponents into line.

The poem 'Did the Woman say?' by Frances Frank is thought-
provoking in this context:

> Did the Woman say, when she held him
> first in the dark of the stable,
> after the pain, the bleeding, the crying;
> 'This is my Body; this is my Blood'?

Did the Woman say, when she held him
for the last time in the dark rain on the hilltop,
after the pain, the bleeding, the dying,
'This is my Body; this is my Blood'?

Well that she said it to him then.
Men ordain that she not say it for him now.[20]

Perhaps the Woman will find the answer in a united christian church.

Priests and Priesthood: Married Priests?

There is a crisis of morale among Catholic priests in many parts of the church. This tends to focus on, but is not confined to, the issues of the appointment of bishops, and the law on clerical celibacy. In fact, priests are just as much affected as anyone in the church, and sometimes more so, by the issues raised in earlier chapters of this book. For instance, the type of leadership in the church, both in its substance and in its style, affects them closely.

Two anecdotes may illustrate. The first relates to a survey on the morale of the priests of a country, conducted on behalf of its episcopal conference. The survey found that morale was low, and that this was attributable in the main to lack of leadership from the bishops. The surveyor believed that there was little the bishops could do about it, because they simply did not have leadership ability. Would they have been chosen as bishops in the first place if they had had it, or would leadership qualities have raised doubts in the minds of the decision-makers in the Vatican as to whether the man in question was a safe pair of hands?

The other was where, in conversation with a group of young seminarians, I asked them what they thought of the new bishop of the diocese. I was prepared for almost any answer, except the one I got: an explosion of laughter, a hearty, honest bellyful of it. I asked no further questions.

A compounding element in the crisis of morale is the widespread perception that significant issues are not being acknowledged, much less addressed with any realism. The issue of the ecclesiastical law on clerical celibacy is a particularly clear example of this. It constitutes a real problem. The official response to the problem is to stone-wall, refuse to call facts by name, restrict the flow of statistical information relevant to the topic and, in short, to refuse to enter into an honest dialogue about it. That is a good example of how *not* to exercise leadership in handling a problem.

I believe that a large majority of Catholic priests are habitually faithful to their vow of celibacy. I also believe in the value of the Gospel charism of celibacy for the sake of the kingdom of heaven. (See Mt. 19:21) The point being made here is not about the value of the charism, but about the practical wisdom of retaining the present church law relating to it. By way of analogy, it is like being in favour of penance, in accordance with the Gospel, without favouring the old-style church laws on Lenten fast and abstinence.

There are at least four good reasons for changing the present law on celibacy:

1. A married clergy, working together with a celibate clergy, (both-and, not either-or) would necessarily give a more complete witness to the full reality of Jesus Christ than a clergy made up solely of celibates. The two types of clergy working together would give more inclusive pastoral service than celibates could give on their own.

2. The right of the baptised to receive the sacraments is, in some places, negated as a result of the present law. Their right to the sacraments has a prior and more compelling claim than that of ecclesiastical discipline.

3. The present law of the church makes celibacy seem like a price to be paid for becoming a priest and therefore not entirely a free choice. If the law allowed a real choice, then the witness value of those who choose to remain celibate would be greatly enhanced: it would be more clearly seen and appreciated that they had chosen celibacy for its own sake.

4. On a case by case basis, those priests who have left the active ministry because of this issue should be shown the compassion which Jesus showed to Peter, the first of the apostles, who denied him three times. They have not denied Christ; for the most part, they are men who needed to affirm their humanity, but could not do so within the framework of celibacy. The role of the church, one could say its definition, is forgiveness and reconciliation; let us show it.

A change in the law would prevent many problems from arising and burdening the lives of these men, their wives, and their families.

There is a counter-argument to the above, in particular to the second point. It is to say that there is no proven causal connection between the law of clerical celibacy on the one hand and the shortage of priests on the other. It says, in effect, 'Prove that the law causes the shortage and then we'll change the law.'

One could respond to that challenge in several ways:

a) No one claims that the law on celibacy is the sole cause of the decline in the number of priests; it is one factor among many.

b) The reasons for changing the law are not based solely on that decline; it is a good idea on its own merits, even if there were no decline.

c) One may question whether it is not inherently impossible to *prove* (the word prove is important) such a causal connection. It is like being asked to prove a causal connection between pornography and sexual violence: it may be impossible to do so, but most people believe it is there. Is it that the advocates of change are being asked to prove something which of its nature is incapable of proof, before any move will be made? That is an effective way of stalling an issue, but is it a good way of facing one? It is clear, however, on the basis of their own evidence, that the very great majority of priests who left the active ministry did so because they wished to marry. (In Britain and Ireland alone there are about a thousand such priests.)[21]

As part of the overall context of this problem, it is worth looking at some statistics.[22] In 1984 there were 375,000 official pastoral units in the church. These are defined for statistical purposes as specific areas, having a christian community, a church building, and normally a resident priest. The most common example of this would be a parish. Of the 375,000 some two hundred and seven thousand or over 55 per cent, did not in fact have a resident priest. In the same year, 58 per cent of the world's priests were living in Europe, and their average age was 52.7 years.[23] And let nobody imagine that the Third World can come to the rescue of the First World: between 1984 and 1994 the number of priests in mission countries rose by 7 per cent;[24] by how much did population rise in those countries in the same period?—by about 28 per cent. In 1971, Zambia had sixty-three locally-born priests, and in 1981 it had exactly the same number.[25] The drop-out rate among priests in the first ten years after ordination in Africa and the USA is about 40 per cent.

And replacements? For every 100 priests who died or left the active ministry in the period 1970–80, the replacement rate was as follows, country by country:

Italy	50 per cent
Ireland	45 per cent
Spain	35 per cent
Germany	34 per cent
France	17 per cent
Belgium	15 per cent
Portugal	10 per cent
The Netherlands	8 per cent[26]

The number of active diocesan priests in the USA is in decline from 35,000 in 1966 to a projected 21,000 in 2005.[27] At present, there are about three thousand parishes in the USA without a resident priest, and some four thousand in France.[28] At present, there are some dioceses which face the threat of being without priests in the not too distant future. And it is estimated that by the end of the century about half the priests of the church will be aged fifty-five or over, and only one-eighth aged thirty-four or less.[29]

Can anyone read those statistics and then fall back on the argument that we must wait until a causal connection between the law on clerical celibacy and the shortage of priests is proven before making a move? The situation is reminiscent of the story of a doctor talking to a patient in hospital and telling him, 'I've got two pieces of news for you, one good and the other bad. I'll give you the good news first. The lab tests show that you've only forty-eight hours to live.' The shocked patient could barely bring himself to reply, 'If that is what you call good news, what on earth is the bad news?' 'The bad news', said the doctor, 'is that the results came yesterday and I forgot to tell you.'

The issue of the law on celibacy has been debated at wearisome length in the church for the past thirty-five years or so. The arguments for change have won the day so persuasively and so massively that the burden of proof has now swung to the other side.

It is the advocates of the present law who now have to establish the validity of their case. How long are we going to continue baptising people into practical excommunication—and that is what we do, because many of those we baptise will rarely, perhaps never, receive the sacraments because of lack of pastoral follow-up after baptism —before we finally decide the time has come to do something about it?

We can learn something from other churches if we want to. For example, the Catholic church in Canada is experiencing a serious shortage of clergy, while the Anglican church there is adequately staffed. In Zambia, the New Apostolic church, which came to the country only in 1953, has already moved well ahead of the Catholic church in the west of the country in terms of numbers, the commitment of its members, and the willingness of its local leaders to accept responsibility for themselves. One reason among several which account for that situation is that those churches have adequate pastoral care because the number of clergy they have is not affected by the insistence on celibacy.

What will happen if the Catholic church does not change this law? One likely result is that we will see more of what has already begun, the slow decay of parish life through inadequate pastoral care, loss of clerical morale, and the simple inability to cope with the demands because of declining numbers. We could respond to that situation by having part-time priests, or priesthood for a fixed period of time. But neither of those is an adequate response to the problem.

If we decide to change now, we still have the time to direct the process of change, to make intelligent, considered decisions, and to be able to think our way through the process. If we delay, we may be faced with a practical collapse of pastoral life in some countries, where the options have run out, and where circumstances impose their own agenda outside our control. Which do we wish to be, a piece of driftwood spun around by the currents, or the canoe carefully riding the waves?

There remains another question. If the situation is as described above, then why has the Vatican not seen the light and changed? One explanation is that the Vatican wants it to happen, that it regards western Europe and North America as lost to the church anyway, washed away by secular humanism, liberalism, and consumerism, and now beyond salvaging. Therefore (so the argument runs), better to let them die out, and then make a fresh start in another generation with 'real' Catholics drawn from groups like the Neo-Catechumenate, Communio e Liberazione, and Opus Dei. It is hard to believe that the Vatican could adopt or even acquiesce in an agenda of such staggering cynicism. But proponents of this theory point to the Netherlands as an example of a place where it has already happened: they say that the Vatican, in the 1970s, decided to write off the Netherlands as lost territory; so it installed bishops at the far end of the conservative scale to rally its supporters, and then simply sat back and waited for the drift of disillusioned liberals from the church to run its course; when it considers that only a reliable remnant remains it will proceed to restore the Dutch church on its own lines, more Roman than Rome.

Another possible explanation for the Vatican's refusal to change the law on clerical celibacy is that it recognises that a married clergy would cost more than a celibate clergy; they would also be less amenable to episcopal control, for example, in transfers; and, sooner or later, there would be scandals involving clerical divorces or polygamy. Seen in this way, money and power seem to be at the heart of the matter, since there are no theological arguments against a married clergy. If that is what it is about, would it not be better to say so and face those questions openly, without sham or pretence; to discuss the matter with full access to relevant information; and in short, to face the problem like intelligent adults? If there is the fear that celibate clergy would come to be seen as the 'real' priests, with those who are married relegated to the second division (though it could be the other way round!), is that not a problem to be discussed through open dialogue and mutual understanding? Surely the above problems are not inherently insurmountable? So why not face them?

What we have in the church at present is not celibacy for the sake of the kingdom of heaven (see Mt. 19:12); it is the kingdom of heaven for the sake of celibacy. The present and future life and growth of the church are being sacrificed for the sake of an ecclesiastical law on celibacy. And that is to turn Gospel values upside down.

8.5 A CHURCH OPEN TO COMMUNION

'The ultimate goal of the ecumenical movement is to re-establish full visible unity among all the baptised.'[30] For the past thirty years the Catholic church has been engaged in a re-evaluation of its relationship to other churches, and a good deal of progress has been made in that time. Perhaps it could be said that a point of no return has been reached, where it will not be possible to return to the attitudes and practices of the past.

Certain basic attitudes of mind within the Catholic church itself are a prerequisite for realistic engagement in the ecumenical process. Among them may be included:

1. Tolerance of diversity: '. . . legitimate diversity is in no way opposed to the church's unity, but rather enhances her splendour, and contributes greatly to the fulfilment of her mission.'[31]

2. A spirit of dialogue: 'Dialogue . . . has become an outright necessity, one of the Church's priorities.'[32]

3. Respect for the person: 'Truth is to be sought after in a manner proper to the dignity of the human person . . . The inquiry is to be free, carried on with the aid of teaching or instruction, communication, and dialogue.'[33]

4. Recognition of the role of *reception* in the development of ecumenical relations: 'We are in fact dealing with issues which frequently are matters of faith, and these require universal consent, extending from the Bishops to the lay faithful, all of whom have received the anointing of the Holy Spirit. It is the same Spirit who assists the Magisterium and awakens the *sensus fidei*.'[34]

5. Working in *communio*: 'All this however must always be done in communio.'[35]

The above statements refer to attitudes of mind, an outlook, a way of looking at things which will shape substantially the content no less than the tone of ecumenical dialogue. Those statements of principle show broadmindedness, generosity of spirit and breadth of imagination. If applied first of all within the Catholic church, they would make a large and necessary contribution to its healing and regeneration.

Looking outwards to other believers in God, there are also statements and actions which give hope of a fresh outlook. Pope John Paul II has written that 'wherever people are praying in the world, there the Holy Spirit is, the living breath of prayer.'[36] And there was generosity, courage and imagination in the action of the same pope in calling leaders of world religions, both christian and non-christian, to Assisi for a day of prayer for peace.

Catholics and Orthodox

It would be impossible in a chapter of this nature to try to cover all the ground on Catholic-Orthodox relations. Instead, only three points will be made, because they have special significance.

The first point is that ecumenism is either the work of the whole church, from top to bottom, or it is not ecumenism. We have good statements of principle on this point, for example, '. . . the quest for unity, far from being limited to a group of specialists, comes to be shared by all the baptised. Everyone, regardless of their role in the church or level of education, can make a valuable contribution . . .'[37] We also have the historical precedent of the reunion between Catholics and Orthodox which was achieved at the general council of Basel-Ferrara-Florence (1431–45), and which fell apart within a few years due to the lack of interest and commitment to it on the part of the great majority of both Catholics and Orthodox. What lessons can be learned from that experience? One is that participation in decision-making is a requisite for reception. A Catholic theologian of the nineteenth century wrote:

> Where there is no participation, there can be no interest . . . No one interests himself in a matter in which he can take no real part . . . The people in our day are submissive only to such ordinances and regulations as they themselves have had a share in establishing, and of which the utility and reason are perceptible.[38]

Where there is participation there is the hope of reception; where decisions are imposed from the top down without consultation, there is rejection, or, even worse, passivity and indifference. It is not possible to create *communio* between churches or within a church by an executive decision. Ecumenical relations require more than doctrinal agreement; they also require *communio* of spirit and practice at the grass roots.

Another point is about respect for legitimate diversity. Are we really serious about it? What do we mean by the word 'legitimate'? —approved by the Vatican, or what? Is the concept of diversity one which is admired in principle as long as no one takes it seriously enough to apply? Admiration in principle, and a bucket of cold water in practice? Take, for example, the experience in Catholic-Orthodox relations of what came to be called the Uniate approach. Sections of the Orthodox churches joined in communion with the pope, the bishop of Rome, while retaining the use of their own liturgy and continuing to exercise many of their particular or local traditions and customs. That approach is not a realistic one for today, and it has been quietly set aside. Why? One reason is that the Vatican did not honour the promise which it gave those churches to respect their legitimate diversity. It steadily Romanised them, so that the Maronites, for example, have lost almost all of their distinctiveness. That breach of trust in the past has closed off the Uniate option for the future.[39]

More recent church documents have taken a different approach. Pope John Paul II has written of a 'unity which . . . is neither absorption nor fusion'.[40] And more recently he has spoken of a new methodology in Catholic-Orthodox relations based on what he calls the doctrine of Sister Churches.[41] Cardinal Ratzinger, the prefect of the Congregation for the Doctrine of the Faith, has written that 'Rome must not require more from the East with respect to the doctrine of primacy than had been formulated and was lived during the first millennium.'[42]

All of these are positive and encouraging, even surprising statements. But central to the issue is the question of whether the Vatican can be trusted to adhere in practice to those principles. Take the concept of *reception* once again. On the one hand, there is the positive statement made by Pope John Paul II that matters of faith require universal consent, extending from the bishops to the lay faithful.[43] But then consider how that is interpreted by the Vatican:

> For the Catholic Church, the certain knowledge of any defined truth is not guaranteed by the reception of the faithful that such is in conformity with Scripture and Tradition, but by the authoritative definition itself on the part of the authentic teachers.[44]

That statement seems to say that reception rests with the bishops, with or without the lay faithful, or priests. It is a good example of a statement of principle being rendered void, simply evacuated of its original sense, by the interpretation put on it. For every step forward in principle there seems to be a corresponding step backwards in interpretation. If that methodology were applied to the five points listed on page 175, what would remain of them? Would they mean anything in real terms?

And if the Orthodox look at the *praxis* of the Vatican today in relation to the internal life of the Catholic church, will they find reassurance of respect for legitimate diversity? The message from the Vatican today to laity, priests, and bishops alike is 'Conform, toe the line, shut up and do as you're told.' And there are significant numbers of Catholics who think that's the way it should be. The phrase 'legitimate diversity' is an example of a noun being subverted by an adjective. The Orthodox would do well to look carefully at the small print of any agreement they make with the Vatican.

The third point relates to the Orthodox themselves. They have a great tradition in the fields of prayer, liturgy, and spirituality. They have serious deficiencies in religious education, pastoral care and missionary work. Perhaps their greatest weakness, however, is their long tradition of subservience to state authority, seeing themselves as national churches. Regrettably, they seem to have learned nothing on this score, and on several others, from the experience of seventy-five years of Soviet rule, and they have squandered a great deal of moral energy and goodwill since the collapse of the Soviet Union in trying to restore the *status quo ante* the revolution, particularly in regard to money, property, and official status. It is well past time for them to cut the umbilical cord to the state and stand on their own feet like adults.

Catholics and Anglicans

Anyone who reads the agreed statements of the first and second Anglican-Roman Catholic International Commissions (ARCIC) cannot but be struck by the large measure of agreement which those statements represent. Not the least of their achievements was agreement on a methodology for working through the difficulties. The end result of those efforts was a reinforcement of the hope that union could be achieved.

The official Anglican response to the statements came after eight years of exhaustive consultation throughout the world-wide Anglican communion. The Vatican response took nine years, after considerably less consultation. One wonders why? And—as mentioned earlier—when the response came, it was not issued in the name of any particular Vatican office, and was unsigned and undated, all of which is very unusual for Vatican documents. The response itself is characterised not so much by a negative attitude as a muddled one. It misquoted and misrepresented statements in the report more than once. While on the one hand containing some modest praise for the report it also, on the other, calls for virtual unconditional surrender, not only in matters of faith but also of theology, and even theological language. This latter point is particularly strange in view of the statement of principle made by Pope John XXIII at the start of the second Vatican Council, and repeated by Popes Paul VI and John Paul II, that it is necessary to keep clearly in mind the distinction between the deposit of faith and the formulation in which it is expressed.[45]

An impression of the role of the Congregation for the Doctrine of the Faith in ecumenical affairs is that it stands apart from them, somehow disengaged, as if it was the work of others to press the accelerator, and its role to press the brake. Every step forward seems to be matched by another step backwards, every sign of progress doused with words of caution. Does the Vatican really want union with the Anglicans, or is it putting them on hold, without saying so, while concentrating on the Orthodox instead?

Catholics could learn a lot from Anglicans, especially about the synodal method of church government, about how to do liturgy, and about pastoral theology. But despite the hopeful possibilities represented by the work of recent years, there is the feeling that much of that achievement is being bypassed by events. In the church of England, the dominant group among younger clergy is evangelical, not Anglo-Catholic, and the influence of the Porvoo agreement with Lutherans, together with the approval by Anglicans in Sydney, Australia, of lay consecration of the Eucharist, suggest that the trend is away from, not towards, union with the Catholic church.

One major issue which is not often addressed in Anglican-Roman Catholic relations is that of the established status of the Church of England. It is more than a historical oddity of merely cultural significance. Recently the British High Court in London ruled that the Church of England, 'as an established religion is subject to state control as regards doctrine, government, and discipline'.[46] That is a shameful and degrading situation for any church, and Anglicans should find in themselves the strength of character to break the establishment link clearly and definitively. It is all the more pressing when one reflects that most British members of parliament are probably not practising christians of any sort. Yet this was the body which, some years ago, had the task of approving the revision of Anglican liturgical texts and the ordination of women!

So where does the future of Anglican-Roman Catholic relations lie? If there is to be forward movement, it will be at the grass-roots, between families, parishes and dioceses, in following the principle that we should do everything together except those things which conscience requires us to do apart. And spirituality may provide common ground for moving forward together.

Avenues to progress

The late John F. X. Harriott, in his book *The Empire of the Heart*, offers reflections on the Catholic church of our time. Much of what he says, though written of the church in general, has a bearing on the ecumenical movement. He speaks of the present crisis in the Catholic church as being the worst in his lifetime. There is in the Vatican, he writes, 'a kind of anticonciliar curial Broederbond bent on disenfranchising most of the national hierarchies as well as the ordinary clergy and laity'.[47] The problem is authoritarianism, not authority.[48] What he objects to in Catholic conservatism is its pettiness: 'A mentality that thinks it, or the Church itself, has God in its pocket, that there is only one ideal social order, one ideal pattern of behaviour, one road to paradise, belittles God and is a lie against the richness of creation.'[49] 'Sometimes', he writes, 'there appear to be two Vaticans, the one persecuting whoever lives what the other preaches.'[50] The church 'cannot preach a God of resurrection by clinging to a dead past'.[51] 'Communication requires trust, and to create trust there must be respect for the individuality and freedom of the other.'[52]

If we are to move forward on the road to unity, we do not need more statements of principle, however good they may be; we need more shared prayer, service and witness at the grass-roots, and the freedom in which they can grow. There are two special areas where more freedom is needed, namely, intercommunion and inter-church marriages.

Intercommunion

The point in question here is that of the reception of Holy Communion at Mass by christians of other churches. At present the discipline of the Catholic church allows this when a christian of another church has Catholic faith in the Eucharist, is properly disposed, is unable to receive the sacrament from a minister of his or her own church, and asks for it on his/her own initiative. It is to be done only by way of exception, such as when the person is in danger of death; in other cases, the bishop will specify circumstances. The thinking behind this discipline is that the Eucharist is a sign of unity, and that unity in faith, worship, and ecclesial life, must exist in fact if the act of receiving the Eucharist is to be true to its significance. To do otherwise would be to profess a unity which does not exist.[53]

In the mid-1970s I was in a situation for a number of years where it was common for non-Catholic christians to come to Mass. They used to ask for Communion. I used to refuse it and explained why by referring to the rules given above, and by saying that when we had agreement in faith, worship and ecclesial life then their reception of the Eucharist in a Catholic church would have its full meaning. I did so out of obedience to the Church, though I found it very hard to do so; a priest does not like refusing Communion to someone who asks for it in good faith, especially when it is clear that the person is thoughtful, reflective and serious about the request.

If I was in the same situation again I would not do as I did then; I would give them Holy Communion. Why? Because the Eucharist is not only a sign but a source of unity.[54] It helps to create the unity we have not yet fully realised. To refuse is to give priority to discipline over the sacrament, to the institution over the person. It inverts priorities, and contradicts the meaning of Jesus' saying that 'The sabbath was made for humankind, and not humankind for the sabbath.' (Mk. 2:27) What would Jesus do? Would he invite someone to his house for a meal and then say, 'You're welcome to the meal but you're not allowed to eat at it; you can watch the others eating.' Should such a person be directed to go instead to a minister of their own church and receive the Eucharist there?—a Eucharist which we do not recognise as valid. And what of the ordinary average Catholic congregation which receives Communion on Sunday morning? Are we sure that there is among them unity in faith, worship and ecclesial life? If not, should they be allowed to receive if we apply to ourselves the rules we apply to others?

As an alternative it would be better if baptised christians of other churches who have Eucharistic faith and devotion were invited to share the Eucharist. It should be offered to them, not given merely in response to their request, and not only when their own clergy are unavailable, but on a continuing basis, especially in an inter-church marriage. (It is necessary to stipulate that *any* recipient of Communion should have Eucharistic faith and devotion; to receive it without that would be meaningless at best.) If there are difficulties about following such a rule they should be left to the person and the priest concerned to resolve, without the need of recourse to the bishop.

Inter-church marriages

The present discipline of the church requires that a Catholic who wishes to marry a christian of another church must sign an undertaking to do all in his or her power to bring the children of their marriage up as Catholics. It would be better to drop the requirement of signed promises. That requirement is widely seen as overbearing, showing a lack of trust, and not without an element of arm-twisting. As to its effectiveness, the resentment which it evokes, possibly from both partners, is likely to make matters more rather than less difficult for the couple.

A Catholic who believes in the faith will want to share that faith with the children. How that will be reconciled with the equally sincere desire of the other christian partner to raise the children in his or her church is one of the challenges of an ecumenical marriage, a microcosm at the level of the domestic church of the effort by the universal church to achieve unity in the family of God. Requiring signed promises does not help in such a situation. It is better to take the risk of trust, and to encourage couples who have already faced such problems to share their experiences together and thereby build up one another in faith.

At one time the church had a rule which prevented what were called 'mixed marriages' from being held in a church; they were to take place in the sacristy with the minimum of ceremony. I once knew an elderly priest who, throughout the fifty or so years of his life as a priest, held such ceremonies in the church with all the trimmings. His explanation was that the sacristy was being painted, and as evidence of this he kept a dried-up stump of a paintbrush, its stubby bristles caked with long-hardened paint, lying in a corner of the sacristy. For all his life the sacristy was being 'painted'.

8.6 A CHURCH REFORMED IN ITS STRUCTURES

God is ever creative. Sometimes dramatically—as in the end of the Soviet Union and other Marxist-Leninist states, or as in the ending of apartheid—sometimes quietly, God works through people, facts, and events to lead the world forward towards the goals he desires for it. There is no need to nudge God along; basically, our job is to get out of the way and not block God's action. There is no need for us to become fussy or excited; God is in charge and knows the world well. Throughout the Bible, it is God who takes the initiative, and our task is to respond.

There are many changes quietly fermenting in the world, some of them with the promise of a better life for people. For instance:

- There is an almost universal longing for peace, coupled with a growing sense of the unity of the human race.
- There is a willingness to work for and insist on human rights.
- There is a slow but real advance in the status of women in society.
- There is a desire by people for participation in decision-making.
- In some places, science is leading people to God.
- New technology, such as in the field of information communication, is bringing a cultural revolution which has potential for good. Information technology is sometimes able to bypass government control and it has contributed already to political revolution, in Iran for instance. What other possibilities does it contain? It may be true that most of what we achieve in life is the unintended by-product of what we set out to achieve. For instance, in the nineteenth century the new technology of the railway had the side-effect of giving a country like India a sense of national unity where before there had only been regionalism. And how many people, when the contraceptive pill was developed in 1954, anticipated the impact it would have on the second half of the twentieth century?

In the church, too, there is a ferment of change. Two examples may help. The drop in numbers entering the priesthood and religious orders has created a new opportunity of developing structures of participation for lay-people. It is an opportunity, no more; we can use it or lose it, the choice is ours. And the world-wide collapse in the practice of confession must be leading somewhere. I regret the change, which seems to result fairly substantially from the loss of a sense of sin, coupled with an unwillingness to admit to being wrong, but God probably has a purpose in it somewhere.[55]

What is the Spirit saying to the church and the world? We will learn the answer to that question if we are willing to engage in intellectually honest dialogue, if we are willing to listen and learn together. That will require the moral courage to climb up out of the trenches and to engage the world as at least a potential partner. That same courage will be needed to enable us to abandon attitudes and structures which are unhelpful or non-viable, and to see beyond the immediate moment to what may lie ahead.

It seems clear that the present structural model of the church is dying. That is nothing to worry about: it is part of the normal cycle of dying, death, and re-birth which we see every autumn, winter and spring. The church itself, the people of God, will not die; it has Christ's promise that it will not die. (Mt. 28:20)

To bring about a renewal of the church requires new and credible structures of participation, decentralisation and subsidiarity, a separation of powers, the free exchange of information and ideas, and, from the bottom up, the creation of democratic structures joined to hierarchy in the service of community.

Adieu to the Vatican

What is meant by the word 'Vatican' in this book is the Roman Curia, the Vatican City-State, and the College of Cardinals. It does not mean the pope, the bishop of Rome, the successor of Saint Peter; the papal office was given to us by Christ, it is an integral part of the life of the church.

The Vatican should go. Why? Here are some reasons:

1. It has no evangelical mandate; it is not part of the hierarchical structure of the church. But it has usurped the role of the bishops, and they have an evangelical mandate and are part of that hierarchical structure.

2. It is hooked on its view of its own power, which it calls 'the authority of the church'.

3. It has become a source of division rather than dialogue, of alienation rather than unification.

4. It does not trust the rest of the church—as its documents show —and that mistrust has evoked a corresponding mistrust from the church.

5. It is stifling the spirit of freedom and creativity in the church through an excess of caution, a dearth of imagination, and, mostly, the fear of losing its power.

6. It is an obstacle to ecumenical relations with Orthodox and Protestants. Many of their fears about the papacy might be more accurately identified as fears of a centralised bureaucracy in the church. A papacy such as we had in the first millennium would be accepted by a great many christians.

7. It costs too much, in credibility no less than cash. A bureaucracy on the scale of the Vatican, with somewhere between two

thousand and two thousand five hundred employees is unsustainable without heavy involvement in the power games of money and politics.

8. It takes up too much personnel, time, and energy.

The church would be a better place without the Vatican. The 'loss' of the Vatican would be like the 'loss' of the Papal States in the nineteenth century—no loss, but a liberation.

Why not reform it instead? Because it is not reformable. As one cardinal put it, 'It's impervious to reform.'[56] Pope Paul VI, who worked in it nearly all his life, tried reforming it from the inside. He brought in fresh blood from outside Europe and delegated some functions to episcopal conferences. That was a setback for the Vatican, but it recovered. The conferences have been sidelined, and the solid core of Vatican staff is still recruited from the same areas as before. More importantly, the mind-set has not changed. Pope John Paul II also tried to reform it.[57] He shuffled the pack and gave some old offices new names. It didn't work.

The Vatican, as we now know it, is substantially a by-product of the counter-Reformation. It has grown steadily in power in recent centuries, and especially in the past thirty years or so, facilitated, unfortunately, by new technology. An example of the growth of its power is that at the start of this century about half the bishops of the church were chosen locally, and the Vatican simply confirmed the local decision. Now scarcely any bishops are chosen at the local level; the Vatican makes the choice, sometimes with little prior consultation, sometimes against the local recommendation. That is only one example of an overall trend to greater centralisation and consolidation of power.

Bureaucracies never surrender power willingly; it has to be taken from them. The people who work in the Vatican are probably as decent a group of people as one would expect to find anywhere. But collectively they have succumbed to the bureaucratic mentality, that is, to a sense of being indispensable, to isolation, and to the desire for control.[58] That frame of mind tends to feed on itself, seeing every expression of dissent as a reason for extending central control still further. One result among many which may follow from such an outlook is that flexibility gives way to rigidity, so small problems tend to develop into big ones. For instance, what began in the 1970s as discontent over the manner in which bishops were appointed had, by the 1980s, developed into discontent about the type of appointee, and now in the 1990s into questioning the role and existence of the Vatican itself. A lot of good may come of that yet.

The Vatican has made a mess of very many of the major issues that it has handled in recent centuries. Almost certainly it will continue to do the same in the years to come because the mind-set which led to those blunders is still there today, and there is not the smallest sign of change—quite the contrary, in fact.

The name of the game is power. When the posturing and the pretence have been removed, the bare fact emerges that power is what it is about. It is not service, though it uses the language of service in self-justification. What relationship does that frame of mind bear to Jesus of Nazareth? It is the opposite of what he stood for. There is only one thing to be done with the Vatican, and that is to remove it, totally and permanently.

What should it be replaced with? Nothing. If something else replaces it, there is no point in removing it in the first place, because the replacement would follow the same path in due time. The alternative to the Vatican is not for episcopal conferences to have their own bureaucracies; if there is anything worse than a Vatican, it is one hundred and fifty or so mini-Vaticans at the regional level. Those that exist already are far from inspiring confidence. The universal church is built on the local church, and it is at that level that decision-making should primarily take place. The local churches should decide what powers, if any, they may wish to delegate to other organisations. At present, the Vatican decides what powers it will delegate to the local churches. The universal church should not follow the pyramid model of organisation, nor that of the multi-national corporation, nor the one-party state, nor seek to be a new Roman empire, but rather a communion of local churches as it was in the first millennium.

There is a reaction against the Vatican in the church at present. The evidence of this is in the departure from the church of many of its members, the loss of morale, the anger, the despair, the passivity, the numb fatalistic resignation, and the switch-off by those who no longer listen. That situation will lead either to reform or revolt. There is a growing credibility and endurance gap between the church and the Vatican. But the Vatican is undermining its own position by using the loyalty of the faithful, including priests and bishops, as a stick to beat them with. That the Vatican should continue so to undermine itself is a consummation devoutly to be wished for, but there is a serious risk that it might bring the papacy down with it. The Vatican would be no loss at all, but we do not need a discredited papacy; there is no benefit to anyone in that. The Vatican has over-reached itself, and the law of diminishing returns has been in operation for some time: the louder it shouts, the less anyone listens; the more power it demands, the more it stokes the smouldering embers of resentment.

A papacy without the Vatican would be a better one. It could again be a source of unity, a builder of bridges, a mediator, a channel of communication, and clearly recognisable as the servant of the servants of God. It would not be a quasi-religious, quasi-political oracle caught up in the power games of money and control.

A church without the Vatican could begin to breathe again; there would be room for freedom and vitality; bishops could begin to be bishops; there would be a voice, a place, a hope for lay-people; and there would be scope for initiative and creativity.

Will the Vatican go, and if so how? One thing is certain, it will not go of its own choice. But it is a bureaucracy, and it shares their weaknesses. Bureaucracies would prefer to be hated or cursed than ignored. What has been happening for some time is that people have been ignoring it. They have switched off, leaving it talking to itself. (One of the delightful ironies of this situation is that I, who criticise the Vatican, read what it says, while its defenders, who are shocked by my views, don't read a word of it!)

Another weakness of bureaucracies is their need of money. They devour it, and cannot last without it. What may happen—possibly has already begun to happen—is that people will not be willing to pay for the Vatican. And it would not last long without money.

Another factor is one that played such a large part in the downfall of that other empire, the Soviet Union, and that is the force of public opinion. Of all people, Marxists should not have made the mistake of underestimating the power of an idea, but they did, and they paid for it by losing power. Public opinion, freely united in commitment to an idea, is a powerful force, and those who ignore it will pay a price for doing so.

The Vatican, if it wishes, can continue in cavalier fashion to dismiss public opinion in the church to Hades, but, as sure as night follows day, that same public opinion will return the compliment.

8.7 A CHURCH MOTIVATED BY MISSION

The church is not in danger of dying. It is in danger of not fulfilling its mission, of not responding to its Christ-given task of bringing the Gospel to all nations, of not making that the focus and motive of all its activities. It has serious credibility problems in being a sign of Christ to a world which needs him. In what ways is this the case? Why is it so? Can the church change and recover a sense of mission? These are questions which call for examination in the church.

'The church should . . . be a sign, a paradigm, a working model of what human society, viewed as a whole, might be.'[59] For some people the church is far from that; its human relations are not those of the Gospel. For others, there is in the church a lot of humbug, hypocrisy, double-talk, and intellectual dishonesty. They reject that, and who could blame them? From rejecting the faults of the church it is not uncommon to reject the church itself, and the christian faith which it represents. For many people, the church is not a good advertisement for christianity, nor is it seen as a paradigm for human society. How can an organisation which effectively excludes over 99 per cent of its membership from participation in decision-making realistically be regarded as a paradigm for human relations?

One reason for this situation is that the church has lost its bearings. It has become inward-looking and self-centred. It talks to itself about itself, and has made itself a substitute for God. But the church is either about God or it has nothing to say. The Vatican is not the centre of the church; Christ is. However platitudinous such statements may seem, they are basic truths which need repetition because they have been lost sight of.

The church today has fallen into the same error that its ancestors, the people of Israel, fell into. They came to identify the kingdom of Israel with the Kingdom of God, and it took the experience of a crushing military defeat and the resulting exile to bring them to learn what God had been trying for a long time to teach them. They had, in fact, fallen into the most condemned sin in the Old Testament, the sin of idolatry. They had, as it were, made God in their own image and likeness; they acted as if God were the puppet on their string; they sought to manipulate and control God.[60]

Something similar has happened in the church today. Although official statements are usually somewhat modest in linking the church to God's Kingdom, as, for instance, saying that 'the Church is the seed and the beginning' of that Kingdom,[61] the assumptions and unconscious reflexes on which the church acts in its day-to-day affairs betray an attitude of mind which indicates a more assertive claim. It is as if it had God at its beck and call, knew exactly what he wanted in any given situation, and had full rights to speak on his behalf. Many have heard of the situation where the wish of any Vatican official is automatically described by him as the 'will of the Holy Father'. There is an analogous situation at another level where the wish of the Vatican on any issue is automatically described as the 'will of God', or 'for the good of the church'. Is that a credible position? Is it an honest position? Does such a procedure foster respect or trust?

The church has become inward-looking, self-absorbed, and quarrelsome. That will continue until there is dialogue, freedom of expression, and participation in decision-making. So we see simple questions which should have been left to the decision of the local church—such as the matter of altar girls—become soured and querulous in twenty-five years of argument. Or the long drawn-out debate about clerical celibacy. Defenders of the present law are like the Flat Earth Society; they will not accept reality and are beyond persuasion. It would be best to change the rule, leave the issue behind us, and go on to issues that really matter.

The pilgrim people of God need to re-orientate their compass, to get their bearings, and to look outwards towards a world that needs us. If we sorted ourselves out internally, we could move from maintenance to mission, and be able to respond to the call of Christ and the needs of the world. To do this we need to lift our consciousness above the level of internal squabbles and look at what God has revealed to us in Jesus Christ. His forerunner, John the Baptist, preached the coming of God's Kingdom (Mt. 3:2), a message which Jesus took up when he began his public life (Mt. 4:17). The concept of God's Kingdom is the all-embracing moral framework of the New Testament. It is both a present and a future reality, extending beyond the limitations of space and time, and it is open to all who surrender to God. As Jesus, who is the King, said to the scribe who had asked him an honest question 'You are not far from the Kingdom of God' (Mk. 12:34). Jesus would say the same to all those who honestly seek what is true, good and beautiful, though they might be far from the church or even hostile to it. And the signs of the presence of God's Kingdom are that 'the blind receive their sight, the lame walk, the lepers are cleansed, the deaf hear, the dead are raised and the poor have good news brought to them' (Lk. 17:21).

It would be a good step forward if we were to make the family the foundation and focus of our efforts to build up the Kingdom of

God. We could learn from our Jewish brothers and sisters who have sustained themselves for 4,000 years by making the family the centre of their religious activity. A church which responds to this challenge will find itself welcomed warmly. But it is a big challenge for the Catholic church since it means turning present ecclesiastical structures and attitudes on their head: it means that married people would teach clergy about the morals of married life, not the other way round; and it means clergy standing back and letting lay-people find a spirituality which meets their needs rather than trying to grow spiritually on a watered-down monastic spirituality.[62] In the Jewish tradition the mother is clearly first in the family; Jewish fathers have a 'priestly' role there. If men were fully integrated into family life, might they not also be fully integrated into church life? There is a challenge there for lay-people, and there are real grounds for hoping that they will meet it if the clergy do not block them by trying to manage or control them.

At another level, we need to take the life of the Kingdom where we find it, that is, at the level where people live and work, where they find some sense of community or belonging. (To say that this may not be synonymous with the parish should be obvious.) In other words, start with people where they are spiritually, morally, intellectually, emotionally, and even geographically, and then build on that foundation. This means that the local church is the church; it is where people are. It means seeing the church as the local community of worship, witness and work rather than as a sacramental service station.

These ideas involve a change of structures and attitudes. By and large, clergy are not ready for this because the control system has been so thoroughly inculcated into church life that we find it almost impossible to conceive of a situation where lay-people have the reins in their hands. But this change will come about all the same, because God is creating new facts to bring it about. The shortage of clergy is becoming acute, intensely so in some places, and this creates the best opportunity of having those conditions which will enable lay-people to take their rightful place in the church. When they are convinced that the church is theirs, that they are the church, they will take responsibility for it.[63]

It is worth looking at some examples from various stages of the history of the church to see what has happened when lay-people were given the chance:

1. In the earliest centuries of the church's life, the missionaries of the Gospel in the Mediterranean basin were mostly lay men, drawn from the unlikely (in present-day terms) ranks of sailors, merchants and soldiers of the Roman army.[64]

2. In more recent times, the Catholic faith was first brought to Korea by diplomats who represented Korea at the Chinese imperial court, where they had been converted by descendants of the followers of the early Jesuit missionary, Matteo Ricci.

3. Japanese Catholics converted by Saint Francis Xavier, persecuted and left without priests for some three hundred years, kept the faith alive among themselves.

4. In Madagascar in the nineteenth century a married woman, Victoire Rasoamanarivo, held the Catholic people of the capital, Antananarivo, together at a time when the missionaries had been expelled during the persecution which took place under Queen Ranavalona I, *La Sanguinaire*. Victoire was beatified in 1989.

5. The martyrs of Uganda were all lay-people, some of whom, at the time when they died for the faith, had not even been baptised.

6. In much of Africa, a great deal of the work of building up the church from the beginning was done by lay catechists.

7. The south Pacific island nation of Kiribati was evangelised by Polynesian sailors from Hawaii who spread the Gospel and baptised before missionaries came.

8. In China, since the coming to power of the communists in 1949, it is lay men and women who have kept the church alive in many places.

9. In many countries today, lay leaders of small, or basic, christian communities are the effective leaders of the local church in a great variety of ways, from conducting Sunday services, to teaching christian doctrine, to helping the poor and needy, and to building churches.

When people see that the responsibility for something they value rests with them, and that they are trusted, there is a very good chance that they will shoulder that responsibility and be faithful to it, especially if they have some support and encouragement.

To think in terms of the Kingdom of God rather than of the church has a number of advantages. It is a move away from something which is often narrowly ecclesiastical to a broader outlook of critical solidarity with the world. It is less open to the risk of reducing christianity to an ideology which is then used as a yardstick by which to judge people's orthodoxy. This is because its focus is clearly on Jesus Christ and how he relates to the human person. (It is significant that the Orthodox churches did not have the witchcraft trials of the Catholic church; perhaps this was because they had a vigorous theology and spirituality of the Holy Spirit which was a counter-weight to any tendency to turn the faith into an ideology.) The concept of the Kingdom of God offers an opportunity for a more comprehensive, complete, integral re-examination of some of the great 'either-ors' which have bedevilled Catholic theology, such as the sacred/secular divide, the divine/human divide, and the natural/supernatural divide.

There is an opening there for a fresh look at things if we have the courage and the vision to use it. 'Strive first for the Kingdom of God and his righteousness and all these things will be given to you as well.' (Mt. 6:33)

8.8 A CHURCH EMPOWERED BY PRAYER

The Catholic faith is not in its essence about creed, code and cult. Its core is a spirituality founded and focused on God the Father through Jesus Christ and empowered by the Holy Spirit. It is this which enables a person to live, as it were, from the inside out, to grow, develop and deepen in a life of union with God. Its motivating source is prayer: it is that which enables, empowers, and gives dynamism.

Christ is the heart of the christian life. When a christian commits him- or herself as wholeheartedly as possible to Christ, without looking for either results or rewards, the by-product, the side-effect, of this is a wholeness or unity in that person's life. 'Blessed are the pure in heart, for they will see God' (Mt. 5:8) means 'blessed are the single-minded,'[65] those who commit themselves totally to God.

A spirituality must have a theological basis; otherwise it becomes directionless, a prey to every subjective whim. Much of our theology is dualistic, while spirituality draws us into unity. Instead of working together they are pulling against each other. Some aspects of our theology need a substantial re-orientation if they are to work towards unity, for example, the inner unity of the individual person, as well as the person's union with nature, with other people, and with God.

We need to overhaul radically our theology of the body and of human sexuality. It is dualistic: one side-effect of this is to leave some married people with the feeling that because of their marriage they are limited to a second class position and role in the church. They sometimes see themselves as the spiritual poor relations of celibates. We have never overcome our suspicion of the body; we still see it as hostile to the spirit even though, as C. S. Lewis wrote, 'The sins of the flesh are the sins which the spirit commits against the flesh.'[66] It would be a step in the right direction if we could come to think of body and spirit, not merely as possible partners but rather as two inseparable yet distinct aspects of one reality. This may be one area, among several, where science can help religion to recover its bearings, where, for instance, neurology may be helpful to theology.[67]

One possible result of this could be to change the way we look at God. Instead of thinking of ourselves as looking out or up to God, perhaps we should recognise God within: 'The Kingdom of Heaven is within you' (Lk. 17:21). This, in turn, could give depth to human experience. We often live on the surface of our lives, we are like ice-skaters, speeding and spinning on a mere film, without daring to face ourselves in any depth. We live fragmented lives, a bit of this and a bit of that, but without inner unity. The source of our unity is God who is with us, God within us. It is 'In him we live and move and have our being' (Acts 17:28).

Another challenge which is a supremely difficult one in this mechanistic, rationalistic, efficiency-orientated world of ours is to reintegrate work into the totality of our lives. I am reminded of the villager I met in Zambia whom I chatted with for an hour or so about odds and ends, while he worked making the heads of fish-spears. For him, there was no boundary between work and leisure; they overlapped. It also brings to mind the UN conference on Human Settlements (Habitat), held in Canada in 1976. During the conference women of the First World expressed their sympathy for Third World women who had to walk long distances to find and then carry home a bucket of water. The women of the Third World rejected this sympathy, saying that when they walked to a well, they chatted and sang as they went along together; when they met at the well they rested and talked of their problems and complaints, and then they returned home at a leisurely pace. They went on to express their sympathy for First World women who commute to work in transport which is often dirty, crowded, and unsafe; who are harried and hassled by a clock from 9 a.m. to 5 p.m., who work in isolation even while in a crowd, and who sometimes find little meaning in the work itself, other than being a meal-ticket, and who then have to return home at the end of the day to face the housework.

The point is not only about trying to integrate work and leisure; it is also about unexamined assumptions, such as being the slaves of a 'standard of living', or being possessed by possessions, or living in the past or in the future while the uninhabited present slides past us. How many people in the First World spend the week living for the week-end, the year living for the holidays, and their working life living for retirement—and their retirement waiting for death? Work may be an expression of service to humanity; it may also be a kind of co-creation with God. But how does a person find meaning or value in work which is mere mechanical drudgery? One of the challenges of life, which spirituality can help a person face, is to find unity in lives which are otherwise fractured and fragmented.

A living spirituality can help to give a person a sense of identity, of self-esteem, of being responsible for oneself. In this context, the late John Main OSB has much that is helpful to offer. For instance, he writes:

> Religious people have so often pretended to have all the answers. They have seen their mission as being to persuade, to enforce, to level differences and perhaps even to impose uniformity. There is really something of the Grand Inquisitor in most religious people. But when religion begins to bully or insinuate, it has become unspiritual because the first gift of the Spirit, creatively moving in man's nature, is freedom and frankness; in biblical language, liberty and truth. The modern christian's mission is to resensitise his contemporaries to the presence of a spirit within themselves. He is not a teacher in the sense that he has provided answers that he has looked up in the back of a book. He is truly a teacher when, having found his own spirit, he can inspire others to accept the responsibility of their own being, to undergo the challenge of their own innate longing for the Absolute, to find their own spirit.[68]

At a time when many feel themselves adrift in a sea of impersonality without community, feel themselves like puppets on strings pulled by money, power, status and pleasure, it can be a liberating experience for people to get in touch with themselves in some depth through the practice of mental prayer. The anonymous Russian pilgrim of the nineteenth century wrote, 'The trouble is that we live far from ourselves and have but little wish to get any nearer to ourselves. Indeed we are running away all the time to avoid coming face to face with our real selves, and we barter the truth for trifles.'[69]

Growing towards God, stage by stage

Traditional spirituality has recognised three stages of spiritual growth in the person's relationship with God, namely, the stages of the slave, the servant, and the son or daughter.

One can visualise the master saying to the slave, 'I'll give you food and shelter; that's my responsibility to you. Your responsibility to me is to be seen and not heard; don't think, it will only get you into trouble; don't take any initiative, that's my affair; just stay out of trouble, shut up, and do as you're told.' The slave's relationship with the master is one of fear: fear of punishment, fear of the uncertainty and insecurity that freedom would bring, fear of having to make decisions and choices if given freedom. The result of this fear is cunning and deviousness, irresponsibility and a refusal to grow up. There are many people who settle for that kind of relationship in their life with God and with other people. It is a stage that God wants to lead us out of. Just as God led the Israelites from slavery in Egypt and brought them to freedom in the Promised Land, despite their *nostalgie pour la boue* (see Ex. 16:1–3), similarly God wants to lead all humanity to a better relationship with him.

'For we are God's servants, working together.' (1 Cor. 3:9) The relationship of the servant-and-employer is a step ahead of the slave-and-master one. On the part of the servant, the relationship is characterised by self-seeking: What's in it for me? What do I get out of it? How can I get the maximum return for the minimum of effort? There may be some scope in it for initiative and responsibility, but it is limited by the fear of taking a risk unless there is the clear expectation of a reward. If the dominant characteristic of the slave is fear, that of the servant is self-interest.

'I do not call you servants any longer . . . I have called you friends,' said Jesus. (Jn. 15:15) And further, 'For you did not receive a spirit of slavery to fall back into fear, but you have received a spirit of adoption. When we cry "Abba! Father!" it is that very Spirit bearing witness that we are children of God, and if children, then heirs, heirs of God, and joint heirs with Christ—if, in fact, we suffer with him so that we may also be glorified with him.' (Rom. 8:14–17) Being a son or daughter instead of a slave or servant means, among other things, growing up to take decisions— and having responsibility for them. (The prodigal son took the wrong decisions, but he remained a son all the same.) It means, not rebellion, which is an adolescent stage, but taking responsibility for oneself and being accountable to God. It is a call to maturity: '. . . until all of us come to the unity of the faith and of the knowledge of the Son of God, to maturity, to the measure of the full stature of Christ.' (Eph. 4:13) The Russian theologian, Khomiakov, wrote that 'the will of God is a curse for the demons, law for the servants of God, and freedom for the children of God.'[70]

Most of us have something of all three stages in us, and there are times when we regress from the more to the less developed. But what God is calling us to is clear: he wants us to be adult sons and daughters after the pattern of Jesus Christ, true God and true man.

How can we do it? We don't do it; it is done in us, when we open ourselves to God through, among other things, the practice of prayer supported by reading and reflection on the scriptures, alone and in community.

When should we do it? It is always now. Sometimes people confuse cause and effect in prayer, by thinking, for instance, that they must prepare for prayer by personal reform and moral change, whereas those are more often the result of prayer than its precondition. And sometimes in our attitude to prayer, we are like Saint Augustine when he said 'Give me chastity, Lord, but not yet.' We don't want to pray because we are not open to the changes it will bring, so we perhaps make the reading of books on prayer or attending courses and retreats a substitute for prayer. The time is now; the place is here; the person is myself as I am, warts and all.

There must also be a community dimension to any christian spirituality. For Catholics the pre-eminent community act of worship is the Mass. In its present form, it is wordy; it needs to be enriched by signs, symbols, and silences. It reaches only the mind, leaving the imagination, the emotions, and the will untouched. It could reach the whole person, as it did for the Russians who visited Constantinople when they were searching, about one thousand years ago, for a faith for the newly emergent kingdom of Rus. First they met Moslems, but were not impressed; then they met Catholics from Germany, with the same result; then they went to the Greeks, and there they found what they had been looking for—in the liturgy. They wrote, 'We did not know whether we were in heaven or on earth. For on earth there is no such splendour or such beauty, and we are at a loss how to describe it. We only know that God dwells here among men . . . we cannot forget that beauty.'[71] The story may or may not be historically true, but there is a truth in it. Liturgy can be beautiful, and when it is it can move people where argument fails. It can communicate a vision of beauty which lifts people above the humdrum and leaves them with a lasting taste of what prayer can be. But more important in this context than any textual or rubrical revision is the recovery among priests and people of a sense of the sacred.

The heart of any spirituality is prayer; it empowers people. It enables them to do and to be what they cannot do and be by themselves. Our greatest need is not for more knowledge, but rather the power to live by the knowledge we already have, for the abstract truths of the intellect to be assimilated by experience into the whole person. That power is made real in us through prayer. 'We do not know how to pray as we ought but that very Spirit intercedes for us with sighs too deep for words.' (Rom. 8:26) Anyone who has ever tried to pray knows the truth of the words 'we do not know how to pray as we ought.' Prayer in the Holy Spirit is to recognise and accept that God is at work in us, that we are redeemed, that what matters is the here and now, and to make room for God without being in the least deterred by the knowledge of our failings.

All of this, and much more, was put by Metropolitan Ignatios of Latakia at a meeting of the Ecumenical Council of Churches in Uppsala, Sweden, in 1968. He stated:

> Without the Holy Spirit, God is far away,
> Christ stays in the past,
> the Gospel is a dead letter,
> the Church is simply an organisation,
> authority a matter of domination,
> mission a matter of propaganda,
> the liturgy no more than an evocation,
> Christian living a slave morality.
> But in the Holy Spirit

the cosmos is resurrected and groans with the birth-pangs of
the Kingdom,
the risen Christ is there,
the Gospel is the power of life,
the Church shows forth the life of the Trinity,
authority is a liberating service,
mission is a Pentecost,
the liturgy is both memorial and anticipation,
human action is deified.[72]

NOTES

PREFACE
1 'The Dry Salvages', *Collected Poems 1909–1962*, Faber & Faber, London, 1974, p. 208.

CHAPTER 2
1 Avery Dulles, *Models of the Church*, Gill & Macmillan, Dublin, 1980.
2 Cited by John Courtney Murray S.J., *We hold these Truths*, London 1961, p. 202.
3 Canon 838.1.
4 The cause of Cardinal Schuster's beatification recently took a step nearer completion.
5 In a document published on 27 April 1996 the Argentine bishops' conference acknowledged for the first time the collusion of the Catholic church in the atrocities committed by the military dictatorship that ran that country between 1976 and 1983. The silence of senior churchmen on the subject had drawn fierce criticism from human rights groups in Argentina, especially as other sections of society, such as the armed forces, had already apologised publicly for their actions. (See *The Tablet*, 4 May 1996, p. 592)
6 On God the Father: *Dives in Misericordia*, 30 November 1980; on God the Son: *Redemptor Hominis*, 4 March 1979; on God the Holy Spirit: *Dominum et Vivificantem*, 18 May 1986.
7 See *The Tablet*, 22 October 1994, p. 1361.
8 See Paul Zulehner, 'Respectable revolt', *The Tablet*, 29 July 1995, p. 959.
9 The 1994 English translation of the 1992 *Catechism of the Catholic Church* comes close to this in n.865 where it states 'it is in her [the church] that the "Kingdom of Heaven" . . . already exists, and will be fulfilled at the end of time.' A more modest statement, borrowed from *Lumen Gentium* n.5, is found in n.567, 'The Church is the seed and beginning of this kingdom'.
10 *A New Catholic Commentary on Holy Scripture*, Nelson, London, 1975, n.735d.
11 Veritas edition, Dublin, 1994. In the edition of Paulines Publications, Africa, the kingdom of God is unlisted.
12 Congregation for the Clergy, *Directory on the Ministry and Life of Priests*, 1994, n.17.

CHAPTER 3

1 Jaques Maritain, *The Rights of Man and the Natural Law*, London, 1945, pp. 14–19.

2 Pierre Mendes-France, *A Modern French Republic*, trans. by Anne Carter, London, 1963.

3 Pastoral Instruction on the Means of Social Communication (*Communio et Progressio*), 29 January 1971, cited by Austin Flannery in *Vatican Council II: the Conciliar and Post-Conciliar Documents*, Dominican Publications, Dublin, nos. 33, 34, 121 and 123 respectively.

4 For another viewpoint from a Catholic journalist see Alain Woodrow, 'Free Speech in the Church', *The Tablet*, 26 August 1995, pp. 1093–5: 'The bishops still regard . . . the independent journalist as a threat, at best a well-intentioned meddler, at worst a dangerous enemy.' (ibid. p. 1094)

5 *Communio et Progressio*, n.116.

6 See *The Tablet*, 17 December 1994, p. 1620.

7 For example, see *The Tablet*: 23 July, 1994, p. 936; 'Rome bars another woman theologian'; 6 August 1994, p. 996, 'Theologian barred by Vatican'; 13 August 1994, p. 1027, 'Teresa Berger's two champions'. In these cases, no reasons were given by the Vatican for decisions which sometimes over-ruled previous decisions by the local bishops, and, according to some, were in violation of the terms of concordats with the states concerned.

8 *Veritatis Splendor*, 6 August 1993, n.80.

9 Ambrosiaster, PC 17, 245.

10 Encyclical letter *Ecclesiam Suam*, n.76.

11 *Ibid.*, n. 78.

12 *Summa Theologica*, I, II, q.105, art.1.

13 The area of the diocese is about 200,000 sq.km.

14 Apostolic letter, *Octogesima Adveniens*, 15 May 1971, nn.22, 47.

15 Encyclical letter, *Quadragesimo Anno*, 15 May 1931, n.79.

16 See Vatican II, *Constitution on the Liturgy*, n.11.

17 Lincoln used this definition in his Gettysburg address on 19 November 1863; and Jacques Maritain adopted it in his *Christianity and Democracy*, London, 1945, p. 47.

18 *Adversus Haereses*, 4, 20, 7: PG 7/1, 1037.

19 'Letter to the Duke of Norfolk' V in *Certain Difficulties felt by Anglicans in Catholic Teaching* II, Longmans, London, 1885, 248, cited in the *Catechism of the Catholic Church*, n.1778.

20 See G. K. Chesterton, *Orthodoxy*, London, 1963, p. 46.

21 *The Catechism of the Catholic Church*, n.1887.

22 This paragraph draws substantially on the *Catechism of the Catholic Church*, nn.1906, 1912–13, and 1904.

23 Canon 223.2. The titles of the Code of Canon Law which deal in Canons 208–31 with the rights of Christ's faithful are far from being a charter of rights. Apart from their limited scope, the Code specifies that the exercise of those rights depends on ecclesiastical authority.

CHAPTER 4

1 Congregation of Religious, *Congregavit Nos in Unum*, 2 February 1994, n.23.

2 The *Decretals of Gratian*, edited by Saint Raymond of Peñafort in 1140, cited by Julio Miró, *Spirituality of Saint Francis*, Sebastián López ed., 1994, Book 1, p. 45.

3 Pope Saint Pius X, cited by Jean Catoir, 'Laity are commissioned by Christ himself as Apostles' in *The Southern Cross*, 29 May 1994, p. 7.

4 Pope Benedict XV, encyclical letter, *Ad Beatissimi Apostolorum*, 1914, in Denzinger-Schönmetzer, n.3625.

5 Vatican II, *Constitution on the Church*, (*Lumen Gentium*), art. 12.

6 'Authority in the Church II', n.25.

7 *Response of the Holy See to the Final Report*, Catholic Truth Society, London, 1991, p. 7.

8 Richard Conniff, 'Ireland on Fast Forward' in *National Geographic*, September 1994, p. 14.

9 The *Catechism of the Catholic Church*, n.1884.

10 See Pope Paul VI, *Evangelica Testificatio*, 29 June 1971, n.39.

11 See Walter Lippmann, *A Preface to Morals*, London, 1929, p. 275.

12 Encyclical letter, *Centesimus Annus*, 1 May 1991, n.44.

13 George H. Sabine, *A History of Political Theory*, New York, 1937, p. 286.

14 See Bishop Reinhold Stecher, 'A better way to choose a bishop', *The Tablet*, 2 September 1995, p. 1122, and Hippolytus in *The Apostolic Tradition*, 'Let the bishop be ordained after he has been chosen by all the people.' The choice of St Ambrose as bishop of Milan provides an example.

15 John O'Brien, *Seeds of a New Church*, Columba Press, Dublin, 1994, pp. 158–9.

16 The three-week course in the Vatican, recently instituted for newly ordained bishops to initiate them into the mysteries of Romanità, is no response to this need. On the contrary, it is another control mechanism.

17 See Moya Frenz St. Leger, 'No Church tax, no sacraments', *The Tablet*, 21 January 1995, p. 66.

18 See James Hogan, *Modern Democracy*, Cork, 1938, p. 55.

CHAPTER 5

1 *Mater et Magistra*, n.219.

2 The 1957 statement on apartheid by the South African Bishops' Conference was perhaps their best for its clarity and forthrightness.

3 See Albino Luciani, *Illustrissimi*: the letters of Pope John Paul I, translated by Isabel Quigley, Fount/Collins, London, 1979, p. 284. For an outstanding example of a Gospel dialogue with Jesus see Jn. 4:5–42.

4 See Ernest Gowers, *The Plain Words*, HMSO, London, 1954, p. 119.

5 This section draws substantially on the encyclical letter *Ecclesiam Suam* of Pope Paul VI in 1964, especially nos. 70–85.

6 The text was published in the *Acta Apostolicae Sedis* 81 (1989) 104–6.
  See also *L'Osservatore Romano*, 25 February 1989, p. 6, and Canon 833
  of the *Code of Cannon Law.*

7 The topic of development of doctrine is examined later in this book on
  pp. 145–7 and 154–7.

8 *Selections from Ancient Irish Poetry*, trans. by Kuno Meyer, Constable,
  London, 1959, p.100. The identity of the King is not in doubt: in Old
  Irish it is In Rí; Sedulius wrote it as Inrí.

9 For Shangombo see Chapter 3, section 1.

10 See *Directives for Mutual Relations between Bishops and Religious in the
   Church*, 23 April 1978, Introduction 1.

11 I am indebted for most of these quotations to a feminist religious
   sister.

12 These quotations are from the same source as the previous citations.

13 For example, the apostolic letter *Mulieris Dignitatem* of Pope John Paul
   II, dated 15 August 1988.

14 Proclamation of Saint Teresa of Avila as a 'Doctor of the Universal
   Church', 27 September 1970. Proclamation of Saint Catherine of Siena
   as a 'Doctor of the Universal Church', 4 October 1970. (See Pope John
   Paul II, Apostolic Letter, *Mulieris Dignitatem*, 15 August 1988, n.1.)

CHAPTER 6

1 Heribert Jone, *Moral Theology*, translated by Urban Adelman, Mercier,
  Cork, 1947 (reprinted until 1961), nn.507–8. The italics are in the
  original. The book went through eighteen editions in French, Italian,
  Portuguese, Dutch, Polish, Spanish and Arabic, as well as English and
  the original German.

2 Bernard Häring's *Law of Christ* and his later *Free and Faithful in Christ*
  are a world apart from the earlier handbooks.

3 John F. X. Harriott, *The Empire of the Heart*, Templegate & Gracewing,
  Springfield & Leominster, 1990, p. 37.

4 *Hamlet*, Act I, Scene III, lines 78–80.

5 Vatican II, Dogmatic Constitution on Divine Revelation, *Dei Verbum*,
  n.10.

6 It may be significant that the official Catholic response when it
  appeared in 1991 was not issued in the name of any Vatican
  congregation, was unsigned and undated.

7 Quoted by Margaret Pepper, *Pan Dictionary of Religious Quotations*,
  London, 1989, p. 322, n.6.

8 *A New Catholic Commentary on Holy Scripture*, Nelson, London, 1975,
  729g.

9 For example, *Donum Veritatis* of 24 May 1990, n.18; and the letter of 28
  October 1995 from the Congregation for the Doctrine of the Faith
  which was a follow-up to the apostolic letter *Ordinatio Sacerdotalis* of 22
  May 1994. 'Creeping infallibility' is also a 'creeping coup' by the
  Vatican bureaucracy against the papal office.

10 Alain Woodrow, 'The beliefs of the French', *The Tablet*, 21 May 1994, p. 643.
11 *Catechism of the Catholic Church*, n.2181.
12 *Ibid.*, n.1861.
13 Pope John Paul II, encyclical letter *Redemptoris Missio*, 7 December 1990, n.39.
14 John F. X. Harriott, *The Empire of the Heart*, Templegate/Gracewing, Springfield/Leominster, 1990, p. 37.
15 The practical 'atheism' of preconciliar moral theology handbooks is well illustrated in Jone's manual referred to on p. 109. Its 43-page index contains no reference either to Jesus or the Holy Spirit, while 'God' manages to get only a toe in the door with two references in 600 pages of text. And the 1917 Code of Canon Law, on which such manuals drew heavily, made no mention at all of God in 2414 canons.
16 The same pope made a similar point in his first encyclical *Ubi Arcano*, in 1922.
17 Cited in the *Catechism of the Catholic Church*, n.1778.
18 *Crossing the Threshold of Hope*, Jonathan Cape, London, 1994, p. 191.
19 Encyclical letter *Redemptoris Missio*, 7 December 1990, n.39.
20 Instruction *Donum Veritatis*, 24 May 1990, n.38. See also n.36.
21 *Crossing the Threshold of Hope*, p. 175.
22 HIV is the virus that causes AIDS.
23 I refrain from naming either of the two men who offered these views.
24 For example, in n.2266 on capital punishment, or n.2385 on divorce.
25 The *Catechism of the Catholic Church*, n.2384.

CHAPTER 7

1 Hymn no. 112 in *The Divine Office*, Collins, Dwyer and Talbot, 1974.
2 Gearóid Ó Tuathaigh in *Ireland before the Famine 1798–1848*, Gill & Macmillan, Dublin, 1974 deals with this topic.
3 A good source on this topic is Joseph Lee, *The Modernisation of Irish Society 1848–1918*, Gill & Macmillan, Dublin, 1974, especially Chapters 3 and 4.
4 Pope Pius XII spoke often of the need for public opinion within the church.
5 Hymn no. 112 in *The Divine Office*, Collins, Dwyer and Talbot, 1974.
6 Denzinger-Schönmetzer, n.563.
7 Neuner-Depuis, *The Christian Faith in the Doctrinal Documents of the Catholic Church*, Collins, London, 1982, n.802.
8 Ibid., n.804 (870, 875).
9 Ibid., n.810: the Decree for the Jacobites (Egyptian Copts). See also Denzinger-Schönmetzer, 1351 where the Council of Florence taught in 1442 that all pagans and Jews would go to hell unless they became Catholics before their deaths.
10 The Council of Vienne (1311–12); see Denzinger-Schönmetzer 906.
11 *Humani Generis*, n.27.

12 *Constitution on the Church,* n.16.

13 An example of this is in the *Catholic Encyclopaedia,* Our Sunday Visitor, Huntington, Indiana, 1991, article 'Salvation outside the Church', pp. 862–3: 'Is there salvation outside the Church? No. Is a person who dies without Baptism in the Catholic Church condemned to hell by this fact? No. Is this a contradiction? No. A proper grasp of the Church's teaching allows an understanding of how this apparent antinomy is resolved.'

14 Encyclical letter *Centesimus Annus,* n.46.

15 Each year an average of 160,000 Catholics in the territory of the former West Germany formally sign a declaration in a local court that they are leaving the church. (See Peter Hünermann, 'A Church in dialogue' in *The Tablet,* 15 July 1995, p. 897.) And in France, the percentage of the population professing themselves Catholic dropped from 81 per cent in 1986 to 64 per cent in 1994. (Alain Woodrow, 'The Beliefs of the French', *The Tablet,* 21 May 1994, p. 643.

16 Cardinal Jozef Tomko, prefect of the Congregation for the Evangelisation of Peoples, reported that between 1984 and 1994 the number of priests in mission countries rose by 7 per cent. (See *The Tablet,* 20 May 1995, p. 646.)

17 See, for example, Raymond Brown, *Priest and Bishop: biblical reflections,* Chapman, London, 1971.

18 Some of these ideas draw on *The Final Report* of the Anglican-Roman Catholic International Commission, CTS/SPCK, 1981, especially pp. 72 and 92.

19 'This holy Synod of Constance . . . declares that, having assembled legitimately in the Holy Spirit, and being a general Council and representing the Catholic Church militant, it has its power immediately from Christ, which every state and dignity, even if it be the papal dignity, must obey in what concerns faith . . .' (Neuner-Dupuis, *The Christian Faith in the Doctrinal Documents of the Catholic Church,* Collins, London, 1982, n.806.

20 See pp. 146–7.

21 Pope John Paul II in the encyclical letter *Ut Unum Sint* of 25 May 1995, n.80, speaks of the reception of ecumenical developments as a new task awaiting the whole church.

CHAPTER 8

1 Winston D. Abbott, *Sing with the Wind,* Inspiration House Publishers, South Windsor, Connecticut, USA.

2 *Catechism of the Catholic Church,* n.760.

3 For example, in his *Letter to Women* of 29 June 1995, n.3.

4 The text is in Austin Flannery (ed.), *Vatican Council II: more postconciliar documents,* Dominican Publications, Dublin, 1982, pp. 331–45.

5 The word 'discipline' is significant; elsewhere the words 'practice' and 'norm' are used: see Introduction and n.4.

6 Ibid., n.5.

7 Ibid.

8 *Ordinatio Sacerdotalis*, n.4.

9 The full text was published in *The Tablet*, 25 November 1995, p. 1529.

10 See Nicholas Lash, 'On not inventing doctrine', *The Tablet*, 2 December 1995, p. 1544.

11 Noldin-Schmitt, *Summa Theologiae Moralis*, Vol. III, n.465. Translation by Kevin Kelly.

12 *Dogmatic Constitution on Divine Revelation*, n.10.

13 Ibid.

14 See Ratzinger's article 'Anglican-Catholic Dialogue—its Problems and Hopes', in Hill and Yarnold, *Anglicans and Roman Catholics: the Search for Unity*, SPCK/CTS, London, 1994, p. 256.

15 Canon 749, nos. 2, 3.

16 *Evangelium Vitae*, n.5.

17 *Letter to Women*, 29 June 1995, n.7.

18 On pages 147–8, under the heading 'Jerusalem'.

19 See Hill and Yarnold, *Anglicans and Roman Catholics: the Search for Unity*, SPCK/CTS, London, 1994, p. 233.

20 See *Irish Missionary Union Report*, March-April 1995, p. 3.

21 See *The Tablet*, 12 November 1994, p. 1458.

22 Statistics on this topic are difficult to get hold of. Those which follow are as accurate as I can find.

23 From the *Annuario Pontificio*, the church's statistical yearbook, for 1986.

24 From Cardinal Tomko in *The Tablet*, 20 May 1995, p. 646.

25 From the *Zambian Catholic Directories* for 1971 and 1981.

26 The *Annuario Pontificio* for 1986.

27 See Richard Schoenherr, *Goodbye, Father*, and 'Numbers don't lie' in *Commonweal*, 7 April 1995.

28 John Joe Spring, 'Opening up Ministry' in *The Word*, July 1995, p. 12.

29 Gerald Arbuckle, *Refounding the Church: Dissent for Leadership*, Chapman, London, 1993, p. 61.

30 Pope John Paul II, encyclical letter *Ut unum sint*, 25 May 1995, n.77.

31 *Ut unum sint*, n.50.

32 Ibid., n.31.

33 Ibid., n.32.

34 Ibid., n.80.

35 Ibid., n.95.

36 Encyclical letter *Dominum et Vivificantem*, 18 May 1986, n.65.

37 *Ut unum sint*, n.70.

38 John Baptist Hirscher, *Sympathies of the Continent*, or *Proposals for a New Reformation*, trans. by A. C. Coxe, Oxford, 1852, pp. 131, 149. Hirscher's work was placed on the *Index of Forbidden Books*.

39 Vatican II went to considerable pains to assure the Orthodox that it had changed its ways. In its *Decree on the Catholic Eastern Churches*, it repeatedly stated its respect for diversity of tradition and practice: see nn.2, 5, 6, 12, 24, 25.

40 Encyclical letter *Slavorum Apostoli*, 2 June 1985, n.27.

41 *Ut unum sint*, n.60.

42 See *Principles of Catholic Theology*, Ignatius Press, San Francisco, 1987, p. 199, and also n.25 of the *Decree on the Catholic Eastern Churches*.

43 *Ut unum sint*, n.80.

44 From the Official Roman Catholic Response to the Final Report of ARCIC I, in *Anglicans and Roman Catholics: the Search for Unity*, ed. Hill and Yarnold, SPCK/CTS, London, 1994, pp. 160–61.

45 For example, *Ut unum sint*, n.81.

46 Cited by Robert Nowell, 'Growing procession on the road to Rome', in *The Irish Times*, 14 October 1995, p.5.

47 *The Empire of the Heart*, Templegate/Gracewing, Illinois/Herefordshire, 1990, p. 7.

48 Ibid., p. 13.

49 Ibid., p. 37.

50   Ibid., p. 40.

51 Ibid., p. 97.

52 Ibid., p. 49. Two especially good chapters are 'My Fears for the Church' and 'Holiness and Humanity'.

53 See *Directory for the Application of Principles and Norms on Ecumenism*, nn.129–31.

54 Ibid., n.129.

55 The Congregation for the Clergy in its *Directory on the Ministry and Life of Priests*, 31 January 1994, n.52, states that experience shows that people come freely to confession as long as there are priests available. That is simplistic, and, by implication, unjust.

56 I refrain from naming the cardinal, or my source of information, so as to spare them harassment.

57 See the Apostolic Constitution, *Pastor Bonus*, of 28 June 1988.

58 Two recent Vatican Directories, on ecumenism in 1993, and the clergy in 1994, are examples of this frame of mind. They are fussy, pedantic, anxious not to leave anything unsaid, and characterised by an almost neurotic fear of losing control.

59 John F. X. Harriott, *Empire of the Heart*, Templegate/Gracewing, Illinois/Herefordshire, 1990, p. 110.

60 See the *Catechism of the Catholic Church*, nn.709–10.

61 Vatican Council II, *Dogmatic Constitution on the Church*, n.5.

62 For example, the English Catholic Truth Society has sold some 16 million copies of *A Simple Prayer Book* since it was first published about one hundred years ago. And the Irish company, Veritas, has sold very large numbers of a series of booklets written by married couples to help parents to prepare their children at home for the sacraments. The point is not about book sales, but about meeting people's needs.

63 For a good presentation of this topic, see *Small Christian Communities: a Pastoral Choice*, Catechetical Department, Catholic Secretariat, Lusaka, Zambia, 1987.

64 See Christopher Dawson, *Religion and World History*, Image Books, New York, 1975, Part 1.

65 In the Bible, the heart is seen as the seat of the mind and the will. See John L. McKenzie, *Dictionary of the Bible*, Chapman, London, 1976, art. 'Heart'.

66 I have been unable to trace the exact source of this quotation in Lewis's writings and rely here on memory.

67 For example, 'the mind is not only in the brain . . . It is also in the . . . glands, and immune system'. (Joel L. Swerdlow, 'Quiet Miracles of the Brain', *National Geographic*, June 1995, p. 26.

68 John Main OSB, *The Inner Christ*, Darton, Longmans and Todd, London, 1994, pp. 37–8.

69 *The Way of a Pilgrim*, Triangle Books, London, 1995, p. 89.

70 Cited by Archbishop Anthony Bloom, *Living Prayer*, Darton, Longmans and Todd, London, 1975, p. 36.

71 See *The Russian Primary Chronicle*, translated and edited by S. H. Cross and O. P. Sherbowitz-Wetzor, Cambridge, Mass., USA, pp. 110–11.

72 *The Uppsala Report 1968*, Geneva, 1969, p. 298, cited by Cardinal Leon Joseph Suenens, *A New Pentecost?*, Darton, Longmans and Todd, London, 1976, pp. 19–20.

17. Zambia & Kaunda's time
31. J.P.I & the CROWDS
35. C.C.C.: CHURCH ⟹ Kingdom of God
43. L'osservatore Romano
47. Dissent eg during Slavery
50. DIALOGUE
56. working for people; working with people.
59. Lay people; their Power & insight.
60. Half-Truth: the Ch isn't a democracy
62. Denying the Principle of Respect for people
    Case of L. Boff.
65. Authority, obedience
68. Reception
74. injustice in Ch institutions
80... choosing bishops

57
30/31
48 "Perfect Love casts out fear" St John
                                   GN 4:18
72 The individual not the "hand-out" but
   the "hand up"
   Family Life